Mitch Feierstein knows the financial industry inside out. For the past thirty years, he has consistently created opportunity and value where others have failed to look. He is a highly successful hedge fund manager and CEO of the Glacier Environmental Fund Limited. Prior to Glacier he was Senior Portfolio Manager of the Cheyne Carbon Fund, part of one of the largest and best-respected hedge fund groups operating in Europe. He has acted as a consultant for a number of governments in their disaster and contingency planning. He divides his time between London and New York.

T0368784

Planet Ponzi

How the world got into this mess

What happens next

How to save yourself

Mitch Feierstein

BLACK SWAN

TRANSWORLD PUBLISHERS
61–63 Uxbridge Road, London W5 5SA
A Random House Group Company
www.transworldbooks.co.uk

PLANET PONZI
A BLACK SWAN BOOK: 9780552778275

First published in Great Britain
in 2012 by Bantam Press
an imprint of Transworld Publishers
Black Swan edition published 2012

A CIP catalogue record for this book
is available from the British Library.

Addresses for Random House Group Ltd companies outside the UK
can be found at: www.randomhouse.co.uk
The Random House Group Ltd Reg. No. 954009

The Random House Group Limited supports The Forest Stewardship Council
(FSC®), the leading international forest-certification organization. Our books
carrying the FSC label are printed on FSC®-certified paper. FSC is the only
forest-certification scheme endorsed by the leading environmental organizations,
including Greenpeace. Our paper-procurement policy can be found at
www.randomhouse.co.uk/environment

Typeset in 11/14pt Berkeley Book by Falcon Oast Graphic Art Ltd.

Printed and bound in Great Britain by Clays Ltd, Elcograf S.p.A.

12

'*I am not a champion of lost causes, but of causes not yet won.*'
Norman Thomas, 1930

I wish my mum were still alive to enjoy and support *Planet Ponzi*. This book is for her; she'd have loved it.

A Ponzi scheme is an investment fraud that involves the payment of purported returns to existing investors from funds contributed by new investors. Ponzi scheme organizers often solicit new investors by promising to invest funds in opportunities claimed to generate high returns with little or no risk. In many Ponzi schemes, the fraudsters focus on attracting new money to make promised payments to earlier-stage investors and to use for personal expenses, instead of engaging in any legitimate investment activity.
US Securities and Exchange Commission

If the maintenance of public credit, then, be truly so important, the next enquiry which suggests itself is, by what means it is to be effected? The ready answer to which question is, by good faith, by a punctual performance of contracts. States, like individuals, who observe their engagements, are respected and trusted: while the reverse is the fate of those, who pursue an opposite conduct.
Alexander Hamilton, first US Secretary of the Treasury, 1790

Either I'm dead right, or I'm crazy!
Jefferson Smith (James Stewart) in *Mr Smith Goes to Washington*
(Sidney Buchman, 1939)

Contents

Part Three: The Wider World

Part Four: Solutions

Acknowledgments

My greatest debt of love and thanks is due to my two brothers Mark and Marty, my sister-in-law Lauren, my dad Alan, my dearest cousins in Australia – Ben, Jen, Jessica, and Abby – and of course Dave and Pat in New York.

My additional thanks to Sally Gaminara, Patsy Irwin, and Janine Giovanni at Transworld, to Harry Bingham for his exceptional editing skills, and to my fantastic yet vastly overpaid agents at AM Heath: Bill and Jennifer – all of whom made this happen.

I also want to acknowledge my supportive friends who have been there for me over the decades – YVV and Melissa, Ben and Marie Vallieres, Dr D. M. Rheims en Paris, Jeff, Donna, Jayme Zwerling (the 'little sister' I never had but always wanted), Frank, Maria, Alessandra and Daniela DeCostanzo; my Finnish pals Mikko Syrjanen and Petteri Barman; and MVF for being MVF. And, of course, Vittorio Grigolo and James Cameron for being true friends!

Finally, a word for many of my golfing pals. Unfortunately, those golden days on the links, when I recorded slews of eagles and torrents of birdies, have largely – bar the odd flash of brilliance – passed away. I am now, it seems, 'the world's worst putter' (thanks, Peter Chalk, for that accolade). So a word of thanks is due to the golfers. For Shar-Pei Sammy, my only room-mate: he never talks back or argues, is always well behaved, and has a handicap lower than mine. Thanks to Leonard Fung for losing loads of money to me 93% of the time, and to Dr Johnny Gaynor – my second oldest friend in the UK, with a lovely family who nobly tolerate his golf and my visits. JG, I await my invite to the Member–Guest tournament at St Andrews or Swinley Forest. And let's not forget a big thanks to Vassar College, and to its fine president, Catherine Hill, a great economist, friend and golfer. I thank Vassar and David Kennett for arousing my now longstanding interest in macroeconomic theory, for teaching how to be different and how to be fearless in questioning authority, and for showing why we should all 'think out of the box'.

ONE

The scheme

NOT MANY MEN have left their names to history. Bill Gates's most famous product does not bear his name. Google is named after a mathematical quantity, not the names of its founders. The most valuable IT company in the world today is named after a type of fruit.

Unlike the entrepreneurs behind these companies, Italian American Charles Ponzi did not allow history to pass him by. In November 1903, equipped with just '$2.50 in cash and $1 million in hopes,' he landed in Boston.[1] He did a series of odd jobs. In one restaurant, he rose from dishwasher to waiter – only to be fired for short-changing customers. He worked for a bank that collapsed. He went to jail for forging a check. He got involved in a scheme that smuggled illegal Italian immigrants into the US and he was jailed for that too. He was a grifter, and not even a good one. He got married. He started an advertising business. The business collapsed.

Then destiny beckoned. One day, Ponzi received a letter from Spain that happened to enclose some International Reply Coupons. The purpose of these coupons – or IRCs, as they are still known today – is to allow somebody in one country to purchase postal services in another. So if you were based in Spain, you could buy IRCs in your local Correos and send them to the US, and whoever was dispatching you your goods could use those IRCs instead of US postage stamps. To most people, this would have seemed like a neat little idea, but one of no particular significance.

But Charles Ponzi was no ordinary person. World War One had just ended. Inflation, debt, war, and flu were wreaking havoc on the old international system – and in the process the prices of these IRCs had become seriously misaligned. Ponzi found that in Italy, for example, the land of his birth, an IRC could be purchased for approximately 25% of the face value of the equivalent US stamps, implying that $10 invested in Italian IRCs would yield over $40 worth of US stamps. Thinking like a financier, Ponzi scented profit.

He quit his job. He borrowed some money. He wired that money to his relatives in Italy and told them to buy IRCs and send them to him. As soon as he received them, he sought to cash them.

And there, alas, is where his trade fell apart. Although the IRCs were technically saleable, Ponzi was thwarted by bureaucracy and red tape. Most men, at this point, would have given up. But not Ponzi. He was only just starting.

He went to friends in Boston and asked to borrow money. He explained the vast wealth available from his IRC scheme, and promised to double their money in ninety days (implying an annual interest rate of approximately 1,500%). Some people thought the offer sounded too good to be true and kept their money to themselves. Others couldn't resist and handed over their cash. Ponzi was in business.

With the money that was now flowing in, he started up the 'Securities Exchange Company' – a grand title for a venture which, after all, was only meant to be dealing in postage stamps. He promised fantastic interest rates. He paid sales agents large commissions for every new client they brought in. In the five months to May 1920, Ponzi made over $400,000 – about $20 million in today's terms. If investors wanted to get their money back, they got it. They weren't paid out because Ponzi was trading in IRCs – in fact, he never made any use of his original scheme. Instead, retiring investors were paid out from the money paid in by new investors. Needless to say, everyone who exited the scheme having made money from it acted as a perfect advertisement to newcomers. Look at those guys, the message went, *they* made money – what the hell are *you* waiting for?

Money continued to pour in. Ponzi deposited $3 million in a Boston bank, then bought a controlling interest in it. He lived luxuriously. He had a mansion, air-con, a swimming pool. When a local writer wrote a piece claiming that there was no legal way in which Ponzi could deliver returns on the scale advertised, Ponzi sued and won. Another $500,000.

So far, everything looked OK. Ponzi was rich. Anyone who wanted to withdraw their money was able to do so, and did indeed get paid out with the promised crazy interest rate. But that's the thing about any such scheme. It looks OK. For a while, it goes all right. But under the surface, the arithmetic is catastrophic.

What were Ponzi's assets? Forget about the IRCs, the 400% profits, the whole postal angle. Those things might have sparked Ponzi's idea in the first place, but they had nothing to do with the way the scheme actually operated. In actual fact, Ponzi just took the incoming money and placed it on deposit at the local bank. Interest rates at the time paid about 5%. Given Ponzi's extravagant expenses, however, those interest rates were no more than theoretical. In fact, the assets were constantly eroded by Ponzi's lifestyle.

Think now of the other side of the balance sheet: the liability side. As the scheme matured, Ponzi was offering 50% returns every forty-five days. That meant that every forty-five days the liability side of the balance sheet expanded by 50%. The asset side, in the meantime, was shrinking as Ponzi raided it.

Naturally, this couldn't go on long – and it didn't. The whole house of cards collapsed. Many people lost their life savings. Many others, who had mortgaged their homes to raise money to invest with Ponzi, lost their money and their homes. On August 12, 1920, Ponzi surrendered to the federal authorities. He was sentenced to (a remarkably lenient) five years in prison. On being released, he was immediately re-indicted by the State of Massachusetts. Having no money for an attorney, he defended himself and, speaking with vigor and eloquence, was almost acquitted. In the end, however, he was sentenced to seven to nine more years in prison – which he served only after a series of further adventures, including a failed escape attempt, a whole new fraud in Florida, and a Floridian jail sentence. He died in poverty, unknown, in a charity hospital in Rio de Janeiro.

His was a useless, wasted, destructive life, but he gave his name to history. A Ponzi scheme is any financial adventure in which depositors can only be paid out by using the money of new investors. As long as the scheme is expanding, everything looks fine. The financial mathematics are bad and getting worse all the time, but you can't tell how bad a Ponzi scheme is by how you experience the ride. It's not the ride that matters, it's the way it ends.

Now, you'd be right to think that Ponzi's investors were dumb. If you think you'd be smarter than them – relax, you would be. But just as investors have become shrewder over time, so Ponzi schemes have become a little smarter too. The most outrageous recent example of a Ponzi scheme was the one operated by Bernie Madoff, under the guise of a hedge fund. When his scheme hit the wall in 2008, investors had accumulated losses of $18 billion.[2] Whereas Ponzi had been sent to federal prison for just five years, Madoff was sentenced to jail for a term of 150 years, the maximum allowed. If he gets time off for good behavior, he can look forward to being released on November 14, 2139. At the time of writing, Madoff is seventy-three years old.[3]

Madoff wasn't some sleazy, undereducated, illegal immigrant. He was as well connected as they come: chairman of the board of the National Association of Securities Dealers, member of the board of the Securities Industry Association, chairman of NASDAQ. Yet though Madoff's scheme had a more polished front than Ponzi's, it was still the same dumb trick underneath. He pretended to achieve wonderful returns, while in fact simply paying any departing investors using money taken from the new ones. Madoff is said to have called his entire scheme 'one big lie.' Although he had been investigated back in 2003, the investigators didn't even do the basics properly. In Madoff's own words, again, 'I was astonished. They never even looked at my stock records. If investigators had checked with the Depository Trust Company, a central securities depository, it would've been easy for them to see. If you're looking at a Ponzi scheme, it's the first thing you do.'[4]

And really, that's the point. The point of this whole book. Ponzi schemes are easy to spot. They're so dumb, so obvious. The asset side of the balance sheet is so full of holes, the liability side so obviously accumulating an unpayable level of debt, you'd have to be nuts not to spot them.

Only people don't. Maybe it's that people don't like to face uncomfortable truths. Maybe it's that people can't imagine anyone could be so crooked, so unsubtle. Maybe they imagine that what looks bad to us really can't be as bad as all that – that policymakers in Washington must be on top of things, that the international financial community must have learned some lessons.

I'm not a psychologist, so I won't extend these speculations. Truth is, I just don't know how people delude themselves. It's not a trick I've ever mastered.

In any case, Charles Ponzi and Bernard Madoff were small fry. Cheap crooks who got what they deserved. They never threatened the financial system. They made some of their investors a whole lot poorer, but the world didn't come crashing down as a result.

For that – for a Ponzi scheme that would threaten to bankrupt capitalism across the entire Western world – you need people much smarter than Ponzi or Madoff. You need time, you need energy, you need motivation. In a word, you need Wall Street. But Wall Street alone doesn't have the strength to deliver a truly cataclysmic outcome. If your ambition is to create havoc on the largest possible scale, you need access to a balance sheet running into the tens of trillions. You need power. You need prestige. You need a remarkable willingness to deceive. In a word, you need Washington.

This book begins with the story of how the politicians in Washington and the bankers on Wall Street jointly created the largest Ponzi scheme in history. The origins of that scheme go way back — at least three decades, if you think only of Wall Street, but arguably as much as sixty years if you think of the federal government.

Naturally, I'm aware that my claim sounds implausible, but I hope it doesn't strike readers as *entirely* implausible. After all, just a few years ago in 2008–9, part of the Ponzi scheme was laid bare for all to see in the shape of the subprime mortgage bust and the consequent banking crisis. That crisis was already the largest Ponzi scheme in history, so the track record is there. As for what's happening today, this book will attempt a patient accounting of the scheme, its debts, its losses, its strategies of concealment. In particular, we'll find ourselves, again and again, running across the following ingredients, key to any Ponzi scheme:

❑ exponentially increasing liabilities — or, in plain English, rapidly mounting debt;

❑ crappy, nonexistent, or inadequate assets;

❑ deceitful or nonexistent accounting;

❑ feeble, inert, or toothless regulators;

❑ a get-rich-quick culture, for preference salted with a whole array of inappropriate incentives;

❑ stupid, ignorant, lazy investors — the greedier, the better; and

❑ an astonishing capacity for self-delusion.

Those things are the bricks from which Washington and Wall Street constructed their castle of debt, and constructed it in plain view of all, and on a colossal scale.

If that edifice hadn't been so utterly destructive, you'd have to admire the ambition and creativity – the whole Dr Evil, death-ray megalomania of it. And sure, Wall Street and Washington have had help. Ordinary Main Street banks did their bit. Households did more than their bit. So too did voters and media companies. The City of London was Wall Street's most willing helper, its evil Mini-Me. Poorly managed states in Europe and the Far East got in on the act. Dumb European savings banks participated. Slothful insurance companies. Crazily inept corporations who felt they had to play poker with Wall Street, not knowing or caring that the dice were loaded against them.

As we've already seen, no Ponzi scheme can last for ever. You can defy financial gravity for months (if you're Charles Ponzi) or for years (if you're Bernie Madoff), but gravity will always claim you in the end.

The first phase of the collapse of our global Ponzi scheme came on September 15, 2008, when Lehman Brothers filed for bankruptcy protection under Chapter 11 of the US Bankruptcy Code. (The earlier failure of Bear Stearns was a warning of cataclysm, but not yet the cataclysm itself.) In Lehman's filing, the bank reported assets worth $639 billion. It owed $768 billion. The bank was insolvent to the tune of approximately $130 billion. In the weeks and months that followed, horrified newspaper readers became inured to ever-greater shocks, ever-greater oceans of red ink. General Motors went bust. Goldman Sachs was seeking emergency funding. Citigroup was crippled. Merrill Lynch was in crisis merger talks. The financial giant AIG was so massively bankrupt that it required $183 billion of government money to bail it out.

Across the world, the story was the same. The British government acquired most of the stock in Royal Bank of Scotland (RBS) and further holdings in various other institutions, thereby accumulating debts about equal to the UK's GDP. The Irish government undertook to guarantee its bank debt, thereby destroying its own creditworthiness. And so on.

The private sector Ponzi scheme had stopped being able to bear the weight of its own creation. Round the world, governments – a cute way of saying you, the taxpayer – were faced with the collapse of capitalism. A system no longer able to pay its way.

That, more or less, brings us to where we stand now. If you believe the story retailed by mainstream financial commentators today, you'll believe that the public sector stepped in to prevent the collapse of the entire global financial system. That austerity measures are now needed to curb government borrowing. That economic growth is likely to be patchy and slow, as it always is after a financial crisis. That regulators are starting to make changes to the system which will diminish the chances of the whole thing happening again. That house prices have mostly bottomed out. That the financial sector is, once again, profitable. That monetary policy needs to remain loose to prevent deflation. That there are risks aplenty, but that the world is fundamentally on the right course. That it was one heck of a crisis, but that we are now slowly picking our way out of the ruins.

These propositions vary from the totally wrong to the hopelessly misleading. We're going to get to the detailed arguments shortly, but for now, let's keep it simple. Ponzi schemes *are* simple, remember. Their crappy hollowness is utterly obvious, if only you choose to look. The mistake lies in not looking.

And if you want the truth, here it is. We are *still* in the middle of a massive Ponzi scheme. Sure, the first phase is over. Governments bailed out the banks. Main Street paid for Wall Street's excesses. But that doesn't mean that the scheme is dead and finished with. It just means that the public sector chose to swallow the private sector's debts. The debts are still there. The bad assets are still there. The same corrupt incentives are still in place. The same degree of profiteering. The same blindness to risk. The same astonishing tolerance for ever-increasing debt.

But don't think all this means that things are as bad as they ever were. They're not. They're worse – much worse. Remember: Ponzi schemes can only operate because of their merry-go-round nature. New dummies providing the influx of funds to pay out the old dummies. But with each cycle, you need more and more dummies – and sooner or later,

Figure 1.1: US federal debt outstanding, 1940–2010

Source: Bureau of Economic Analysis, US Treasury,
www.usgovernmentspending.com. Data for fiscal year 2010 estimated.

you'll be all out of idiots. And when you reach that point, the mountain of debt will only have gotten higher, the clean-up operation more horrendous.

If you think I exaggerate, let's take a quick tour of the first of our Ponzi scheme ingredients: exponentially increasing liabilities. If you ever see a set of figures which suggests exponentially increasing liabilities, you should think hard about whether or not you might be looking at a Ponzi scheme. A set of figures like those in figure 1.1, for instance.

This graph shows debt issued by the US federal government. It's adjusted for inflation, so you're seeing a real increase in total indebtedness, not simply an artificial effect generated by a rise in prices. But really, for the moment, I'd encourage you to put all such technicalities out of your head. If you don't have an economics degree, don't worry. If you aren't a financial expert, it doesn't matter. Just ask yourself whether this graph suggests that:

(a) the finances of the US government are under control, which is what the government would want you to believe, or
(b) that a Ponzi scheme is approaching its final death-rattle.

If you need a little help in answering that question, take a look at figure 1.2, which shows the federal deficit over time. In the Clintonian 1990s, the deficit hovered either side of the axis. Sometimes the government needed to borrow a little, sometimes it operated in surplus and repaid some of its borrowing. For present purposes, we don't need to worry too much either way. The point is, net government spending was under control. Over on Wall Street, the first revolutions

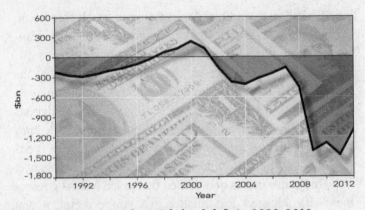

Figure 1.2: The US federal deficit, 1990–2012

Source: Congressional Budget Office. Data for 2011 and 2012
represent CBO projections.

of the Ponzi scheme were getting under way, but in
Washington, money was still reasonably sound (though
there were, even then, huge accumulating liabilities which
we'll explore more extensively in a later chapter).

In the George W. Bush years, things got worse. The
federal government became habituated to borrowing. Taxes
never covered spending – but still, even in 2004, the worst
of those years, federal borrowing never breached the $500
billion level. And just as well: $500 billion is a lot of money.

Then came the credit crunch. Lehman, AIG, General
Motors – the first, most colorful phase of the current credit
crisis. In 2008, the deficit hovered close to $500 billion. The
following year, it was approaching $1,500 billion, or $1.5
trillion if you prefer.

Just pause for a moment to consider how much money
that is. Numbers that large become difficult to comprehend,
because of the absence of obvious comparisons. So let's look

at some big numbers. Table 1.1 sets out some compiled by *The Economist*. Instead of thinking about the current US deficit in pure numerical terms, think about it in terms of what you could buy for $1.5 trillion. You could buy the entire global stock of monetary gold (that is, excluding gold worn as jewelry and the like). You could get close to buying all the farmland in the United States. Or maybe you'd prefer to diversify a little, in which case you could snap up the whole of Manhattan, the whole of Washington DC, all the military hardware owned by the US armed forces, the fifty most valuable sports teams in the world – and still be able to buy a controlling interest in Apple, Microsoft, IBM, and Google.[5] That's what $1.5 trillion is worth. And remember, that's not what the government owes (it owes way more than that): it's how much the government expanded its borrowing *in one single calendar year*. That was 2009. In 2010, it did the same thing – give or take the odd hundred billion – all over again. And 2011 is predicted to be worse.

	$
Value of global oil production, 2011 [est.]	3,410,000,000,000
US farms	1,870,000,000,000
Sovereign debt of Spain, Portugal, Greece and Ireland	1,510,000,000,000
Monetary gold	1,430,000,000,000
Apple, Microsoft, IBM, Google	916,000,000,000
US military hardware	414,000,000,000
Manhattan real estate	287,000,000,000
Washington DC real estate	232,000,000,000
50 most valuable sports teams	50,000,000,000

Table 1.1: What you can buy for a trillion dollars or three

Source: 'Who wants to be a triple trillionaire?,' *The Economist*, April 14, 2011.

In the years after 2011, the deficit is forecast to come down – we'll look at whether it truly will in a later chapter – but remember, it's not enough for the deficit to come down. For as long as the government is a net borrower, its debt is expanding. So for things to really start improving, the deficit has to turn negative. The approximately $1.5 trillion which the federal government borrowed in each of the years from 2009 to 2011 will need to be repaid. If it's not repaid, it's a Ponzi scheme – and a Ponzi scheme only ever ends one way.

But let's broaden the scope of our enquiry. This book isn't about the US federal debt, or even about the US government. It's about the global economy: Planet Ponzi, not Potomac Ponzi. After all, maybe the federal government is in a mess, but perhaps the monetary authorities have a firm grip on things. Or perhaps things are in a mess in the United States, but they're in better order elsewhere. Or perhaps the public

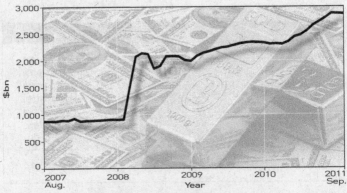

Figure 1.3: Total assets of the US Federal Reserve, 2007–2011

Source: Federal Reserve.

sector is in poor shape, but the private sector is doing fine.

So let's take a look. Let's consider monetary policy. Figure 1.3 shows how the balance sheet of the Federal Reserve has changed over recent years.[6] For a good long period, things were completely stable. The Fed's assets burbled along at a shade over $800 billion. (Its liabilities, of course, are somewhat notional – unlike regular banks, the Fed can print money. Its biggest 'liability' is simply notes and coins in circulation.) Then, when the credit crisis struck, the balance sheet started expanding rapidly. From $800 billion to over $2,800 billion. That's an increase of $2,000 billion – $2 trillion – in less than three years: more than enough to buy all the farmland in the US, or to buy yourself nearly five times as much military hardware as the American military possesses. Where does that increase come from? What financed it? The answer is that those assets were produced by magic. By printing money. The huge increase in the Fed's balance sheet came from unelected officials choosing to spirit new dollars out of nowhere. And please notice one more thing. The biggest one-off increase in new money came in the immediate aftershock of the Lehman crisis, but the response has not been a one-off. The Fed's balance sheet has been creeping up from late 2010 right through to mid-2011. Item one on our list of Ponzi ingredients was exponentially spiraling debt – and please tell me that you can look at these graphs and see any other pattern emerging.

As for the world beyond the US: there is a crisis in Europe. Greece is bankrupt, Ireland and Portugal not far behind. The bond market is currently raising serious doubts about the ability of Italy and Spain to fund themselves. Uncertainty has even started to lap at the shores of France, long seen as a 'strong' market and now just starting to be reappraised.

Perhaps North American readers will feel insulated from these uncertainties, but they shouldn't. If one of the three most vulnerable countries – Japan, Italy, or Spain – detonates, the consequences will be felt globally. Bear in mind that Lehman Brothers owed only $0.77 trillion when it went under, and it had assets of over $0.6 trillion. Those sums are trivial in relation to the amounts now in question. Italy owes more than $2 trillion, Japan around $10 trillion. Italy is, as you may have noticed, a low-growth, poorly governed, somewhat corrupt country with an organized crime problem and a wholly untested and unelected government. Japan is, as you may have noticed, an earthquake-prone country with an aging population, a stagnant economy, a two-decades-old problem with deflation, no energy security, no raw materials, a huge and increasingly assertive neighbor, and a political class that seems perennially unable to implement radical change. Oh yes, and a nuclear mess that isn't cleared up and seems all set for a tragic replay.

As for the purported health of the private sector: don't be fooled. At the time of writing, Bank of America, which is the largest bank by assets in the United States, has a stock market capitalization equal to just 25% of its book value.[7] A company's book value is the total accounting value of its assets less the total accounting value of its liabilities. The value of its liabilities is relatively uncontroversial: a company owes what it owes. The value of its assets, however, is much more uncertain. A bank may claim that (let's say) its mortgage book is worth $10 billion, but perhaps impending delinquencies and defaults mean that its true value is nearer $9 billion, or $8 billion. The fact that the stock market's coldly calculating eye values Bank of America at just one-quarter of its supposed financial worth speaks volumes about how little faith the market truly has in the firm. And Bank of America is far from unique. Citigroup and JP Morgan Chase also trade at a substantial discount to book value. In Europe, RBS is valued at less than a fifth of book value, Deutsche Bank and Paribas at little more than half. It's being reported that RBS is in line for a fresh injection of government funds.[8]

In short, in the course of this very brief introductory review we've found that the US government has exponentially spiraling debts, that the monetary authorities appear to be slaves to the same Ponzi-ish gods, that the debt crisis in Europe is profound and growing, and that some of the major pillars of the global financial sector are worth a fraction of what their accounts would seem to imply. I hope that those reflections at the very least give you pause for thought. Though my central claim is a big one, it's hardly without evidence.

Naturally, however, we're going to have to examine these things in more detail. We're going to take that list of ingredients for a Ponzi scheme and tick them off one by one. Overvalued assets? Check. Deceitful accounting? Uh-huh. Slothful regulators? You betcha. Nor will we confine ourselves to the US. The Ponzi scheme in America may be bad, but it's a whole lot worse elsewhere – among major nations, I'd say that Japan, Italy, and Spain are far less creditworthy, France and Britain not much better. Even China, with no significant debt at a national level, suffers from an opaque banking system, poor incentives, booming asset markets, and dangerously flawed accounting. We'll look at all these things in due course.

But that lies ahead. The rest of this book is divided

into four sections. The first three parts go through the grim accounting of Planet Ponzi. We'll look in turn at Washington, at Wall Street, and at the wider world. We won't only look at mounting debts – the liability side of our global balance sheet; we'll look at the asset side too. Ponzi schemes are reliant on an ever-swelling basket of hopelessly misvalued assets. When we turn to look at some of the major markets around today, we'll see misvaluation or bubbles on a gigantic scale. Misvaluation in the housing market. Misvaluation in the equity market. Misvaluation to a dangerous degree in the bond markets. Those things might sound dryly technical, but then things can't get more dryly technical than CDO-squared structures in the subprime mortgage market. Those technicalities, however, ended up wrecking your economy and trampling your future. Sometimes technicalities matter.

Finally, Part Four looks at 'Solutions.' That's a bad title, actually: there are no solutions. You don't solve a Ponzi scheme; you end it. That means huge deleveraging resulting in huge losses: the resulting wrenching dislocations are inevitable. There was no way the authorities could make right what Charles Ponzi did, or what Bernie Madoff did. People lost mountains of money, and all you can do at that stage is send the perpetrators to jail and start to repair the damage.

All the same, there are things that policymakers could do right now to limit the coming carnage. There are also things that you personally can do to protect yourself and your family. They're things that I'm doing too. This book holds back no secrets. There's been too little candor for two decades and more, and truth remains the single best antiseptic. At the end of this book, I'll set out a personal action plan for you to follow. But because books move more slowly than the financial markets, I'll also keep you updated on my website, planetponzi.com. We're in this together.

This book is about some complicated things, but I'm going to avoid complexities in talking about them. Unlike the magicians of dodgy accounting, I can say everything I want to say in clear, plain English. If you can handle the graphs we've already looked at, you can handle everything else that follows. (Well, OK, full disclosure: when we talk about financial derivatives or pension accounting, I do get a little technical, but not overly so. Those who are interested can explore the sources cited in the endnotes, which will supply greater detail, but there's no need to do so. It's your call.)

What's more, I'm not going to throw any strange numbers at you. I'm going to source my data from impeccable official sources. In most cases, you can go straight to the internet and check my facts. Indeed, I *invite* you to do just that. The scheme has arisen because not enough people used their native common sense to check up on the claims of so-called experts. If we're to escape the scheme with the minimum amount of damage, we need to change mindset. People need to become skeptics. We need to learn how to challenge authority, how to get a plain answer to a plain question and not rest until we're entirely satisfied. At the beginning of this book there are three quotations. One of them is spoken by Jefferson Smith, the Jimmy Stewart character in *Mr Smith Goes to Washington*. Addressing the US Senate, Smith says:

I'm sorry, gentlemen. I know I'm being disrespectful to this honorable body, I know that.

> A guy like me should never be allowed to get in
> here in the first place. I know that. And I hate to
> stand here and try your patience like this, but
> either I'm dead right or I'm crazy!

You and I are the same. We've never run the government, a major bank, or the Fed; we've never borrowed a trillion dollars or ten. Yet by writing this book (for my part) and by engaging with its arguments (for yours), we're doing as Jefferson Smith did: bringing common sense to bear in an arena that asks us to dispense with it. We're right to insist. Either we're dead right or we're crazy.

In that Smithian spirit, let me tell you more about me and my qualifications. I'm a hedge fund manager, currently raising a new $500 million fund. I've been active in the global financial markets for almost three decades. I've never touched subprime mortgages – I thought they were total crap the first time I encountered them, and I haven't changed my mind since. As a matter of fact, my personal interest has long been in environmental investing – creating and trading in financial securities that help governments and corporations pursue an ethical environmental stance. I also have an interest in investing in proven technologies that can help cure the Western world's addiction to planet-endangering fossil fuels sourced from the hostile and unstable nations that produce them. A number of major international corporations have gone carbon neutral, through their own strenuous energy efficiency and reduction efforts and by using some of the carbon management tools which my colleagues and I have developed. I'm proud of that work.

But you don't need to know or care about my

environmental views. You aren't required to share them. For the purposes of this present book, you need to know that I can foresee a crisis when it comes. And, yes, I did make the correct call on Credit Crunch 1 and made money by buying puts on global stock markets (a way of betting on a coming stock market crash). I also bought gold when it was at $377 per ounce. It's now at approximately $1,800. I'm not claiming to be unusually smart in making these calls correctly. I'm just claiming that, unlike far too many of my peers, I wasn't stupid. When the first waves of the credit crunch started to lap round the markets in 2007, I began to think more systematically about where it had begun and where it had to end. Almost five years on, this book is the result.

Finally, it would be easy for you to assume that my position is an extreme one. That, much as the current political class might have gotten it wrong, the real truth probably lies somewhere in the middle. Yet the views I express in this book are nowhere close to the extreme. As a matter of fact, I'd say my views represent a fairly cautious, middle of the road opinion. Take, for example, those statistics I gave you about the stock market values of various major banks in relation to their accounting values: those numbers summarized not my view, but the view of the markets in relation to those huge firms. And it's not just the markets that are worrying about these things. As we'll see in due course, there are plenty of sober academic economists who share my views. Those economists say bluntly that the US is bankrupt. In the words of Laurence Kotlikoff, whose debt calculations we'll review in a later chapter:

Uncle Sam's Ponzi scheme will stop. But it will stop too late. And it will stop in a very nasty manner . . . This is an awful, downhill road to follow, but it's the one we are on. And bond traders will kick us miles down our road once they wake up and realize the U.S. is in worse fiscal shape than Greece.[9]

That moment of awakening is getting closer – and so is the kicking. But before we figure out how to handle that moment when it comes, let's turn back to the origin of everything. How the Ponzi scheme started. What keeps it going. How the whole thing is still in place, still revolving, still expanding – and getting ever closer to the final showdown.

We start with government.

PART ONE

Washington

TWO

The price of liberty

THE SEMINAL MOMENT in the history of public finance was a sea battle fought in 1690 by a French fleet under Admiral Tourville and an Anglo-Dutch fleet under Admiral Torrington. The French fleet boasted seventy-five ships of the line and a further twenty-three fireships. The Allied navies were scattered over a variety of duties and could muster only fifty-six ships, a huge disadvantage. Following direct orders from the Queen of England, Torrington's Allied fleet sailed against the French – and was crushed. Almost a dozen Allied ships were destroyed. Torrington fled and was later court-martialed. The French were left in total control of the English Channel and, for a while, a French invasion seemed not merely possible but likely.

That unaccustomed naval defeat shook England to the core. The country needed funds for rearmament, but the nation lacked any sophisticated way to attract them. So, in 1694, the decision was taken to create the Bank of England, intended from the first as a means to raise funds for the English state. In effect, that moment marked the start of the modern era in public finance. Private subscribers to the Bank's capital raised £1.2 million in twelve days. All that money was lent to the King, and half was immediately used to rebuild the Royal Navy. It was money well spent. The English (later British) government would come to enjoy almost two centuries of unchallenged naval dominance; the country would never come close to invasion again.

And that's why countries have debts.

It's so they can borrow money in times of national emergency. Not it's-a-national-emergency-that-so-many-kids-are-flunking-out-of-high-school. Not it's-a-national-emergency-that-our-elderly-are-facing-mounting-medical-bills. I'm talking about real emergencies. The War of Independence. The Civil War. World War One. Pearl Harbor and World War Two. Crises that threaten the fabric of the nation are unarguably powerful reasons to take on debt. In 1790 Alexander Hamilton, the first Secretary of the Treasury of the new United States, wrote that the country's public debt, incurred as a result of war, was 'the price of liberty.'[1] He was perfectly correct. He also, however, made it clear that to incur debt was an emergency response to an emergency situation. In ordinary times, no government should seek to take on debt. On the contrary, during times of peace and prosperity it makes sense to pay down past debt as a protection against future shocks, creating room for maneuver.

Indeed, it's not even clear that a peacetime government has any moral authority to incur debt. On what basis can one generation choose to saddle its successor with a financial burden? In times of safety and prosperity, government debt should either be close to zero or moving toward that level. There's no other ethical, wise, or prudent alternative.

As you can see from figure 2.1, until recently – very recently – the United States obeyed this logic to the letter.[2]

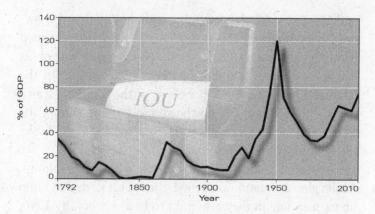

Figure 2.1: Gross US federal debt since 1792

Source: Author's calculations from various sources, esp. Christopher
Chantrill's website www.usgovernmentspending.com.

The nation's founding war left it with debts somewhat in
excess of 30% of GDP. That debt (with a little blip for the
War of 1812) was paid down to $0.00 in 1835. In 1836 –
there was no new debt. The country was at peace and
unthreatened. The country had no reason to borrow, so it
didn't. A little later, the Civil War bumped up the debt,
before it started to run down again. The same pattern was
followed during and after World War One.

Indeed, prior to 1980, the only time that the United
States increased its borrowing when it faced no existential
threat was during the Great Depression. From a low of 16%
in 1929, public debt increased to a high of almost 41% in
1934. If you're a Keynesian, you can defend this increase on
the basis that the country would have been in worse
economic shape without it. If you're not, you might feel that
the economy would have fared just as well with balanced

budgets and moderate federal spending. Either way, however, debt increased by just 25% of GDP and remained
within highly sustainable levels. If Roosevelt got some of his
decisions wrong, he didn't get them *badly* wrong. In the
country's worst ever depression – the market crash,
the unemployment, the dustbowl and farming slump, the
collapse of trade – the government response never broke
the bounds of a cautiously managed public debt.

Alas, that caution soon had to give way to other things.
As the global situation darkened, the nation started to ramp
up its spending in the years prior to Pearl Harbor. By 1946,
debt had hit a high of more than 120% of GDP. The nation's
finances had gone through the meatgrinder; but the country
had fought and won wars across two continents and was
beyond question the moral, financial, and industrial leader
of the free world. The grind had been worth it.

Over the decades that followed, debt retreated. In 1980,
at the outset of President Reagan's first term of office, debt
stood at a shade over 32% of national income. For every
dollar that the nation created in income that year, the
government owed just 32 cents. It had been a long way back
from those wartime debt levels, but the road had been
steadily trodden nonetheless.

And then – something happened. Wall Street started to
innovate. Leveraged buyouts funded by junk bonds became
fashionable. The stock market soared. These were the years
when the communist system collapsed; peace and
prosperity reigned supreme. By all past standards, these
conditions should have ensured a huge *decrease* in public
debt. There was absolutely no reason why the nation needed
to borrow. Yet it did. Like crazy. After three terms of
Republican rule between 1980 and 1992, gross debt had

risen to a startling 63% of GDP. After a pause under Clinton, debt started to rise again.

Since then, the US has experienced two insanely expensive wars. Nobel Prize winning economist Joseph Stiglitz estimated the cost of the Iraq war at $3 trillion.[3] The Joint Economic Committee of Congress placed the cost at closer to $3.5 trillion, or approximately $31,250 for each household in America.[4] If you care to add the cost of the Afghanistan war to the total, you can add another trillion or so, or around $10,000–15,000 per household. Perhaps the war in Afghanistan had some strategic necessity – no one wanted to witness another 9/11 launched from Afghan soil – but the war in Iraq was unquestionably a war of choice. A choice which, if you are a taxpaying US householder, will cost you over $30,000 once all the bills are in.

We've also witnessed the insanity of the $3 trillion tax cuts under George W. Bush. That's something we'll talk about more in the next chapter, but just bear in mind that those tax cuts were made *when the budget was in deficit*. That's not a reduction in tax at all. It's an *increase*, because future generations will need to pay back not just the amount borrowed, but the interest on the borrowings. Those 'tax cuts' were engineered by a president who claimed to be a fiscal conservative, yet was surely the least conservative president in history.

And he didn't stop there. As part of his effort to hand on the worst in-tray in American history, President Bush also left the incoming administration a catastrophic banking collapse, a vicious recession, and a bailout program which Obama implemented broadly in line with his predecessor's policies. That program was so extensive, so multifaceted, it's hard to place a precise cost on it – or even to describe

it accurately. The best 'simple' guide to the cost of
the crisis is probably Christopher Chantrill's website
usfederalbailout.com, whose current accounting is summarized in table 2.1.[5]

One of the problems with representing costs in a table
like this is the way it removes all drama from the numbers.
It's easy to read the totals as being a little under 15,500 for
guarantees, about 3,400 for net outlays. The table feels
orderly and precise rather than frightening and chaotic. But
remember: *these figures are in billions of dollars*. If you took a
million dollars in hundred-dollar bills, it wouldn't look like
all that much. You'd have a stack approximately 4 feet high
and light enough to be picked up by a single person without assistance. But that's a mere million bucks. A trillion is a

	Gross Outlays $ billion	Net Outlays $ billion	Guarantees $ billion	Major components
Troubled Asset Relief Program (TARP)	873	265	–	Capital Purchase Program, auto industry finance, systemically significant failing institutions, etc.
US Treasury, non-TARP	527	510	3,355	Acquisition of Fannie Mae and Freddie Mac pref. stock, ABS purchases, student loan purchases, Money Market MF Program
Federal Reserve	3,142	2,632	2,018	CP Funding Facility, purchase of GSE-backed MBSs
Federal Deposit Insurance Corporation	0	0	2,475	Temporary Liquidity Guarantee Program
Other	26	17	7,621	FHFA, FHLB guarantees
Totals	4,568	3,424	15,469	

Table 2.1: The cost of the bailout

Source: Christopher Chantrill, www.usfederalbailout.com.

million million, so three trillion dollars – which is what that 'net outlays' figure really means – would form a tower well over 12,000,000 feet high. That's a tower approximately 10,000 times as high as the Empire State Building; a tower whose middle and lower sections would risk damage from satellites in low earth orbit – and whose upper sections would lie well out of their range.[6]

Additionally, of course, the complexity and non-transparency of the various bailout programs make it hard to keep tabs on their cost. Take another look at that table. In the last row, you'll notice that $7,621 billion has been guaranteed primarily via the FHFA and the FHLB guarantees. Do you even know what those things are? I don't mean: Do you know the acronyms? (Respectively, the Federal Housing Finance Agency and the Federal Home Loan Bank.) I mean: Someone has decided to issue a guarantee for $7.6 trillion, which is equivalent to more than 50% of US GDP. If you're one of the 310,000,000 people living in the United States, you're on the hook for your share of that amount: it works out at approximately $67,500 for each US householder. Unless you're remarkably relaxed about your household finances, you probably aren't in the habit of issuing guarantees for that amount without a certain amount of consideration. So do you actually understand what those FHFA and FHLB guarantees are for, when they might be called upon, and whether the economic justification for making them is remotely solid?

If you're a little hazy in your answers, I don't blame you. In July 2009 Neil Barofsky, a special inspector general for the Treasury's Troubled Asset Relief Program (TARP), tried to make sense of the numbers and concluded that US taxpayers could be on the hook for as much as $23.7 trillion, or almost 170% of national income. Barofsky also stated that the Treasury has 'repeatedly failed to adopt recommendations' to increase transparency and accountability in the way the money is being spent or committed.[7]

These things ought to cause mass protests in the streets of Washington; but because the underlying issues are so technical, they tend to be buried in the finance pages of newspapers instead. Still, $23.7 *trillion*? Sure, it's highly unlikely that all those commitments will be triggered at the same time. But the nature of a commitment is that you're on the hook whether the world is as you expect it to be or not. It is simply beyond belief that the governing class could authorize pledges on this scale and that taxpayers could know essentially nothing about them.

Meanwhile, as I write, the politicians in Washington have just agreed to raise the federal borrowing ceiling to $16,700 billion. If you took that tower of hundred-dollar bills and laid it out flat, you could loop $16,700 billion one and a half times round the circumference of the earth. In theory, the increase in the federal borrowing limit comes in exchange for $2,400 billion in deficit reduction measures but, as we'll see, that deficit reduction is somewhat theoretical. It's a reduction counted in future-money, a strange currency which can mean pretty much anything you like. The one solid, unarguable reality is that the deficit for 2012 will be over $1 trillion, or about 7% of GDP. Our politicians will go into the 2012 presidential race talking about austerity measures and budget cuts and vast savings and tough decisions . . . yet they're still borrowing 7% of our national income to fund their spending. The reductions they're talking about haven't yet kicked in and maybe never will. Obama came into office promising change and an end to big spending and big government. We got change all right: an *acceleration* of the rate at which we're accumulating debt. Somehow, I'm not sure that's what voters thought they were voting for.

Absolutely everything is wrong with this picture. We're going to analyze it piece by piece in the chapters that follow, but the main point is really simple. *Government borrowing is an option to be used in time of war or other mortal danger.* In the three decades we have lived through since 1980, that sober logic has expired. The logic of Planet Ponzi has come to reign supreme. Soviet communism has collapsed. America's existing allies in Europe and Japan remain strong, free, and supportive. Economic growth has been dependable, innovation impressive. Older companies have found new strengths, new companies have built global businesses at an astonishing pace. All this ought to have meant that we paid off our debt. Watched it disappear completely.

That's not some weird theoretical feat that never happens in practice. It does. It happens in oil-rich countries like Norway and Saudi Arabia, which have net *asset* to GDP ratios of 156% and 50% respectively. It also happens in ordinary, well-run, but oil-free countries like Chile (net assets of 11%), Sweden (15%), and Finland (57%).[8] Those countries are piling up savings in the good times as a precaution against calamity down the road. And, of course, those savings generate interest income, so that teachers can be paid, soldiers trained, and medical bills taken care of through savings instead of through taxation. That's the position we in the US ought to be in. It was the position we achieved in 1835–6. But when Planet Ponzi came to Washington all such rational aspirations flew out of the window – and our creditworthiness with them.

While you probably already know that the US government is highly indebted, I'm willing to bet that you have no idea how deeply bankrupt it truly is. What's more, you probably aren't aware that the government is effectively bankrupt *even on its own* (alarmingly optimistic) figures. The grim arithmetic of that bankruptcy is where we turn next.

THREE

Future-money in happy-land

FOLLOWING A PERIOD of heated and acidly partisan debate in Congress, in early August 2011 the House and the Senate voted to raise the US government's debt limit, thereby staving off a situation in which the government would have become unable to meet its obligations. The US Senate passed the Budget Control Act by 74 votes to 26. Commentators on both sides of the aisle explained how tough the decisions had been, how difficult the compromises, how much the US economy would benefit in the long run. As part of the same package, the deficit had been, we were repeatedly told, cut by $2.4 trillion.

Now, I'm not fond of the deficit and I'm not fond of the mountains of debt that currently burden the US economy. So you might reasonably think I'd be elated to hear that the deficit had come down by $2.4 trillion. You probably think I'm already figuring out how high a tower I could build from $2.4 trillion in hundred-dollar bills, or how many times such a tower would wrap round the world.

But I'm not. The trouble with that huge deficit reduction is that it exists only in the mind of Washington. It has no bearing on the planet that you and I are living on.

Let's start with the idea that our courageous politicians have just voted for cuts. According to the agreed plan (along with the raising of the debt ceiling, all part of the Budget Control Act), federal discretionary spending has just been 'cut' by $741 billion. The impact on the deficit, we are told, is even better than that because borrowing less money means we owe less interest, and so we need to borrow less money. Taking those interest savings into account, and some small additional adjustments to mandatory spending, that $741 billion cut becomes a total deficit cut of $917 billion. That's pretty good news. News of the sort that ought to cheer me up.

Except that here in figure 3.1, using publicly available data from the Congressional Budget Office, is how federal discretionary spending is projected to alter over the next decade, after taking those $917 billion cuts into account.[1]

Please study the graph very carefully. You may want to look at it under bright light, or make an enlargement, or enter the data into a computer program of your own devising. Once you've conducted any checks that occur to you, I'd like you to list any cuts you can see. You know: cuts. Where spending gets *smaller* from year to year. I don't see any such thing in that graph. What I see is a federal discretionary spend that *increases in every year*. Not all that much to start with, but then at an increasing pace. That's not cutting anything. It's certainly not cutting $917 billion. In fact, it looks an awful lot like spending money. Money which the government does not have and will need to borrow.

But let's continue, because our brave congressmen and congresswomen magnificently managed to save a further $1.5 trillion over the same ten-year period. That's an impressive sum of money. If someone in my firm managed to

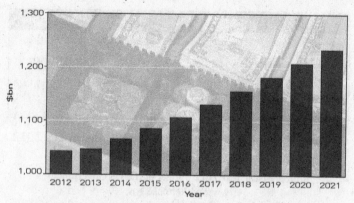

Figure 3.1: US federal discretionary spending limits, 2012–2021, under the Budget Control Act 2011

Source: Congressional Budget Office.

save even 1% of that figure, I'd give him or her a nice rise and maybe even a corner-office.

Unfortunately, no one knows where that $1.5 trillion is going to come from. The Pentagon budget? Social security? Medicare? Food stamps? Please don't ask me, because I don't know. Nor does anyone else. What's more, we don't even know *when* these savings are going to happen. Not 2012, that's for sure. But 2013? Or 2021? Or sometime in between? We don't know. The money being saved is in a currency called future-money. It's easy to save future-money. You just decide to spend $5 trillion in 2025, then change your mind and decide to spend $4.5 trillion instead. If you can manage that, you can save half a trillion future-dollars any time you like. Once you get good at it, you can do it five times before breakfast.

But it gets better. The $1.5 trillion which is being saved we-don't-know-how and we-don't-know-when also

	2012	2013	2014	2015	2016
Real growth in GDP	3.6	4.4	4.3	3.8	3.3
Civilian unemployment	8.6	7.5	6.6	5.9	5.5
Consumer price inflation	1.8	1.9	2.0	2.0	2.1
Interest rate on 10-yr bonds	3.6	4.2	4.6	5.0	5.2

Table 3.1: Principal economic assumptions in US 2012 budget (%)

Source: Fiscal Year 2012 Budget of the US Government, www.whitehouse.gov.

includes an unknown quantum of interest savings. That's interest being saved on money we haven't spent and haven't borrowed. It's future-interest on future-money, which is being saved at a random time and from unknown sources. It's imaginary savings on imaginary interest created by imaginary cuts against a theoretical baseline. That's how you save future-money. You should try it sometime.

Meantime, back in reality, the 2012 budget will still show a deficit of $1 trillion and the deal agreed with such fanfare on the Hill will cut 2012 spending by just $22 billion from a total spend of $3,600 billion. *That's* the cut.[2]

All this 'cutting' is absurd enough, but the fun has only just started – because future-money is a currency that works best in happy-land, a place known only to economic forecasters working in Washington. Here in table 3.1 are the economic assumptions which underlie the White House budget for 2012[3] (and on which the numbers above are also based).

In happy-land, the economy races away, unemployment tumbles, inflation remains low, and interest rates creep up a little but stay affordable. In happy-world, taxation is strong, because all those companies are booming away. Federal obligations on such things as food stamps and housing benefits will diminish for the same reason. It's easy putting budgets together in happy-land, because all the nasty things (inflation, unemployment) do all the right things, and all the nice things (GDP growth) go skipping away like spring lambs.

Sadly, happy-land doesn't look much like the planet I live on. On my planet, unemployment has stayed relent-lessly high. Leading indicators of mood such as the ISM index show consistently negative results.[4] Growth is constantly being revised downwards.[5] Inflation is burden-some. The highly depressed yields on US Treasury bonds – currently at historic lows and likely to be among the lowest we see in our lifetimes – reflect the bleak outlook for the US economy.

The simple fact is that the US government is making no real cuts in spending or borrowing. It has no credible austerity plan for the medium term. Its budgeting is based on economic nonsense. And our politicians don't want a truthful debate about any of these things.

That's the bad news.

There is, however, good news too. Around the world, governments have faced precisely these kinds of problems and have responded in exactly the right ways. Sweden had a huge banking bust in the early 1990s. It managed to force the costs of bailout almost exclusively on to shareholders, with such success that the costs ultimately borne by tax-payers were somewhere between 0 and 2% of GDP.[6] In the meantime, however, the government was left with a fiscal deficit amounting to 12% of GDP and public debt projected to reach 128% of GDP unless something was done. So something *was* done. Cuts were made, taxes raised, and the necessary adjustments communicated clearly and honestly to citizens. There was, in addition, broad political consensus about the need for all this. In a time of crisis, the political class worked together and the Swedish people recognized that, little as they might enjoy the austerity process, it was nevertheless essential.[7] The harvest of all this difficult work was both predictable and golden. Sweden currently boasts strong growth and sound banks, and holds national assets in place of a national debt. There is no reason why that happy future should not come to America too. All it takes is common sense.

Taxes

I'm a hedge fund manager and a business owner. I have an income which is well above the median national income. So you might expect me to be a strong supporter of the Bush-era tax cuts and of those Republicans in the House today who vow never to raise a tax. And in part, you'd be right. I believe in a small state, with low government spending and strong incentives to invest, work, and take risks.

But tax cuts made when the budget is in deficit aren't really tax cuts at all. All you're doing is borrowing money, which will one day have to be repaid with interest. You might receive a $10 tax rebate today, but you'll pay $12 for it in the future. That's not a tax cut, it's a tax *increase*. It's the opposite of what any fiscal conservative should recommend. In the scathing words of a blogger for *The Economist*:

> Basically, in the grip of careless enthusiasm about

the economic future, we borrowed $3 trillion
from bond markets and handed it out to citizens
in rough proportion to how rich they already
were. In the middle of a recovery. This is not a
useful thing for the government to do.[8]

Damn right it isn't. It's madness. Given that China is
now the major holder of US Treasury bonds, the Bush
administration in effect decided to borrow heavily from a
fast-emerging communist power in order to fund a con-
sumption splurge that was most pronounced among the
wealthiest 1% of Americans.[9] Figure that one out, if you can.

To be fair to President Bush, however, his approach to
revenue was not a new one. In 1980, the year when Planet
Ponzi started to turn, the average effective federal tax rate on
the median American household was 11.4%. By 2010, that
rate had plummeted to just 4.7%.[10] That is not a reasonable
amount for the average family to pay in exchange for
defense, social security, Medicare, Medicaid, homeland
security, the Department of Education, environmental protection, and various other services besides.

The results are all too predictable. If you want to understand why we have a deficit in the US, look at figure 3.2.
The graph is unusual in that it aggregates *all* sources of
government revenues: not just taxation but other fees,
charges, utility revenues, rents – any money that leaves your
pocket and ends up in the government's.[11]

The blunt truth is that government revenues haven't
been this low for fifty years. To return to the taxation levels
we experienced back then would be fine – I like low taxes –
but in the 1960s we were steadily paying down the national
debt. Low taxes (and other charges) were justified by

Figure 3.2: Total US government revenue, 1965–2010

Source: Christopher Chantrill, www.usgovernmentrevenue.com.

prudent finances. You have to earn the right to cut taxation, and we haven't: we've spent three decades having fun and racking up debt in the process.

In any case, American taxation is already low. If we consider only the OECD group of rich countries, taxes in the US are lower than they are in Canada. Lower than in Britain or any European OECD country. Lower too than they are in Australia and New Zealand. Lower than in Israel. In fact, there are just two 'rich world' countries with lower tax rates than ours: Chile and Mexico.[12] I'm not sure that most US citizens would willingly swap places with citizens of either of those countries.

We don't simply have a problem when it comes to the amount of tax collected. We have a huge problem when it comes to the way we collect taxes. Take corporate taxes as an example. We impose taxes at the second highest rate in the rich world (35%), yet the corporate tax code is riddled with incentives, subsidies, exemptions, and loopholes.[13] The result is crazy. We give firms a huge disincentive to earn money at home (because our basic tax rate is so high), while giving them huge incentives to play the system. And remember: the United States boasts some of the world's most innovative and entrepreneurial companies. If we give those guys an incentive to find ways around our tax code, they'll turn out to be world-beaters.

World-beaters like General Electric, for example.[14] GE earned $14.2 billion of profit in 2010, of which $5.1 billion was generated in the US. I'm guessing that you earned less than $5 billion that year, but I'm damn sure you had a more painful settlement with the taxman. In 2010, GE's net corporation tax obligation to the US government was sub-zero. The firm actually derived a net benefit from the government. In the five years to 2010, GE accumulated $26 billion in American profits and booked a net benefit of $4.1 billion from the IRS. That's completely insane. You don't, however, need to be GE to outperform in this way. Big Oil can play the same game to almost equal effect. According to a Citizens for Tax Justice report out in 2011, 'Over the past two years, Exxon Mobil reported $9,910 million in pretax US profits. But it enjoyed so many tax subsidies that its federal income tax bill was only $39 million – a tax rate of only 0.4%.'[15] It's true that to some extent these ultra-low figures are affected by the correction of prior year estimates; but a tax system that was not riddled with gamesmanship, loopholes, and exemptions would not see corrections on this scale – or the resulting wildly low tax outcomes. And, unsurprisingly, Exxon is not alone in experiencing such results. In 2008, the Government Accountability Office said that 72% of foreign corporations with businesses in the United States paid no federal income tax at all for at least one year between 1998 and 2005.[16]

There are countless other examples of huge, profitable

companies paying far less in tax than they would do in almost any other jurisdiction in the world. Our tax system ought to be giving companies incentives to invest, to innovate, and to grow. Instead, we're giving them incentives to hire tax lawyers – and generating compliance costs estimated at a staggering $163 billion a year.[17] The inevitable result: we collect far less in tax than we ought to. In 1952 – a year when, by the way, the United States led the world on every conceivable measure of industrial and commercial success – almost one-third of all federal tax receipts came from corporations. Today, that figure is under 10%.[18] It's bananas. And the answer is so obvious. We need a low rate of corporation tax – Ireland levies its rate at 12.5%, for example – and then we need to collect it. Like, actually knock on GE's front door, and say, 'Sorry, guys, but since you live here would you mind contributing?'

Similar problems affect the taxation of individuals. Nina Olson, the National Taxpayer Advocate, estimated in a December 2010 report that taxpayers spend a total of 6.1 billion hours a year complying with tax-filing requirements.[19] That's the equivalent of 3 million full-time jobs which could be spent doing something productive – like building cars or writing program code – and are instead used to generate paperwork. Because that paperwork is insanely complex, individuals end up caught in a vicious Catch-22. Taxpayers who honestly seek to comply with the law often make inadvertent errors and consequently make overpayments or suffer IRS enforcement action. Since that's not a particularly attractive option, many taxpayers seek instead to become sophisticated tax experts, constantly seeking loopholes, shelters, and exemptions. The result: everyone is stressed, financial incentives are muddled and contradictory, taxpayers spend way too much time and money on paperwork – while the government collects far less than it ought to.

Again, the answer is unbelievably simple. The number of exemptions needs to be slashed. At present, the US Treasury gives away about $1 trillion in exemptions and tax breaks.[20] That's the budget deficit right there. Meantime, our overall tax *rates* need to stay the same or come down. The incentives to play the system would be hugely reduced as a result. Fairness would improve and the rewards to hard work and enterprise would increase. It's so simple – but it isn't even in prospect.

The Pentagon

Since I've just enraged the Tea Party movement by supporting higher taxes, I may as well drive any remaining conservative readers into a fury by advocating that we also cut the defense budget. (If it's any consolation, I'm about to enrage liberals too. Either I'm dead right or I'm crazy.)

Our defense budget is a mess. I'm all for a strong military. I'm proud of all that they do for their country and proud of the decisive way that America has led the free world over the past six decades. I'm proud of the resolution with which we hunted for and then took out bin Laden. But that doesn't mean it makes sense to turn a money-hose on to the Pentagon and leave it running at full blast. No organization in the world will thrive under those conditions.

Let's start with the big picture. In 2010 the United States spent $698 billion on defense, 43% of the global total. That may sound like a high proportion, but it *under*states our position of dominance. For one thing, our oldest and closest allies also spend a lot on security. Britain, France, Japan, Germany, and Italy are all there in the top ten defense spenders, and neither India nor Saudi Arabia is exactly hostile. The United States and its closest allies account for just shy of 70% of global defense spending.[21] Are we expecting assault from outer space? Terrestrial enemies such as Iran, North Korea, and Syria are vastly outgunned by their neighbors, let alone by the United States.

What's more, the Department of Defense is called that for a reason. It isn't called the Department of Protecting the Entire World. Still less is it called the Department of Looking After African Fishermen, yet the DoD's AFRICOM command reports that its responsibilities

> include piracy and illegal trafficking, ethnic tensions, irregular militaries and violent extremist groups, undergoverned regions, and pilferage of resources. This last challenge includes oil theft, as well as widespread illegal fishing that robs the African people of an estimated $1 billion a year because their coastal patrols lack the capacity to find and interdict suspicious vessels within their territorial waters and economic exclusion zones.[22]

Excuse me? The key phrase in that bizarre paragraph is 'their coastal patrols.' Not ours. Not our patrols, not our coasts, not our fishermen, not our fish. A billion dollars a year is a lot to lose, but since when did the welfare of African fisherfolk become a US strategic priority? Why are ethnic tensions and pilferage of resources in Africa something that American citizens should spend their money on? And these things are expensive. In 2010 AFRICOM enjoyed a budget of $302 million, up from just $125 million in 2008/9.[23] Although these sums are small in the context of our runaway budgets, they're also indicative. At a time when you'd think the government would be thinking hard about every dollar it had to spend, it vastly increased the budget of a command structure which believes its remit includes limiting illegal fishing activity in Africa.

The same culture of spending and poor cost control runs rampant throughout the Pentagon. Take, for example, the F-35 Joint Strike Fighter. The program started, as so many of these things do, with a good idea: build a relatively cheap aircraft, produce it in large numbers, ensure it's versatile enough that – with a few tweaks – the same basic plane can serve for army, navy, and marine corps. The idea started out as a way to save money.

And then . . . the Pentagon went to work. Estimated costs per plane almost doubled. Including research and development costs, the anticipated procurement cost per aircraft currently stands at over $150 million.[24] The jump-jet version of the aircraft intended for the marine corps currently doesn't work and probably never will. Even the version intended for the navy is of questionable utility. The plane has a maximum range of 600 miles. China's fast-advancing missile technology means that our carriers will be pushed out into the western Pacific where they'll be able to threaten a few Pacific islanders and absolutely nothing else. Oh, and to ensure the right degree of stealthiness, the plane carries just *two* air-to-air missiles.

Now I'll admit I'm not the go-to guy for commentary on air combat effectiveness, but I'm not alone in questioning the F-35. Senator John McCain, hardly a security wimp, called the project a 'train wreck.' The head of the air dominance branch of the Air Combat Command says he wakes up 'in a cold sweat' thinking about it. *The Economist* reckons the plane will probably be obsolescent within 'a few years' of entering service. The lifetime cost of maintaining and operating this train wreck – a cost which American taxpayers will bear in full – is currently estimated at $1 trillion.[25]

Or take our aircraft carriers. A Ford Class carrier with a full complement of aircraft costs approximately $15–20 billion in hardware alone. (Manning, operating, maintaining, and controlling the ship costs far more again.) The United States boasts eleven such carrier groups. No other country possesses even one. Yet we're currently planning to maintain this huge overmatch, despite the fact that those multi-billion-dollar craft are ever more vulnerable to fairly cheap and increasingly sophisticated ballistic missiles. As Secretary of Defense Robert Gates caustically put it: 'You don't necessarily need a billion-dollar guided missile destroyer to chase down and deal with a bunch of teenage pirates wielding AK-47s and RPGs.' You do if you're the Pentagon.[26]

Cost extravagances of this kind are inevitable when there has been a longstanding culture of budgetary indiscipline. They arise in any organization that has been exposed to too much easy money for too long. (I should know: I've worked on Wall Street.) What's needed is a period of retrenchment. A focus on costs. A reformulation of strategic purposes and priorities. If these things are done right, the result will be a re-energized military. Leaner, stronger, more purposeful, more focused. Better able to carry out the tasks we assign it, less distracted by nonsense.

Obamacare

The Pentagon, however, is like some kind of budgetary Walmart, some fuel-sipping Japanese mini-car, in comparison with the beast which is health care. Even in those far-off days before Obamacare, the situation was appalling. Over successive administrations, through countless reforms, despite constant legislative attention, health care in the United States failed to deliver.

Take, for example, the most basic duty of a healthcare system: that it extends life. Of course we want other things too: we want our healthcare services to reduce pain, to respect our dignity, to discuss clinical choices. Heck, we probably want free coffee, comfortable waiting rooms and a short walk to the parking lot. But when it comes right down

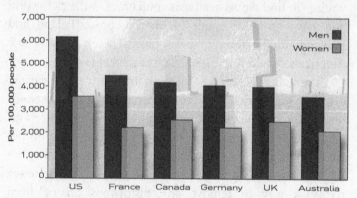

Figure 3.3: Potential years of life lost, per 100,000 people, selected countries

Source: OECD (figures for 2009 or most recent year available).

to it, we want our doctors and nurses to give us more years of life. Figure 3.3 sets out the potential years of life lost through premature death for the men and women of various major countries. The way this statistic works is by comparing actual age at death with expected age at death. So if you could, on the whole, expect to live to 75, the death of a 25-year-old would count as 50 years of life lost, the death of a 74-year-old as a single year only. On this measure, and considering all 29 countries for which the OECD has data, the United States scores worse than every nation except Hungary and Mexico for women. For men, the US scores worse than every country except those two, Poland, and Slovakia.

There's no way to excuse or explain away these figures. The American healthcare system allows far too many Americans to die early. No doubt we have better hospital coffee, some wonderful parking lots, some caring nurses, and some terrific doctors – but too many Americans die too young. To find worse healthcare outcomes in the rich world you have to travel south to Mexico, or to Poland and Hungary in the former Soviet bloc. There's no way any American should find these results acceptable.

Then there's the cost. The extraordinary, eye-watering, economy-destroying cost. No economy in the world spends on health care the way America does. We spend over twice what the British, Japanese, Italians, and Australians do per capita, and almost exactly twice what the French do. (The figures shown in figure 3.4 are based on purchasing power parity, a way to remove any distortions arising from constantly moving market exchange rates.)

Defenders of US health care like to point out that ours is a private sector system, true to the red-as-blood nature of

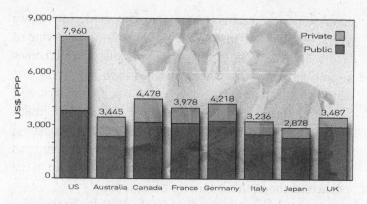

Figure 3.4: Healthcare spending per capita, selected countries

Source: OECD (figures for 2009 or most recent year available).

American capitalism. Yet if you look only at *public* spending on health care, we still outspend all those other countries I've just mentioned. Measured in the only way that matters – in dollars and cents – our government is *more* involved in health care than any other government in the world, with the one exception of tiny, socialist, oil-rich Norway. In effect, we pay for our health system twice over: once indirectly through taxes, once directly through insurance. (Most people will find that their employer picks up the tab, but that simply means that the employer has less money available for salaries. There are no free lunches.)

And of course, it's not just doctors and nurses we're paying for. We're paying for the massive administration costs arising from insurance company bureaucracy. We're paying for the huge costs of medical litigation, for all the cover-my-ass medical tests conducted as a protection against that litigation. We also pay in uncertainty and worry. You may have paid your healthcare premiums regularly for twenty years, but that won't necessarily stop your insurer trying to dodge a claim or chisel you out of your due when it comes to settling your bills. These anxieties inevitably come just when you least need them: when you're feeling sick and financially insecure. The exponentially rising cost of health care over recent decades has a lot to do with the stagnating incomes of ordinary American families. The economy has grown, but far too much of that growth has ended up in the pockets of the health insurance behemoth.

Although these things affect us all individually, they also have an impact at a corporate level. One of the reasons why the Big Three auto makers struggled against foreign competition was their legacy health costs: their obligation to fund the spiraling health costs of retirees. Those costs, which amounted to as much as $1,700 for every vehicle produced, handed a huge competitive advantage to Japanese and European auto makers seeking entry into the US market, a competitive advantage that Detroit was powerless to counteract.[27] And any global company considering where to build a new factory or research facility has to factor those costs into the equation. Build in the United States and face a huge healthcare bill? Or build elsewhere and let the government take care of those costs? For many companies, the answer will be obvious. And there's part of the explanation for the US's current high levels of joblessness and underemployment.

That was the background in 2008 when President Obama swept into power with a mandate for change. He had the inbox from hell already – Iraq, Afghanistan, banking crisis, recession – but the pressing need for healthcare reform dumped another huge problem on to the To Do list.

Right at the top of the reform agenda should have been the topic of cost. There was no other sane priority. In case you should doubt that, take a look at the projected costs of Medicare and Medicaid over the next seventy years in figure 3.5.* The data are drawn from a 2011 study conducted by the nonpartisan Congressional Budget Office. They present the CBO's 'alternative fiscal scenario,' which is in fact its core simulation, as it reflects various changes in the law which are widely expected to take place. In essence, the data in the graph represent the CBO's best guess of the future, assuming that there is no fundamental shift in policy.

That graph is one of the single most scary graphics in this book. It's not too much to say that Medicare and Medicaid are starting to kill the federal budget. Indeed, the CBO acknowledges precisely that. Its report includes a projection of federal debt out to only 2036, even though the projections for healthcare spending run all the way to 2085. Why? Because beyond 2036, the government's debt rises to more than 200% of GDP. To put it simply: within the space of a single generation, on current policies, as measured by a nonpartisan government statistical bureau, the government is going bankrupt. That's what the CBO data are telling us. The coming old age of the baby boomers is like a cost tsunami, still a few miles offshore but moving fast and heading straight toward us. Faced with this clear and present danger, the government needed to act. It needed to get a grip on costs first, deal with universal coverage second.

What we got was the inverse of that. In Obamacare, we

* Medicare is a federal insurance program, primarily there to help the elderly. Medicaid is an assistance program for those on low incomes (of any age), and bills are paid from a mixture of federal, state, and local funds.

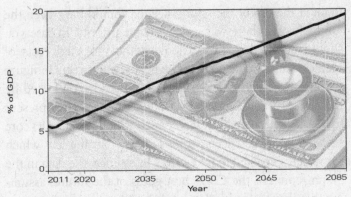

Figure 3.5: Projected spending on Medicare and Medicaid, 2011–2085

Source: 'CBO's 2011 long-term budget outlook,' Congressional Budget Office (www.cbo.gov), June 2011.

got a plan that aimed to ensure near-universal health coverage for Americans but one in which cost control was nowhere to be seen. It wasn't even part of the design. In frank comments made after he had left Capitol Hill, David Bowen, the former health staff director of the Senate Health, Education, Labor, and Pensions Committee, said: 'This [Obamacare] is a coverage bill, not a cost reduction bill. There is stuff here that will begin to address the issue of cost, but this is not a cost reduction bill with a bit of coverage on it – it is really trying to get coverage first.'[28]

Increasing the scope of health care before tackling the critical question of cost was always bound to be expensive, yet the CBO estimated that the reform would *reduce* the budget deficit by $119 billion over ten years.[29] Now that makes no sense. You can't expand healthcare coverage to reach some 30 million or so extra Americans and yet not experience a hike in costs. Needless to say, the reform does increase costs; it merely tries to balance those costs with additional taxation. Seeking to estimate those costs, the CBO placed the total burden of Obamacare at $940 billion over ten years. So, according to the plan's promoters, the cost tsunami which was heading our way before is still heading toward us, only this time it's swollen by another trillion dollars.

Unfortunately, those statistics make no sense. The true costs of Obamacare don't really kick in until around 2015.[30] So when the CBO projects a cost of $940 billion over the decade that runs from 2010 to 2019, it's actually projecting a relatively modest cost for the first five years (a total of $80 billion) and a huge cost ($715 billion) for the five years from 2015 to 2019: an average of $143 billion per annum. That's a huge sum of money.

Because the numbers in this book are frequently so vast, it's essential that we keep giving ourselves a sense of scale. Over four of those five years, the $143 billion annual costs of Obamacare amount to $572 billion, or, if we add a little interest, $600 billion. That's more than the entire national debt of Canada.[31] If our national finances were in a strong state, you could argue that this price was a price worth paying. At a time of funding crisis, it's an additional burden of insane proportions.

And then there's the question of whether the government's numbers are dependable. After all, those in charge of the planned reform had every incentive to massage the numbers down. And it so happens that we don't entirely need to trust the government's numbers, because we can review what happened to Mitt Romney's healthcare reforms in Massachusetts – effectively a prototype for President Obama's federal version. The experience in Massachusetts has been a double disappointment. First, the number of uninsured people remains stubbornly higher than was projected (and most of the uninsured who have taken out insurance have only done so thanks to extensive subsidy). Secondly, and more alarmingly, the costs are out of control. It is now estimated that 'Romneycare' will cost the state some $2 billion more than predicted. At the same time, health insurance premiums, which had increased more slowly than the national average, are now increasing 5.8% faster. The average employer-sponsored family health plan costs almost $14,000 a year, the highest rate in the nation.[32] In short, the likely effect of Obamacare, based on the closest statewide model in existence today, is that public costs will be substantially larger than anticipated while private costs will also grow more rapidly.

In short, Obamacare has taken the single worst-controlled area of government (and private) spending and severely exacerbated the problem, in the midst of recession and unrelenting funding pressures. It's insanity cubed.

The themes explored in this chapter – the fantasy figures on which the federal budget is based, the too-low taxes, the colossal waste of the Pentagon, the fearsome costs of Obamacare – these things go a long way to explain why we are currently spending a trillion and a half dollars more per annum than we are raising in tax. They explain why the US budget deficit is in the red and why, after three broadly peaceful decades, the US government has managed to end up owing $14 trillion while countries like Sweden have somehow managed to accumulate net assets.[33]

We'll explore in a later chapter just why politicians have

allowed this position to arise, but we can't quite leave the topic of the federal deficit without talking about the last-minute deal struck to raise the federal debt ceiling in July 2011. It's truly difficult to know who emerged from those negotiations with more dishonor. The Democrats needed to get specific about cuts to entitlements. The administration needed to get real about the need for austerity. The Republicans needed to put tax increases (or at least a bonfire of tax exemptions) on the table. None of them acted with any responsibility on their 'core' issues. Yet in deliberately threatening default, the Republican party took things one step further. They pointed a loaded weapon at the very heart of American prosperity and threatened to pull the trigger if their unreasonable demands weren't met. The bargaining tactic was as low, as stupid, and as destructive as I've witnessed in thirty years of trading the financial markets. Even Berlusconi has never behaved as badly.

When the ratings agency Standard and Poor's (S&P) promptly reduced the US credit rating by a notch to AA+ with long-term negative outlook, the firm came in for furious attack on every side.* But S&P was right. If anything, it was too cautious. The creditworthiness of any borrower rests principally on a test of *character*: the borrower's iron determination – or otherwise – to repay his debt. By posturing in Congress, and by evincing delight at the success of that posturing, the Republican party deliberately created doubt as to the fundamental character of the United States.

---

* Warren Buffett reacted angrily to the S&P downgrade, commenting that the US would be AAAA rated if such a rating existed. But Warren Buffett doesn't know his history. The US government has defaulted twice, in 1790 and in 1933. If something has already happened twice, it can happen again.

Would the US pay its debts come hell or high water? Or would it risk default because of a petty squabble? For a period of weeks, no one knew the answer. And though the immediate deadlock has been overcome, the answer is still as unclear as ever. That is a shameful fact.[34]

The problem runs deeper yet. A corporate borrower repays debt by earning profits. If its profits disappear, so too does its creditworthiness. A sovereign borrower has no business to operate, no profits to make. Ultimately, the creditworthiness of a sovereign borrower depends on its ability to levy tax and on the willingness of the populace to pay those taxes. The Tea Party movement and its leaders in Congress are deliberately corroding the government's legislative and administrative ability to levy tax. Every new impediment to that tax-raising ability is a further proof that S&P, alone among its peers, has recognized the grim truth about US politics today. Character matters, and our leaders are all out of the hard stuff.

All this sounds like a serious position for the country to be in, and it is. Unfortunately, however, it's only the beginning of an outline of the problem. The whole picture is so very much worse, it's hard to put numbers on it. Back in 2005, economists Jagadeesh Gokhale and Kent Smetters produced a careful study which estimated the value of the US fiscal gap – in effect, the country's true national debt – at a stunning $65.9 trillion, or about four and a half times American GDP. More than the GDP of the entire planet, in fact.[35]

That figure sounds so extreme, you might think it was based on some strange assumption, or some totally inappropriate manipulation of the data. Unfortunately, the exact opposite is the case. Gokhale and Smetters' data are based on *the same accounting standards that any private sector firm is obliged to employ every time it draws up a set of accounts*. Those are accounting standards that make perfect sense, that drive the investment patterns of businesses and individuals across the world, the ones you would adopt if you went into business.

And it gets worse, because that $66 trillion number is now six years out of date. Eagle-eyed readers may have noticed that the US economy has deteriorated rather sharply since 2005. Economic prospects are worse, federal entitlement programs still hopelessly overblown. The consequences for US indebtedness are catastrophic. The only good news is that, in a way, once you're bust you're bust and it doesn't make too much difference just how bust you are. Unraveling that whole sorry tale is the subject of the next chapter. (There is some good news in this book, by the way, but you'll have to wait for it a while. Ponzi schemes create a lot of things, but warm and fuzzy good-news stories aren't among them.)

FOUR

A hole as big as the world

ABALANCE SHEET IS in essence so simple that you don't need to be an accountant to understand one.

On the left-hand side, you have your assets. Stuff you own. Cash, other financial assets, inventories, property, equipment. If you own it, it's an asset. The liability side is simple too. Here you write down all the money you owe. That includes money you've borrowed from banks or the bond markets. It also includes obligations you incur in the normal way of running a business: money you owe to your utility suppliers, your landlord, your raw material providers, and so on. And it includes pension obligations.

Now, before we start to talk about the government's Ponzi-ish approach to pensions, we need to define some terms. There are two main ways in which an employer can offer a pension. The prudent method is for the employer to commit to a certain level of pension contributions for each employee. So if a given employee earns a salary of $50,000, the employer might agree to contribute $5,000 each year into a pension fund for the benefit of that particular employee. Because this type of plan fixes the employer's contribution, it is known as a 'defined contribution' plan and – if the employer keeps current with its contributions – there's no reason why any pension liability should mount up. He or she just needs to pay the agreed amount into the pension fund and that's it for the year. As you might predict, this type of pension is popular with employers, because it's so simple. If the payments are sufficiently generous, employees can be well provided for, while employers understand precisely what the cost of their obligations is.

Because defined contribution plans are simple, clear, and fiscally responsible, they have proved highly unpopular with government. Instead, the US government at every level – federal, state, and municipality – has preferred to award 'defined benefit' plans to its employees. From an employee's perspective, these plans are great: they eliminate risk. Instead of knowing how much money will be *contributed* to your pension scheme, you know the income you will end up *receiving* in retirement. The risky business of how much money has to be put aside to create that income has shifted from employees to employer.

That's only the first move of the government's Pension Ponzi scheme, however. After all, defined benefit schemes used to be very popular in the private sector too, and private sector employers were generally careful to ensure that their plans were properly funded. In order to figure out whether a plan had enough cash in it or not, employers simply made the following calculation. Step One: they figured out the stream of pensions they would be paying out in the future, based on the number and age of their employees and on estimated life expectancies. Step Two: they calculated how much money they would need in their pension schemes today to fully fund those future payments.

Carrying out those calculations is not an exact science, but it is a science. You know that your employees won't, on average, all drop dead one year into their retirement. You also know that they won't all live to be a hundred. Maybe your calculations will be a little out, but you should expect, more or less, to hit the target.

Which brings us back to the concept of pension obligations and how they ought to figure on a properly drawn up balance sheet.

Let's say that you and your professional advisors have figured out you owe your current and future retirees $10 million. Let's also assume that you've already put aside $8 million to cover those obligations. That means your net pension liability is $2 million. That's your best estimate of the money you owe to cover those pension liabilities. It might be a little more or a little less, depending on how you work those calculations, but the approximate number is hardly a mystery.

Please also note that there is nothing fictitious about that $2 million debt. You have made a legally binding promise to your employees. You must meet your pension obligations or face court action and, if necessary, bankruptcy. Although pension obligations may not fall due until well into the future, that's true of countless other liabilities too. The Massachusetts Institute of Technology recently issued a 100-year bond, for example, and ten- and thirty-year obligations are commonplace. In other words, though the exact amount owed may be a little unclear, you owe real money to real people and that debt can be enforced through the courts. It's called a liability because it is a liability. A debt. Money owed.

Public employee pension liabilities

So much for concepts. A prudent government led by wise men and women and blessed with thoughtful and farsighted legislators would do the obvious thing. In each and every year, such a government would put money aside so that its future obligations were properly funded. It might, let's say, run up liabilities of $2 trillion, but it would take care to set aside an equivalent amount in assets. Net liability: $0. Such a government would be looking after its retirees *and* its taxpayers; its present *and* its future.

That is not the government that we have, and it's not one we have ever had. The government we have has taken two huge leaps away from financial common sense. Each leap has plunged the country further into debt – and this is a debt that isn't even counted in the government's $14 trillion debt figure.

The first leap is simple: countless state and municipal governments simply don't set aside what they need to. Even by their own calculations, their pension funds are grossly underfunded. According to a definitive 2009 study of 116 state pension schemes conducted by Robert Novy-Marx and Joshua Rauh, the total amount of assets in those funds was $1.94 trillion.[1] The total reported liabilities were $2.98 trillion. In other words, even if you trust the accounting methods used by these pension schemes, there was a funding gap of over a trillion dollars.

Most places, a trillion-dollar hole would get a little airtime, but not on Planet Ponzi. On Planet Ponzi, a trillion-dollar hole is a lovely thing. It's a place where you can hide your debt, allowing dangerous liabilities to accumulate out of sight, out of mind. On the other hand, a trillion-dollar hole, nice as it is, has one big disadvantage: it isn't larger. Which brings us to the government's next great leap away from financial responsibility.

When you're looking at your future pension obligations, you have to figure out what those obligations are worth *today* – what they're worth in 'present value' terms, according to the jargon. Making that calculation involves choosing a discount rate. What the government *ought* to do is to use bond yields to derive their discount rates. That's what the private sector does. That's what normal accounting standards require. It is, for reasons I won't get into here, what common sense requires. (Wikipedia has a useful entry on 'net present value' for anyone wanting to understand the arithmetic a little better.)

Trouble is, using bond rates would make the government's pension liabilities look frighteningly large. So the government essentially plucks its figures from thin air. It deliberately cheats on its discount rates, employing a system where *the more risk it takes, the smaller its obligations appear*. The system sounds so close to criminal fraud, I wouldn't blame you if you didn't believe me, so here's a quote from pensions expert Novy-Marx giving testimony to the Congressional Committee on Oversight and Government Reform:

> If I take a dollar out of my right pocket, and put it into my left pocket, I presume that you all will agree that doing so has made me neither richer nor poorer. The idea that moving money from one pocket to another could somehow make you richer insults common sense.
>
>   Yet ... [under government] rules a plan's reported financial status improves when it takes

on more investment risk. When a plan moves a dollar from its right pocket (bonds) to its left pocket (stocks), it magically gets 'richer' (less underfunded).

This logic is clearly flawed.[2]

Flawed? It's insane.

Using proper accounting methods, Novy-Marx and Rauh calculate the true value of the state and municipal pension liability at $5.20 trillion. When you deduct the $1.94 trillion of pension assets that have already been set aside, you get a net liability of $3.26 trillion. That trillion-dollar hole just got three times bigger.

You can call this kind of financial management flawed or insane; the truth is that the management of government pensions in the US is a fraud. It's a fraud committed on state employees, whose pension plans aren't properly funded. It's a fraud committed on voters, because the financial ill-health of our country is being deliberately concealed. And it's a fraud committed on US bondholders, because our public debt figures pretend that our liabilities are $3 trillion smaller than they actually are.

These things might sound calamitous, but abstract. I doubt, however, they'll sound that way if you happen to be a government employee in Ohio. If you do, the pension benefits that have been promised to you and your colleagues are projected to end up costing the state more than 50% of its future total tax revenues. Do you truly believe that your pension is safe, given that fact? And if you're a government employee in Colorado or Rhode Island, you'd better not be laughing, because your pension is in the same precarious position.

In New Hampshire, California, Oklahoma, Illinois, Oregon, South Carolina, New Jersey, Kentucky, Mississippi, South Dakota, Missouri, Alabama, and New Mexico, pension benefits are projected to swallow between 30% and 40% of future state tax revenues – a liability so extreme that, from a purely financial perspective, these states are probably best seen as bankrupt, thereby threatening countless past and present employees who depend on them for their retirement income.[3] That's the thing about Ponzi schemes: when they collapse they hurt people, and the bigger you build the scheme, the more people you're going to injure.

If you're a federal employee, by the way, the news is both good and bad. It's good in the sense that military and other federal employees have pension schemes that are generally better funded than those elsewhere in government. It's bad in the sense that they're funded exclusively with US Treasury bonds. That means, in effect, that your pension fund depends entirely on the generosity of future generations of taxpayers, and on the federal government's ability to manage down its debt without default. Neither of those things seems very dependable at present.[4]

Social security

These are somber thoughts. The federal debt is $14 trillion and growing fast, yet it excludes a further $3.3 trillion which the states owe to their public servants – owe, and in many cases, cannot pay. Consequently, as a nation, we owe over $17 trillion, which is substantially more than the $15 trillion or so we earn in a year. If we all worked hard for the next 365 days and handed over every single penny of our earnings to the IRS, the country would still be in debt afterwards.

But, serious as the state-level pension crisis is, it's only the tip of a vastly larger iceberg. The pensions owed to public servants are legal, enforceable, courtroom-ready obligations, but that's not the only kind of obligation a government can create for itself. As a nation, we have also made public promises to *all* our current and future retirees, telling them that if they contribute to social security via the Federal Insurance Contributions Act (FICA) taxes, we will make pension payments to cover their old age. That's not a legally enforceable promise, as it happens, but it is quite clearly a promise of immense financial and ethical weight. Along with defense and medical support for the poor or the elderly, it's an undertaking that lies at the heart of the contract between government and citizen. If the government dishonors that insurance pledge, it will be breaking its faith with huge numbers of Americans, many of whom will have planned their life journeys on the assumption that they can trust their government's word.

It's a rash assumption.

Every year, the board of trustees of the Federal Old-Age and Survivors Insurance and Federal Disability Insurance Trust Funds produce a report. Since OASDI is the key component of our social security programs, and since those programs account for the single largest slice of federal spending, that report should be of some interest to us all. The trouble is that most of us don't wait eagerly for the board of trustees of the FOASI&FDI Trust Funds to produce their next report and, even if we did, we'd have to know to flip straight through to table IV.B7 on page 67, because that's how far you have to go before you get to the juice.[5] Which is a pity. Because what you find in that table is enough to make you fall off your chair. In a calm, dry, technocratic presentation, that table tells you that the social security program is $18.8 trillion underfunded.

Nineteen trillion dollars. That's a hole so huge it dwarfs everything else we've looked at so far. I would start to compute what 19 trillion dollars actually looks like (a tower of money reaching far out into space, a coil of money looping round the globe) or figure out what 19 trillion dollars could buy (at current prices, the entire US stock market plus the entire Chinese one), or seek to compute, in thousands of negative IQ points, just exactly how dumb our politicians must be to have gotten us into this hole . . . only there's no point in doing that, because we haven't finished reckoning up the damage. Sad to say, there's worse to come.

Medicare and fiscal gap accounting

Medicare also boasts a board of trustees. That board also issues an annual report. That report is also somewhat dry, somewhat technical, somewhat hard to read. Which, again, is a pity, because it too tells you things you really, really ought to know.

The two parts of Medicare with huge implications for the budget are Part B (medical insurance) and Part D (prescription drug plans). Because of the way the relevant laws are written, it's impossible for the board of trustees to record any unfunded obligation since any deficit has to be filled from general tax revenue. Which is a nice idea, except that the general tax revenue actually needs to be there. Someone has to pay it. And the greater the liabilities racked up on the entitlements side, the bigger the burden on future taxpayers. So if you're curious about the burden which the government is choosing to create on your behalf, you might want to turn to table III.C15 on page 130 and table III.C23 on page 146 of the board's 2011 annual report. If you do that, you'll find that the Part B burden is expected to be $22.4 trillion. The Part D burden is expected to be $16.1 trillion.[6]

By this point your head may be reeling, so I've set out the key numbers you need to know in table 4.1.

The GDP of the entire world is about $60 trillion. The US government owes over $75 trillion. In 2009, the median household income in the United States was approximately $50,000.[7] Remember, that's household income, not individual income, so it requires you and your spouse or partner to generate it together. If the two of you patriotically decided to put your shoulders to the wheel and pay off that accumulated debt all by yourselves, it would take you 1,498 million years to do so. (I'm ignoring interest payments here, because even patriotism has its limits.) I don't know how the world will look in 1.5 billion years' time, but 1.5 billion years

	$trn
US financial debt outstanding	14.6
Unfunded state and local pension liabilities	3.3
Social security unfunded obligation	18.8
Medicare Part B tax burden	22.4
Medicare Part D tax burden	16.1
Total debt and unfunded obligations	75.2

Table 4.1: US debt and unfunded obligations (various dates)

Source: See discussion in text.

ago, the planet was in the middle of the Proterozoic Eon. The planet hadn't too long ago encountered its first multi-cellular organisms and the big new thing was fungi. There were no plants. No vertebrates or invertebrates. Dinosaurs lay way, way into the future. Ditto mammals. Double ditto humanity. Triple ditto the invention of agriculture, the first cities, the origin of writing. And from that unimaginably distant point to this, you and your partner would need to toil away, earning $50,000 a year, not one penny of which you could keep, in order to generate the funds needed to pay off the US government's debt.[8]

At this point, however, I need to come clean. I don't believe these stats. With one exception, every element in the table above comes from official government data. Those data are publicly available online. You can verify them yourself with a few clicks of your mouse, and I encourage you to do so. The sole unofficial element is the $3.3 trillion funding hole in those state and local pension schemes. The official figure there is around $1 trillion and is based on obviously false accounting, but you can use it if you prefer.

Yet no matter how impeccable the sources of my data, I don't believe them. The truth is that once you start to look at the crazy mathematics of our government spending, you start to disbelieve everything. When the Bush tax cuts were brought in, they were, technically speaking, temporary. They were meant to expire. Yet the Bush administration created them knowing that future legislatures would find it almost intolerably hard not to extend them. So temporary came to mean permanent. Yet when the Congressional Budget Office drew up its forecasts, it was constrained by the terms of its mandate to base its numbers on the assumption that existing law would be implemented in full

– that is, assuming the Bush tax cuts would expire. Although government statisticians themselves are honorable and truthful people, the dodges forced on them by government mean that we can't trust their data. Or rather, we can trust it in one direction only. We know that the true position of the United States is at least as bad as that $75.2 trillion statistic implies – it's certainly not going to be better than that – but broader, less optimistic estimates imply that the true position is very much worse.

Guarantees and other contingent liabilities

For one thing, when the mortgage giants Fannie Mae and Freddie Mac were taken into conservatorship, their debts were effectively nationalized. While those two misshapen twins had always enjoyed an implicit guarantee, that guarantee now came bound in iron. The conservatorship therefore added around $5.4 trillion of financial debt to the government burden.[9] When S&P (quite rightly) down-graded the US Treasury it also downgraded the debt of Fannie Mae and Freddie Mac, recognizing – again quite rightly – that the performance of those debts is entirely dependent on government support.[10]

It's true, of course, that both Fannie and Freddie come with plenty of financial assets alongside their debts. Yet it's not appropriate simply to cancel one off against the other. In the first place, debts are debts are debts. You have to pay them off, no matter what happens to the assets. The debts are unconditional. And secondly, just think about why Fannie and Freddie find themselves in conservatorship in the first place. They're there because, as part of their contribution to Planet Ponzi, they piled up heaps of crappy subprime assets, whose true value stands far below historic cost. What's more, as we'll see in a later chapter, the American housing market remains acutely vulnerable. To date, there has been carnage in the subprime market, but relatively little blood spilled in the prime or commercial markets. That precarious calm, however, is unlikely to last. Further dips in the price of housing will start to generate huge cracks even in the prime market. Those cracks will, in turn, cause a wave of distress sales – foreclosures, and homeowners seeking to escape the burden of negative equity – and those sales will force prices lower still.

In short, though the government's housing debts are unquestionably real, the associated assets are anything but. So we should strike out $75 trillion and replace the figure with something over $80 trillion . . . but even this total still represents only *actual* liabilities, not *contingent* ones. A contingent liability is one that may or may not be incurred, depending on how things pan out. As you would by now expect, the federal government has been notably promiscuous in incurring contingent liabilities, tending to treat its guarantees as effectively costless to the taxpayer.

And that's a nonsense. Guarantees are never costless. Take, for example, the Federal Deposit Insurance Corporation (FDIC), which is the federal body that insures bank deposits in insured institutions up to a limit of $250,000 per depositor per bank. Pretty much any bank on Main Street is an insured institution and, if you step into such a bank, you will see a notice stating that 'deposits are backed by the full faith and credit of the United States Government.' No depositor supported by this guarantee has ever lost so much as a dime since the FDIC came into being in 1933.[11]

That's a creditable record, yet you can't judge the future by the past. Financial shocks tend to be violent, not gradual; abrupt, not predictable. And the mathematics behind that FDIC guarantee look frightening. Insured deposits total some $6.2 trillion. The insurance is legally binding (unlike the promises made with respect to social security or Medicare, for example), so that $6.2 trillion can't simply be withheld if it were ever called upon. That colossal commitment is currently supported by just $10 billion, or around 0.16% of potential liabilities.[12] In an era of banking crisis, of concerns about liquidity and capital sufficiency, that's an insanely low level of support. Indeed, the FDIC's own financial statements reflect the likely insufficiency of funds, with the fund balance in negative territory for 2009 and 2010. And bear in mind that deposit insurance represents just one of the government's implicit or explicit guarantee programs.

The true picture

In the end, there is no single precise measure of the US government's indebtedness. That's partly because it's hard to compute liabilities, partly because any projections are necessarily very long-term and uncertain. Nevertheless, the Congressional Budget Office itself recognizes the catastrophic state of the country's finances. Departing from its normal carefully neutral language, it commented in a recent update document that 'beyond the 10-year projection period, further increases in federal debt relative to the nation's output almost surely lie ahead if certain policies remain in place . . . [If current policies remain intact] the resulting deficits will cause federal debt to skyrocket.'[13]

'Skyrocket' is correct. Whether that debt will stop at the stratosphere or whether it's going to keep on going into outer space we don't yet know. What we do know is the scale of the problem we have already accrued. One economist who has made a lifetime study of fiscal gap computations is Laurence Kotlikoff of Boston University. He uses CBO data to determine the present value of our unfunded commitments – that is, he uses government data to model the country's true level of indebtedness. That type of computation is the *only* mathematically and financially complete way to calculate overall debt. On this basis, Kotlikoff puts the true level of US indebtedness somewhere in the region of $202 trillion.

The blunt truth, of course, is that the US is bust. It cannot, even remotely, fulfill its obligations. In the first chapter of this book I quoted Kotlikoff's sobering words about the coming crisis, but at that stage you didn't have enough background to understand precisely what was involved. You do now. And what Kotlikoff had to say was this:

> Let's get real. The U.S. is bankrupt. Neither spending more nor taxing less will help the country pay its bills . . .
>
> How can the [$202 trillion] fiscal gap be so enormous?
>
> Simple. We have 78 million baby boomers who, when fully retired, will collect benefits from Social Security, Medicare, and Medicaid that, on

average, exceed per-capita GDP. The annual costs of these entitlements will total about $4 trillion in today's dollars. Yes, our economy will be bigger in 20 years, but not big enough to handle this size load year after year.

This is what happens when you run a massive Ponzi scheme for six decades straight, taking ever larger resources from the young and giving them to the old while promising the young their eventual turn at passing the generational buck.

Herb Stein, chairman of the Council of Economic Advisers under U.S. President Richard Nixon, coined an oft-repeated phrase: 'Something that can't go on, will stop.' True enough. Uncle Sam's Ponzi scheme will stop. But it will stop too late.

And it will stop in a very nasty manner. The first possibility is massive benefit cuts visited on the baby boomers in retirement. The second is astronomical tax increases that leave the young with little incentive to work and save. And the third is the government simply printing vast quantities of money to cover its bills.

Most likely we will see a combination of all three responses with dramatic increases in poverty, tax, interest rates and consumer prices. This is an awful, downhill road to follow, but it's the one we are on. And bond traders will kick us miles down our road once they wake up and realize the U.S. is in worse fiscal shape than Greece.[14]

There is, weirdly, some good news buried in this avalanche of disaster. If a system is broken, it has to be fixed;

and this system is broken so completely, so absolutely, that the fixing is closer now than ever before. What's more, it's obvious what needs to be done. Tax revenue has to increase. Entitlements have to be cut. There is no alternative. If a politician tells you there's some other solution available, he or she is either lying or stupid.

It also becomes obvious that those politicians who pretend there are other solutions don't truly care about the things they pretend to care about. If Democrats genuinely cared about protecting the elderly, the poor, and the sick, they would want to reform welfare programs so they weren't headed for bankruptcy. They would be promoting bills to rein in entitlements, for the longer-term benefit of the constituencies they claim to represent. If Republicans genuinely cared about fiscal conservatism, they would recognize that current tax revenues are hopelessly insufficient to deal with our obligations and would be bringing forward measures to slash tax exemptions, loopholes, and other dodges. (Those things are all more important than raising rates, though some tax rates may also need to rise.)

Well, if Republicans don't, in fact, care about fiscal responsibility and Democrats don't, in fact, care about the poor, sick, and elderly, who *do* they care about? That question is the one we turn to next.

FIVE

How to win friends and influence people

ONE OF THE NOTABLE features of Ponzi schemes – the point of them, in fact – is that they make their promoters very, very rich. Charles Ponzi bought a bank and thought about buying a battleship. (He wanted to turn it into a floating shopping mall.) Bernie Madoff wasn't daft enough to buy a battleship; he was simply content to live the gilded life of New York's super-rich, without a care for those whose stolen money he relied upon. If we're claiming that the US government and (as we'll come to see) Wall Street are running huge Ponzi schemes, we should expect to find some beneficiaries: the Charles Ponzis, the Bernie Madoffs.

Following the collapse of the mortgage market in 2008, it's been common enough to point an accusing finger at the bankers who caused it. I don't disagree with that accusation – quite the opposite – but a Ponzi scheme as wide and as deep and as old as the one we're considering is hardly likely to have been promoted by a mere handful of bankers working in one subsection of the financial markets. We'd expect to see a broader group of individuals involved – and reaping some stunning rewards. Any data that suggested such a group existed would be powerful evidence contributing to the overall hypothesis.

Evidence such as the graph in figure 5.1, for example. This chart plots the income (including capital gains) of the top 1% of US earners as a proportion of total national income. What it shows is that, from the late 1970s onwards, the income share taken by the super-rich has grown enormously – so much so that their share of total income today is nearly two and a half times what it was in the mid-1970s. And that's just their *share*: naturally, since total incomes have grown substantially over the same period,

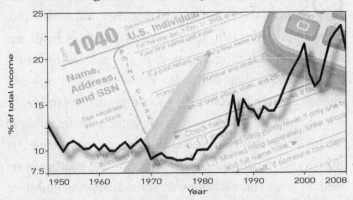

Figure 5.1: Income of the top 1% earners in the US, 1950–2008

Source: Thomas Piketty and Emmanuel Saez, 'Income inequality in the United States, 1913–1998,' *Quarterly Journal of Economics*, 118 (1), 2003, pp. 1–39. A longer and updated version is available in A. B. Atkinson and T. Piketty, eds, *Top Incomes over the Twentieth Century: A Contrast between Continental European and English-Speaking Countries* (Oxford University Press, 2007). The tables have been updated to 2008 and made available online at
http://g-mond.parisschoolofeconomics.eu/topincomes/.

their incomes measured in absolute terms grew very much faster than that.

The increase in the incomes of the rich has been widely noted, widely reported. Yet the appropriate political conclusion to draw is hotly contested. Trickle-down theory, for example, suggests that if the rich are left to get very rich, their efforts will benefit the poor and middling in society. That explanation, unfortunately, is not a very good one. As figure 5.2 overleaf illustrates, the poorest in society have seen the lowest income growth, a mere 11%, across the entire 27-year period since 1979. Those in the middle – the second, third, fourth, and most of the fifth quintiles – have done OK. They've worked hard, gotten a little richer, seen a little improvement in their standards of living. But those at the top, the putative 'Ponzi class,' have grown vastly richer. In real terms (that is, adjusted for changes in the cost of living) the richest 1% have seen their annual after-tax income rise from a (prosperous) $337,000 to an astonishing $1,200,000.[1] Bear in mind that that's an income figure. Not a lottery win. Not some one-time bonus or payoff. Those who make their nests in the very top branches of the American income tree expect $1.2 million each and every year – well, how else would you keep up the payments on your yacht?

At this point, the trail starts to get quite interesting. In previous chapters, we've noted that the US government has run up debts of somewhere between $75 trillion (if you believe the government's figures) and $202 trillion (if you believe independent experts). The data presented so far in this chapter show that a very small group of people have become very, very rich indeed. If we were sleuths – if we were playing Columbo, or Marlowe, or the invincible Poirot – we would, however, be forced to note that the coexistence

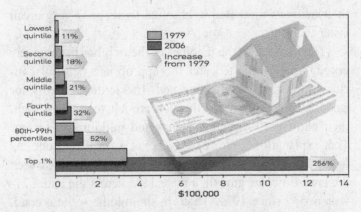

Figure 5.2: Average annual US household income after taxes and benefits, 1979 and 2006 (2006 dollars)

Source: Congressional Budget Office.

of a serious crime (the bankrupting of America) and the presence of some possible beneficiaries (the very wealthy) doesn't itself prove that the two things are connected. So we need to dig a little further.

Fortunately, some of that digging has already been done. The nonprofit and nonpartisan Center for Responsive Politics has patiently compiled statistics on political lobbying since 1998, using data made available by the Senate Office of Public Records. The sums involved are not small and, as you'd expect from the accelerating nature of any Ponzi scheme, are growing fast. At the start of the millennium, the amount of money spent lobbying Washington every year was around $1.5 billion; over the following ten years it's more than doubled, to around $3.5 billion annually. The total spend increased right through the banking crisis, right through the recession. As you'd expect, our friends on Wall

Street are more than happy to play their part in keeping the pressure on legislators: the securities and investment industry has invested some $874 million in lobbying between 1998 and 2011, the insurance industry a further $1,617 million.[2] (We'll explore some other curious facts about these industries in a later chapter.)

More important than the sums of money themselves is what they buy you. In 2010, researchers Hui Chen, David Parsley, and Ya-wen Yang systematically explored the effect of lobbying on the financial results of major corporations.[3] Their raw data are interesting enough. Take, for example, the simple question of which companies spend the most on lobbying. Chen et al.'s top ten, listed in table 5.1 overleaf, include a number of interesting names, many of which are already familiar to us.[4]

We haven't yet arrived at Chen et al.'s punchline, yet the data are already eye-opening. General Electric has the gall to pay no tax in the United States, yet outspends all rivals on influencing our legislators. (Oh, and it thinks its status in the US business community buys Jeff Immelt, GE's chief executive, the right to be part of President Obama's inner circle. A perfect choice, right? If the company paid any taxes, it might have a conflict of interest. As it is – no conflict.)

Next on the list, Altria (the owner of Philip Morris) makes its money by selling lethal and addictive products to American citizens, and spends a lot of it on ensuring it is given a hearing by our lawmakers. Lockheed is wildly over budget on a critical weapons program but shame, apparently, doesn't stop it from buying favors in Washington. As for the bailout twins AIG and General Motors, I have to admit that no investment I've ever made has come close to matching the stunning multiyear returns

Rank (2005)	Firm	Lobbying spend ($m)	Comment
1	General Electric	18.8	Doesn't like paying tax.
2	Altria	13.6	Makes cigarettes. Which kill you.
3	Northrop Grumman	13.6	Arms manufacturer. Multiple violations of Arms Export Control Act, International Traffic in Arms Regulations. Multiple allegations of overcharging the US government and concealing serious faults in equipment.
6	AIG	8.5	Received $183 billion in federal bailout support 2008/9.
7	General Motors	7.8	Received $52 billion in federal bailout support 2008/9.
9	Lockheed Martin	7.3	Makes the F-35, a $1 trillion 'train wreck.'
10	Exxon Mobil	7.0	Doesn't like paying tax.

Table 5.1: America's best lobbyists

Source: Hui Chen, David C. Parsley, and Ya-wen Yang, 'Corporate lobbying and financial performance,' April 28, 2010, available from the Social Science Research Network (www.ssrn.com).

which they managed to generate. For an entry ticket that cost just $8.5 million in 2005, AIG secured funding of $183 billion just four years later, an *annual* return of 1,111%. The folks at General Motors, poor saps, obviously played their hand badly, because they received federal funds of just $52 billion, an annual return only just over 800%.[5] General Motors, by the way, has still not repaid its loans to the US government, and I for one am skeptical that it ever will.*

---

* You're confused? Perhaps you thought GM had already paid back its loans. Well, yes, so it has – using one pot of bailout money to repay another pot of bailout money. Neil Barofsky, the inspector general charged with overseeing the Troubled Assets Relief Program (TARP), commented: 'Remember that the source of this money is just other TARP money.' That's how you repay a loan on Planet Ponzi.

You might well be tempted to dismiss some of these comments. You could argue that the banking crisis was unique, a once-in-a-century disaster that demanded and received a once-in-a-century response. You could argue that Lockheed Martin and Northrop Grumman are makers of weapons, and therefore certain to be tied closely to their major customer, and inevitably involved in a number of large, costly, and complex projects, some of which will go wrong. Well, perhaps. But it's striking how successful lobbying can be, across a very broad range of industries and issues. Take for example this story, reported by the *Washington Post* in 2006:

> A few years ago, a coalition of 60 corporations –
> including Pfizer, Hewlett-Packard and Altria –
> made an expensive wager. They spent $1.6
> million in lobbying fees – a hefty amount even by
> recent K Street standards – to persuade Congress
> to create a special low tax rate that they could
> apply to earnings from their foreign operations
> for one year.
>
> The effort faltered at first, but eventually the
> bet paid off big. In late 2004, President Bush
> signed into law a bill that reduced the rate to 5
> percent, 30 percentage points below the existing
> levy. More than $300 billion in foreign earnings
> has since poured into the United States, saving
> the companies roughly $100 billion in taxes.[6]

An investment of $1.6 million? A payoff of $100 billion? That doesn't sound like any commercial or financial investment I've ever made, or ever come across in the normal, ethical course of business. That's the kind of return which has the whiff of a Ponzi scheme to me. The same whiff hangs around *Fortune* magazine's estimate that Lockheed earned a return on its political investment of 163,536% since 1999, or that Boeing clocked up returns of 142,000%.[7] And bear in mind that the $100 billion which Pfizer and others saved in tax was money that the US Treasury did not have. Remember that the costs of the weapons contracts achieved by Lockheed and others have to come from the public purse. No wonder federal tax revenues are at a fifty-year low, that the deficit is at an all-time high. No wonder corporations play an ever smaller part in contributing to the welfare of Americans. No wonder the federal government has a debt crisis of planet-swallowing proportions.

Either we're dead right or we're crazy.

But let's get back to Chen's study. Rather than extrapolate from individually astonishing anecdotes, Chen and his colleagues systematically explored the question of whether lobbying was associated with better-than-expected financial returns. The researchers were careful. They explored various different measures of financial return and specified their model in a number of different ways. But their conclusion was robust no matter which way they chose to look at things. In their words, the data 'are consistently positive and continue to support the conclusion that lobbying expenditures are statistically significantly positively correlated with financial performance.' Bluntly put, lobbying works. It boosts profits and stock prices. Chen's data also demonstrate that the more you lobby, the more money you make. This is an arms race where the more you spend, the more you win. Poor old Exxon Mobil – suffering under the lash of its 0.4% corporate tax rate – simply made the mistake of not spending enough. No doubt the folk in its executive suite are currently figuring out how to do better.

Companies, however, are not the ultimate beneficiaries of all this hard work. Companies, after all, are merely legal entities, obligated to pass their profits through to their stockholders in the form of dividends and capital appreciation. It would, therefore, be natural to presume that ordinary shareholders end up gaining from all this lobbying effort. Though US citizens might lose the benefit of corporate tax revenues and find themselves overspending to a crazy degree on weapons programs and the like, at least they might expect to see their share portfolios and pension funds blossoming. What the left hand loses, the right hand gains.

Only, strange to say, that isn't what happened. If you invested $1,000 in the S&P index on January 1, 2000 and took it out on August 17, 2011 (the day I'm writing this paragraph), you'd find it was worth just $812. If you'd reinvested dividends as you received them, that would have bumped up your return, but you'd still be looking at a strangely small amount after more than a decade of investment. (By way of comparison, gold has returned over 525% in that time frame.)

One of the rules of poker – and of the bond markets, and of life – is that if you don't know who the sucker is, it's you. Take a look again at figure 5.1 at the start of this chapter. The rewards of our modern American economy flow to a tiny subset of people. If your household is in the 90th income percentile (if, in other words, you do better than 89% of all households in America), your income over the last three decades will only just have kept pace with the average.[8] According to data released by the Census Bureau, real median household incomes in 2010 haven't budged from where they were in 1996. Indeed, because healthcare costs have increased by some $5,400 over and above the rate of inflation, you could argue that real income has effectively declined in the period.[9] It's a truly terrible record. Understanding exactly where the money went will pre-occupy us for much of this book, yet some clues are so obvious they hardly need a Poirot to decipher them.

Take tax, for example. We live in an era of fiscal crisis, yet it's a crisis in the midst of abundance: high company profits, exceptional incomes among the very rich. Plenty of people are suffering in this recession and will suffer more before it's over, but Wall Street bonuses are still huge, executive pay still riding high. In any rational political system, taxation revenue would flow from all that abundance to mitigate the distress elsewhere. But that's no longer how politics operates in Washington. We've already seen how successful corporations have been in avoiding tax. The same is true of the very rich. Over the same period in which their incomes were quadrupling in real terms, they saw their effective tax rates come down by vastly more than the seven percentage points or so by which median house-holds saw their tax rates fall. Around 50% of those with incomes over $200,000 face tax rates of less than 20%.[10]

In a time of rapidly mounting federal debt, those figures are bad enough, but I suspect them of being somewhat less than accurate. Anyone earning more than $1 million a year has ways to shelter their income from the taxman's scrutiny. Just as corporations find ways to shift their profits to the most friendly overseas location, so too do the very wealthy. Banks on Wall Street and in the City of London create elaborate schemes to ensure that the bonuses they pay aren't taxable or can be tax-deferred. And those schemes relate to onshore money – the stuff the taxman has some chance of learning about. Meanwhile, the International Monetary Fund estimates that some $18 trillion in assets are being held in offshore tax havens beyond the reach of any tax authority.[11] The result is that the tax rates visible from the official statistics are almost certainly overstated. The rich are richer than we think and pay less tax than we can credit.

The position has become so extreme that even the billionaires are protesting. In a bold, truthful, un-Ponzi-ish op-ed for the *New York Times*, Warren Buffett wrote:

> Our leaders have asked for 'shared sacrifice.' But when they did the asking, they spared me. I checked with my mega-rich friends to learn what pain they were expecting. They, too, were left untouched.
>
> While the poor and middle class fight for us in Afghanistan, and while most Americans struggle to make ends meet, we mega-rich continue to get our extraordinary tax breaks . . .
>
> Last year my federal tax bill . . . was only 17.4 percent of my taxable income – and that's actually a lower percentage than was paid by any of the other 20 people in our office. Their tax burdens ranged from 33 percent to 41 percent and averaged 36 percent . . .
>
> Since 1992, the I.R.S. has compiled data from the returns of the 400 Americans reporting the largest income. In 1992, the top 400 had aggregate taxable income of $16.9 billion and paid federal taxes of 29.2 percent on that sum. In 2008, the aggregate income of the highest 400 had soared to $90.9 billion – a staggering $227.4

million on average – but the rate paid had fallen
to 21.5 percent . . .

My friends and I have been coddled long
enough by a billionaire-friendly Congress. It's
time for our government to get serious about
shared sacrifice.[12]

He's right. Of course he is. No one who looks without
prejudice at the facts could draw any other conclusion; yet
Congress still shows no sign of listening. In any case, our
billionaire-friendly tax regime is hardly the most egregious
offence against common sense and decency. Take, for
example, the case of AIG, an insurance company that took
to insuring various financial risks on a humungous scale
without making any realistic provision against possible
losses. When those losses were realized in the course of
2008, the firm became insolvent. As far as I've always understood things, the rules of the capitalist game are simple: if
you lose, you lose. Anyone who takes a credit risk on a failing firm will lose money and deserves to do so: it's those
losses which act as a reminder that credit risk matters.

Hank Paulson, the Secretary of the Treasury, presumably
knew those rules, since before coming to Washington he
had been the CEO of Goldman Sachs. (In 2006, Forbes
estimated Mr Paulson's personal holdings of Goldman stock
at $632 million. Luckily he wasn't obliged to live off his
dividend checks, however, as his compensation over the
previous five years amounted to some $40 or $50 million.[13])

Yet in 2008–9, the rules suddenly changed. AIG was
reprieved, thanks to some $183 billion of taxpayer support.
AIG took that money and used it to pay off its creditors, who
would otherwise have incurred serious losses. Chief among

those creditors were Goldman Sachs, Merrill Lynch, Société Générale, Deutsche Bank, and UBS. Collectively, those five banks received payments worth $32.7 billion from the US government at the munificent rate of 100 cents on the dollar.[14] Some of that money was passed on to further counterparties, but some appears to have stuck to those firms themselves, thereby bolstering profits and making it easier for them to pay huge bonuses. Goldman Sachs alone paid out $16.2 billion for its 2009 fiscal year.[15]

So, to summarize: when a group of investment banks make errors of judgment that threaten to cost them or their clients $32.7 billion, a Goldman alumnus funnels enough government money their way to cover their costs in full, supporting the banks' efforts to maintain their extravagantly large bonus payments. And all this takes place at a time when the US Treasury is tipping over into insolvency, in significant part owing to a crisis precipitated by those self-same banks.

And yet no one involved in this whole process did anything illegal. It all happened in plain view; no one ended up in jail or being hounded from the country. This is just how things work on Planet Ponzi. It's the classic Ponzi three-step. Step One: You create phony profits (in this case, via the mortgage markets) and pay yourself huge bonuses. Step Two: You push the accumulating losses on to another firm (in this case, AIG) and pay yourself huge bonuses. Step Three: When that firm goes bust and those losses look like returning to haunt you, you cash in your lobbying chips and push the losses on to the (insolvent) US government, thereby allowing you to pay yourself some more huge bonuses. Even Bernie Madoff himself was never that barefaced.

Goldman itself has contended that it did not benefit directly from the government bailouts.[16] Since we can't inspect their books directly, it's hard to be sure; but the bailout money was only one of the ways the government supported these institutions. According to documents obtained by Bloomberg, Morgan Stanley received a stunning $107 billion in loans from the Federal Reserve, Citigroup almost $100 billion. Goldman Sachs itself was in debt to the Fed for a total of 438 days and to a maximum of $69 billion.[17] That money was repaid, but it might not have been. Your money was placed at risk to protect Wall Street bonuses. How do you feel about that?

These tales point to one further moral. Ponzi schemes are, by their nature, vastly wasteful; it's almost as though their boastful extravagance provides them with camouflage. In AIG's case, the US taxpayer found $183 billion, so that $32.7 billion of payments could be made to Wall Street, so that Goldman Sachs and its peers could pay out billions in bonuses. Three of the five beneficiaries named above are foreign-owned. Compared with the economic waste involved in these payments, the Pentagon looks like the world's most penny-pinching spender, Obamacare like the Scrooge of healthcare plans. And AIG, of course, will never repay its bailout money.

But it's time to step away from the federal government and fiscal policy, and turn to the Federal Reserve and monetary policy. If you're anything like most people, even the words 'monetary policy' will be sufficient to induce mild drowsiness, but this is not a soporific story. It's about the prices in your shopping basket and the value of the currency in your pocket. Those two things are moving fast, neither in the way you want.

SIX

The $50,000,000,000 egg

On JULY 18, 2008, the British *Guardian* newspaper reported that ordinary hen's eggs were selling at an average price of $50 billion. These eggs were not particularly expensive, however, since the dollars in question were issued by the Reserve Bank of Zimbabwe. In US dollar terms, each egg was retailing for a perfectly reasonable $0.32.[1] Even in Zimbabwe, it wouldn't be long before Z$50 billion would seem strangely cheap for an egg. In January 2009 the Bank of Zimbabwe, making a determined effort to address the country's hyperinflation problem, issued currency in a new range of denominations, of which the most valuable was the new $100 trillion note. I have one of those notes beside me as I write. Valued at about US$30 when it was issued, it's essentially worthless today, except as a curio.[2] You can buy them on eBay for around US$5.

If the first duty of any government is to protect the country, the first duty of any central bank is to protect the currency. Particularly when a government's treasury department has lost hold of the reins, the central bank needs to act as a fierce guardian of value. For it to do so effectively, it needs an accurate measure of the value destruction being inflicted on the currency by inflation. In Zimbabwe, accuracy in measuring inflation simply meant figuring out the right number of zeroes. In the United States, however, you'd expect the measurement of inflation to be simple, uncontroversial – and right. Yet to say there's room for doubt on the US government's figures is to be far too kind.

Inflation, at root, is a simple concept. If you buy a basket of goods in March for $100, then buy the same basket the following month for $101, you'd want to say that inflation had been 1% over the course of the month. (The annual inflation rate, of course, would be higher.) That, surely, is what we think inflation is: the rate at which a basket of goods increases over time.

But that's not how the US statistical department (as guided by Congress) cares to measure it. The issue is as follows. Let's suppose that in March, your selected basket of goods contains a carton of orange juice, priced at $1.00. In April, you find that that carton has increased in price to $1.20. Because you aren't a passive consumer, obliged to buy the same items you bought last month, you're likely to reject that carton as being unacceptably expensive. Perhaps you trade sideways and buy grapefruit juice at $1.10. Or if all juices have risen in price, maybe you leave them aside and just add candy or a pound of apples or bag of salad. Naturally, consumers are astute shoppers. If they notice a good deal on apples, they'll likely stock up on apples. If there's a buy-one-get-one-free offer on salads, they'll walk out of the store with plenty of salad in their bags.

The problem for statisticians is how to handle this consumer behavior. The older, more rigorous methodology was clear. If the price of a fixed basket of goods went up by 1%, then inflation was 1% over the period in question. Government statisticians prefer to avoid this clarity and this rigor, and *reweight* the basket of goods each month in a way that reflects consumer efforts to avoid price increases.[3] In effect, we have a measure of inflation which deliberately exploits the inflation-avoiding behavior of consumers to generate an inflation rate far lower than the one we actually experience. In the words of economist and statistician John Williams, a long-time critic of official statistics, 'The fact that switching the CPI concept to a substitution-based basket of market goods from a fixed-basket violated the original intent, purpose and concept of the CPI, never seemed to be a concern to those in Washington.'[4] Let's be more frank. Washington chose to switch in order to conceal the truth. That's how you do things on Planet Ponzi. Needless to say, a host of other methodological adjustments have been made, which cumulatively tend to reduce the extent of reported inflation – to the bemusement of consumers, who know things are getting dearer faster than they used to.

Fortunately, however, the politicians don't have it all their own way. Williams has attempted to reconstruct US inflation data as they would have appeared if the old rigorous methodology still operated. According to his results, inflation is currently running at over 10% and has been consistently higher than government figures for as far back as he's been able to measure.[5] I haven't been able to review his precise calculations, so I can't say for certain that his data are correct. Nevertheless, there's no question that consumers don't *feel* like they're in a low-inflation environment any time they go to the grocery store or gas station. Inflation is fierce and rising. We can mitigate the effect of that inflation rate through ever more careful shopping, but the reality is brutal and getting worse.

Mention of the grocery store and the gas station raises another presentational concern. Government figures like to focus our attention on 'core' inflation, a measure which excludes the 'volatile' components of food and energy prices. And sure, those things are volatile – the way Wall Street bonuses are volatile: variable, but heading upwards. In February of 2011, food prices experienced the highest monthly increase for almost forty years. A Department of Agriculture spokesman – presumably too low down in government to have had the memo from the White House – commented bluntly: 'Food prices have been rising a lot faster, because underlying costs have really shot up. You're seeing some ingredients up 40%, 50%, 60% over last year. When you see wheat prices close to 80% up, that's going to ripple out to the public.'[6] He's completely right, except in his choice of metaphor. An 80% increase in the price of wheat isn't going to feel like a ripple to less well-off consumers. It's going to be yet another economic wave, breaching defenses, ruining lives.

It's the same with oil. In November 2008, in the wake of economic meltdown, oil briefly traded for less than $50 a barrel on the New York Mercantile Exchange. By April 2011 the price had doubled, to over $110. It's come back a few dollars since then, but it's still acutely vulnerable to upward pressure. As I write, there's revolution in Libya, civil war in Yemen, violence in Syria, brittle peace in Iraq, tense (and possibly nuclear-armed) calm in Iran, simmering unrest in the Gulf kingdoms, increasing militancy in Nigeria, and worsening maladministration of oil assets in Venezuela.[7] Those are not, to put it mildly, conditions which suggest that the oil price is likely to float gently back down to its historic levels.

And it's the same again, more broadly, with commodities. I'm looking at a screen that reports twelve-month changes in major commodity prices. The good news is that fishmeal and oranges are both cheaper than they were this time last year. The bad news is that the prices of crude oil, coal, diesel, gasoline, natural gas, jet fuel, heating oil, coffee, tea, barley, maize, rice, wheat, beef, pork, shrimp, sugar, coconut oil, palm oil, peanut oil, soybeans, wool, logs, sawn wood, hides, rubber, aluminum, copper, gold, iron ore, lead, nickel, silver, steel rod, reinforcement steel, tin, uranium, zinc, fertilizer, potassium chloride, rock phosphate, urea, and various other commodities related to those on this list have increased by at least 10% and in many cases much more than that over the course of a year. To a government statistician, these data provide firm evidence of the need for a fishmeal-and-oranges inflation index. To the rest of us, they're evidence of a serious, underreported, and dangerous tide of inflation.[8]

Threat is one thing; response is another. There are some inflationary pressures not even the most vigorous action by the Federal Reserve can just wipe out – China's rapid growth and consequent demand for raw materials, for example. You can't expect Ben Bernanke, chairman of the Fed, to be able to do anything about that. On the other hand, the Fed's response to the rapidly declining value of the dollar has been to assist that decline in every way possible. I pointed out in chapter 1 that the Fed has allowed its balance sheet to inflate by some $2,000 billion, largely as a result of quantitative easing (to use the technical term) or printing money (to use the descriptive one). This 'easing' has taken place at a time when the Fed has already forced down short-term interest rates as low as they can possibly go, lower than they've been for generations.[9] It has come at a time when long-term interest rates are as low as they've been since Japanese bombs were falling on Pearl Harbor.[10] In addition, it's come at a time when the threat of deflation (an admittedly serious possibility) has long, long retreated.

I'm not the only one to worry about these matters. Here are the wise words of one other worried soul, Richard Fisher, head of the Dallas Fed:

> I was skeptical about many of the presumed benefits of further asset purchases [i.e. printing money]. I was more certain of some of the potential costs.
>
> One cost is the risk of being perceived as embarking on the slippery slope of debt monetization [i.e. printing money to support government borrowing]. We know that once a central bank is perceived as targeting government debt yields at a time of persistent budget deficits, concern about debt monetization quickly arises.
>
> I realized that two other central banks were engaging in quantitative easing – the Bank of Japan and, most notably, our friends at the Bank of England. But the Bank of England is offsetting an announced fiscal policy tightening that out-Thatchers Thatcher. This is not the case here. Here we suffer from fiscal incontinence and regulatory misfeasance. If this were to change, I might advocate for accommodation. But that is

not yet happening. And I worry that by providing monetary accommodation, we are reducing the odds that fiscal discipline will be brought to bear.[11]

Fisher puts his finger on precisely the right issue. If the federal government were hacking back at spending – if it were seeking to 'out-Thatcher Thatcher' in its fiscal rigor – the Fed might well want to soften the blow of the ax. But as we've seen, the government in Washington is acting with so little fiscal discipline that the president of the Dallas Federal Reserve Bank can speak openly of 'fiscal incontinence and regulatory misfeasance.'

It's a shame the Fed doesn't possess more Richard Fishers. Since the departure of Paul Volcker in 1987, the Federal Reserve has the unwelcome record of having gotten every single major decision wrong. Every time there has been a hint of a crisis, the Fed has acted like some senior court advisor to the Emperor of Planet Ponzi. The 1987 stock market crash, my liege? I'll pump in liquidity. Asian financial crisis, sire? I'll flood the place with dollars. A major hedge fund, LTCM, has gone bust, your majesty? I'll organize a bailout. Dotcom bubble? Let's watch it inflate. Even the September 11 terrorist attacks – surely a matter for the US security apparatus rather than its monetary authority – were taken as an excuse for monetary loosening.

Little wonder that inflation has been racing away. Little wonder that the Washington establishment has been ever more anxious to manipulate the data. Little wonder that we've seen crazy bubbles in the markets for housing, for shares, for mortgage assets – for pretty much anything that Wall Street can stick a price on. Governor Rick Perry, a

Republican contender for the presidency, said, in response to a question from an Iowa voter,

> If this guy [Bernanke] prints more money between now and the election, I don't know what y'all would do to him in Iowa but we would treat him pretty ugly down in Texas. Printing more money to play politics at this particular time in history is almost treasonous in my opinion.[12]

If Governor Perry considers that threatening the chairman of the Fed is a way to advertise his suitability for high office, he has a few things to learn. But his anxieties are not as overblown as his rhetoric. Printing money destroys value. I have a bank note on my desk which confirms it.*

So much for the US government's money management. But before we turn to the second engine that has powered the Ponzi scheme we're examining – Wall Street – we should step across the pond to take a quick look at how public finance in the UK has fared in those years since the Bank of England was founded to fend off national disaster.

---

*Indeed, Governor Gideon Gono of the Bank of Zimbabwe has recently warned against money-printing in the US, advising that the effect is likely to be excessive inflation. And he should know. (See John Carney, 'Zimbabwe bashes Bernanke – on inflation!', CNBC, Dec. 2, 2011.)

SEVEN

After Beachy Head

IN WRITING ABOUT the United States, I happened to mention that modern public finance started with a sea battle fought by England against France beneath the white cliffs of the south coast. What I didn't go on to discuss, however, was the longer-term implications of that sea battle for public finances in the UK – and for mastery of the modern world.

We start, as ever, with the data, shown here in figure 7.1 overleaf. In the long century which followed the Battle of Beachy Head, Britain would experience a succession of wars with France, culminating in the defeat of Napoleon at Waterloo. Those wars were – or felt like – wars of existential importance. Whenever the country was at war, its debt shot up in relation to GDP. As soon as the war ended, debt began almost immediately to moderate. The one real exception was in 1815, when a long economic slump kept debt high for a few years, even though the country was, finally, at peace. Even then, however, once Napoleon was gone and the French threat with him, the country was eventually able to get on with running the world and paying back its debt. In 1913, just as that debt seemed all ready to disappear for ever, war came again – and then yet again in 1939. The 'Hitler peak' didn't match the 'Napoleon peak,' but it came close. That's what it costs to win wars for European dominance.

Then, with the world war won, indebtedness started to decline. By 1991, the debt-to-GDP ratio stood at around 25%. The country faced no threats to its existence. The Soviet Union had collapsed. There were no French fireships in the Channel, no archdukes being assassinated in Sarajevo. The entire history of Britain since the time of William III suggested that the national debt would now vanish. It had come into being because of military crisis and been kept alive through three turbulent centuries by a succession of wars and alarms. But the country was now at peace; its economy was prospering; there was no famine, plague, or pestilence. The debt should have vanished.

But it didn't. It ticked along, growing when it should have shrunk. The thinking of Planet Ponzi came to affect government, banks, and consumers alike – and debt grew on every front. That debt came to seem acceptable: an aspect of reality every bit as normal as delays on the Underground or summer

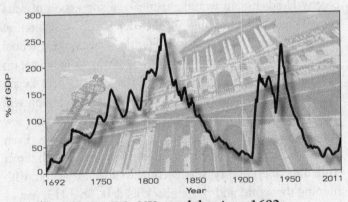

Figure 7.1: UK net debt since 1692

Source: www.ukpublicspending.co.uk.

drizzle. By 2007, the government deficit was running at 2.7% of GDP. That ought to strike you as a shocking fact. The government in power had presided over a decade of continuous economic growth. What possible justification could there be for borrowing money to sustain public spending? Yet the reckless spending of 2007 would soon seem like prudence itself.

When financial crisis struck, those seeds of indebtedness bloomed at an astonishing rate. In 2008, the deficit more or less doubled. In 2009 and 2010, it was running at more than 10% of GDP. In other words, for every £10 produced by an entire national economy, the government was borrowing more than £1. That's a figure that makes sense if you're in a life-or-death struggle to defend the nation – but to fund bailouts for the banks? To maintain bonuses in the City of London? To protect bank creditors, many of whom are foreign? It's lunacy. Except perhaps in America and Ireland, no democratic country has ever imposed so great a burden on its ordinary citizens, for the benefit and protection of that country's wealthiest elite. The worst kleptocrats of Africa and Asia must be watching in astonishment. They never knew it could be this easy.

You don't have to take my word for these things. In his testimony to the House of Commons Treasury Select Committee in spring 2011, the Bank of England Governor, Mervyn King, commented: 'The price of this financial crisis is being borne by people who absolutely did not cause it. Now is the period when the cost is being paid. I'm surprised that the degree of public anger has not been greater than it has.'[1] He's right. The country has grumbled, but it's kept its anger largely in check. There are no gallows at Marble Arch, no mobs baying for blood in Belgravia. Not one of the multimillionaires who led their firms, and their country, into disaster have paid any meaningful price for their actions – either in fines or (my strong preference) in jail time.

What's more, King went on to say – also correctly – that the impact on living standards would be long-term and severe. 'The research makes it clear that the impact of these crises lasts for many years. It is not like an ordinary recession, where you lose output and get it back quickly. We may not get the lost output back for very many years, if ever.'[2] It's also inevitably true that the cost of fiscal austerity falls far more on the poor than on the rich.[3] Mervyn King's 'lost output' will be causing pain in Tottenham and Toxteth for years and probably decades after those in Chelsea and Cheltenham have forgotten about it.

Because these things are now well known, I won't labor the point further. What I would add, however, is that the problems of lobbying are as entrenched in the UK as they are in the US – arguably more so. The Labour Party of Tony Blair and Gordon Brown was notoriously banker-friendly. The 'light touch regulation' on which those politicians prided themselves ended up doing unspeakable damage to the national finances. Yet the contemporary Conservative Party is more or less owned by the finance industry. According to the Bureau of Investigative Journalism, the financial sector is the source of more than half the Tory Party's political funding. If anything, that ratio has been increasing. Unsurprisingly, and according to the same source, the Tory-led coalition's first year in office has seen a slew of tax changes all intended to help the most prosperous individuals in society.[4]

This shouldn't come as any surprise. For all the apparently tough measures being taken to restrict the destructive power of the financial sector, money speaks louder than words. The fact is, when a single industry sector has governments so deeply in its pocket, it remains highly improbable that those governments are going to injure their donors. The Labour Party foolishly chose to sup with the devil, but may at least have learned its lesson. The Tory Party doesn't simply sup with the devil, it owes him board and lodging. The next financial crisis is already brewing today.

That's the bad news. Yet, as we'll see in a later chapter, the British government of today is well off in one crucial respect: it has a plan for deficit reduction – a plan which, to a large extent, is accepted across the political spectrum and the country at large. It's well off in another respect, too. In the United States, a huge portion of the federal budget is taken up with mandatory expenditures: spending required by laws passed by a previous Congress. Since you need all the stars in alignment to alter those laws – you need dependable and simultaneous control of the House of Representatives, the Senate, and the White House, which rarely happens – political leaders are stuck with the implementation of laws they themselves might not have passed. I'm not against that. The Constitution of the United States worked pretty well for two hundred some years; but for two hundred some years, Planet Ponzi wasn't in existence and wasn't wanted. Naturally Congress would, from time to time, pass some dumb laws, but those laws didn't threaten the basic solvency of the United States. In the last three decades, however, those mandatory expenditures have come to bankrupt the US. If you take seriously the unfunded liabilities on pensions and health care, the country is ruined: utterly unable to fulfill its future obligations.

Britain is not in that position. Parliament does not generally write laws that bind future parliaments, and if it did, the government – which almost always has a functional majority in the House of Commons – can simply change the law. So although the British government debt is absurdly high, although the deficit is a standing insult to every ordinary British citizen, although bankers must still be blinking with astonishment to find that they've got away with their heist, huge unfunded liabilities of the kind which are crippling the United States do not exist – or do not exist in the same way – in the United Kingdom. Unfunded liabilities that arise from mandatory healthcare spending in the US amount to almost $40 trillion, or about two-thirds of global GDP. The equivalent figure for the UK government is £0.00. There is no such liability. The same thing, more or less, with pensions. Though there will be a cost as the population ages, the government of the day won't be bound by laws that it didn't create and cannot change – and governments from Thatcher onwards have proved remarkably willing to make the necessary tough decisions on keeping pension spending down to sane levels. (It won't surprise you to learn, however, that the government's pension provision for its own employees is woefully under-funded to the tune of some 86% of GDP.)

Yet perhaps the most important point of this whole section of the book is the one with which I began this chapter. Planet Ponzi is an aberration. In the three hundred years since the Battle of Beachy Head, there have been good governments and bad governments, reckless spenders and cautious skinflints. Yet throughout the period, the only real increases in national indebtedness arose because of war. Not itty-bitty conflicts in faraway places, but conflicts that threatened the integrity of the nation. When the country wasn't at war, it was paying back its debt. That's how it ought to be and that's how it always was. The mindset of Planet Ponzi is a new phenomenon, a temporary one, and one we need to destroy for ever. The country that once defeated Napoleon and Hitler deserves nothing less.

PART TWO

Wall Street

EIGHT

A statistical anomaly

ASSUMING YOU HAVE even the vaguest interest in the world beyond your door, you'll be familiar with the concept of GDP or gross domestic product. It's the basic measure of national income, the total value of goods and services produced in a given period of time. Nearly always, GDP is quoted as an aggregate figure, offering us a measure of the value created by an entire economy over a given quarter or year. Underpinning that aggregate figure is a massive amount of detailed data about every sector and subsector of the economy in question. These data are churned out, with an impressive degree of timeliness, by government statisticians, and large quantities of data are published or made available online. Yet these data have for a long time now contained an anomaly, whose nature lies at the heart of this book.

We begin with the concept of value added – a term of jargon, which just so happens to mean exactly what you think it ought to mean. So, for example, if a manufacturer sells a widget for $1.00, and the cost of his various inputs (raw materials, power, etc.) amounted to $0.40, his value added is equal to $0.60. In effect, it's how much extra value the manufacturer and his staff added to those raw materials by processing them into finished goods and successfully marketing them to the end user. The concept allows us to explore who contributes what to economic value, and because government statisticians have compiled broadly the same types of data in broadly the same ways for a long time, it's possible to see how those contributions have shifted over time.

Back in 1947, the US economy looked much as you'd think it would look. Agriculture was still a significant sector, contributing over 8% to national output. Manufacturing contributed more than a quarter of the total. Even transportation and warehousing chipped in almost 6%. By comparison, the finance industry wasn't particularly important. Finance and insurance contributed just 2.4% of national prosperity. Their role – in supplying credit, handling cash, dripping a little oil on to the wheels of capitalism – was important, but humble.[1]

As time went by, the finance sector grew in importance. In the late 1940s, many people had no access to banking facilities. Many firms were only local. Credit markets were restricted. The sector needed to grow, and it did. By the late 1970s, finance and insurance were contributing around 4.7% of total economic output. The sector was still a small one, but no longer puny. Finance was starting to grow up.

In 1977, government statisticians responded to the changing makeup and complexity of the economy by introducing a set of more finely grained economic categories. Finance and insurance *as a whole* accounted for some 4.7% of the economy, but it was now possible to tell where that 4.7% came from. As you'd expect, ordinary retail and lending banks – 'Main Street' banks, if you like – made up the largest single chunk of the sector, responsible for 2.45% of overall GDP. Insurance contributed 1.86%. The sector called 'securities, commodity contracts, and investments' – what we know as Wall Street – accounted for a mere 0.34% of economic output. A sector that creates just 0.3% of a nation's income is, evidently, tiny. The trucking industry was three times as important. Forestry and fishing were more important. In 1977, Wall Street made a few people rich. It raised some capital and it made some markets. But it did not contribute much to the economic pie.

Then things started to change, and change fast. By the early 1990s, the finance industry as a whole was generating over 6.5% of economic output, while Wall Street's share of GDP had *tripled* to around 1%. Wall Street was still a minor player in the scheme of things, but a feisty one, a growing one. No other sector had grown at that rate. Even the computer industry, in the age of the PC and the mass-produced silicon chip, had not grown that fast.

That turbocharged growth was fueled by two principal ingredients. First, the advent of floating exchange rates in 1971 had gradually led to the dismantling of international controls on the movement of capital. As capital started to become ever more mobile, Wall Street firms were ideally placed to skim a little froth from the river of money as it passed on through.[2] Secondly, Wall Street had perfected the art of 'disintermediation.' The term is ugly and obscure, but its meaning is startlingly simple. In the old days, if large borrowers – industrial companies, for example – wanted to borrow money, they were, on the whole, obliged to get it from banks. Banks, for their part, acted as middlemen: taking money on deposit from investors, lending it on, making a spread. That old system had worked well enough for a long time, but it was inefficient. New methods of accessing the international bond markets made it possible for would-be borrowers to go direct to investors. Investors got a better deal than they had done from the banks. So did borrowers. Traditional corporate lending was a business in trouble, but Wall Street – the people who so energetically sold the benefits of securitization – was booming.

Naturally, because this was Wall Street, there were bound to be a few little hiccups along the way. The 'mezzanine debt' market – that's the junk bond market to you and me[3] – provided a great way for poor-quality borrowers to reach investors. Unfortunately, Drexel Burnham Lambert, the firm that created the market, went bust and its star, Mike Milken, went to jail. So too did Ivan Boesky, an insider trader who was also fined an eye-popping $100 million. And one of the leading banks of the era, Salomon Brothers, was caught bilking the US Treasury and fined $290 million for its pains. And yes, the landmark deal of the era, the takeover of RJR Nabisco by KKR, a leveraged buyout outfit, was unwound after little more than ten years in a haze of cost and disappointment. But all this time Wall Street was booming.

The growth of the securities market was enthusiastically assisted by the regulators. In 1999 Congress and President Bill Clinton repealed the Glass–Steagall Act, which had, for seventy years, maintained barriers between lending banks and securities houses. Although there had been a small but growing market in credit-based derivative products in the 1990s, the rule changes of 1999 laid the groundwork for massive growth in that market. To regulators this looked like another win: furious innovation, big fees on Wall Street, new products for investors and corporations alike.

Now, of course, we know what that win turned into. A

massive increase in leverage. The sale of crazy products to the wrong buyers supported by bankrupt counterparties. Weapons of mass financial destruction indeed, to quote Warren Buffett's all-too-accurate description. By 2009, the last year for which we have complete data, Wall Street contributed 1.2% of total US economic output. The entire finance industry, including insurance, contributed 8.3%, more than three times what it had done in 1947. That's a larger proportion of the total than you see in highly production-oriented economies, like Germany's, but not hugely so. The financially oriented economies of Switzerland and Britain both have banking and insurance sectors relatively larger than their US counterpart.[4]

So much for the background. Now for the anomaly – the anomaly which lies at the heart of Planet Ponzi.

Over the period 1998–2010, Main Street banks have contributed about 3.6% to total economic output, and they have made about 3.6% of all profits in the US economy. That's more or less what you'd expect. The banks do a job. They make some money, but not vast amounts. They simply earn a regular slice of profit by way of reward for doing what they do.

The same tedious logic, however, stops applying when it runs up against the 'other financial' sector – the term given by the government's statisticians to Wall Street and insurance companies. That 'other financial' sector contributed just 4.3% to economic output over the same period, *yet took a staggering 28.9% of all American profits.*[5] That fact is so astonishing it bears repeating. Just under 30% of all profits made in the US economy were being made either on Wall Street or in insurance. And there's more. Wall Street pay is notoriously lavish, bonuses exceptionally large.

Those things are counted as expenses, deductions against profit. If pay on Wall Street were halfway normal, the sector's profits would be even higher. And, of course, I've quoted an average figure. In the boom years of 2002 and 2003, that 'other financial' sector generated profits equal to 40% of the total. *Two-fifths*. From a sector that represents about one-25th of the nation's output.

There is, let us remember, nothing inherently sinful or suspicious in people making profits, even big ones. For example, if you scraped around in your backyard and found some rich and easily accessible gold deposits, you would quite likely make some extremely large profits. Those profits would last as long as your gold deposits remained rich and easily accessible. You wouldn't have done anything unethical in exploiting them; you'd just have been very lucky.

And you don't need to stumble across an oil well or a gold mine to strike it rich. Google and Microsoft are examples of firms smart enough and lucky enough to have created virtual gold mines of their own. The nature of computer operating systems and search engines appears to favor the largest player. You couldn't say that either firm is immune from competition, just that the forces of competition don't work to drive down prices in the way that they do for more ordinary markets, like the ones for pressed steel, or cookies, or handsaws, or haircuts.

There are other ways to create gold mines. Cartels – price-fixing agreements among supposedly rival suppliers – are a classic way for firms to boost their profits at the expense of consumers, which is why cartels are generally illegal. Any government regulation that makes it hard for new firms to enter an industry always boosts the profits of the protected firms. So, in one notable recent instance, the Italian government (then led by Silvio Berlusconi) proved curiously unwilling to allow free competition in the TV industry – much to the advantage of the sector's dominant player (which just so happened to be owned by Silvio Berlusconi).

All these examples – gold in the backyard, Google, cartels, inappropriate government regulation – have one thing in common: an absence of ordinary competition. In normal industries, any profit windfall is soon winnowed away by the rush of incoming competitors. That's why, as it happens, it's not worth your while scraping around in your backyard for gold. Any such easy gains were scooped up a long time ago. That's why the gold rush was a rush, not an amble.

So far, so obvious – so what are we to make of those financial profits? Wall Street may be greedy, blind, duplicitous, dishonorable, and a thousand other things, but one thing it is *not* is uncompetitive. Quite the reverse. It's difficult, indeed, to think of any industry where competition is more vigorous. Firms compete furiously for talent. They steal talent from other firms. They pitch hard, market hard, price keenly, incentivize massively. There are plenty of big firms generating competition all by themselves, and there are always plenty more competitors, from both the US and overseas, ready to enter the market and snatch whatever business they can from the better-known incumbents. Barclays, RBS, UBS, Deutsche are only some of the more prominent would-be entrants to this golden industry; the truth is that every sector of finance – every sub-sector, even – is a seething mass of firms struggling to get an edge over their peers. Wall Street may not be pretty, but it's Competition Central and it has been for years.

But competition *erodes* profit. It drives it down to the level where firms earn a fair return for their commitment of capital and energy, but no more. As far as all economic logic is concerned, those pumped-up Wall Street profits shouldn't exist. What's going on?

So far, our discussion has assumed that the commercial world splits neatly into two: financial firms on the one hand; nonfinancial ones (the truckers, the widget-makers, and so on) on the other. We've assumed that firms in the second group make money in pretty much the way you'd expect them to: carrying things on trucks, making widgets, and so forth. But that's not quite accurate. Certainly the finance guys don't get involved in things that might make their hands dirty, but those in the regular economy are by no means averse to picking up financial profits themselves.

In a remarkable 2005 study, Greta Krippner sought to explore the degree to which profits now accrue 'primarily through financial channels rather than through trade and commodity production.'[6] In particular, she measured the ratio of portfolio income (interest, dividends, and capital gains) to total corporate cash flows. In effect, she was looking at the degree to which *nonfinancial* firms were earning their money through *financial* means.

Her results were extraordinary. From 1950 to 1970, financial profits averaged less than 10% of the total. Naturally, widget-makers might find they had some cash on deposit and would earn some interest from it, but broadly speaking they made money the good old-fashioned way: by making something for $0.90 and selling it for $1.00. Then, in 1970, something started to change. The key ratio started to rise and rise. By the end of the 1980s, nonfinancial firms were earning more than 40% of their total through financial means. After a slight dip in the 1990s, the ratio returned to that 40% level in time for the millennium.

These figures are disconcerting in the extreme. One of the most obvious features of the financial system is its theoretical symmetry. If I lend you twenty dollars and charge you a dollar in interest, that dollar is my income, but your expense. They cancel out. Aggregated over an entire economy, we should find that there is no *net* interest at all, except to the (relatively modest) extent that it comes in from overseas. Something similar applies to dividends and capital gains. If I grow a business and sell it for a good profit, I'll earn a capital gain. Yet such gains – and, indeed, any dividends – arise ultimately from growth in ordinary, regular, run-of-the-mill profits. If those profits have become ever less important to the overall economy, what on Earth is keeping those financial profits afloat?

These questions are not easy to answer, but the more you reflect on them the more you realize you are left with only two possible options. When it comes to those bizarrely high Wall Street profits, you can choose to believe one of the following two propositions:

❏ over the last couple of decades, Wall Street has become the first industry in the history of capitalism to have consistently super-sized profits despite continual aggressive competition; or

❏ those pumped-up profits are a mirage – or, in plain language, a Ponzi scheme.

Your choices are broadly similar when seeking to account for the bizarrely large proportion of financially derived profits found in the accounts of nonfinancial corporations.

Perhaps even the second conclusion doesn't go far enough for you. Indeed, it's quite possible that a further reflection has already occurred to you, namely:

❏ Of course Wall Street has pumped-up profits; its activities have no social utility at all and it basically exists only to steal money from the rest of us, so why wouldn't it make monster profits? That's what thieves do.

If that's what you're thinking, then I like your style. As it happens, though, I don't think that Wall Street is *only* about theft. Companies do need to raise capital. Bonds and equities do need to be tradable in liquid markets. And so on. The core of Wall Street's traditional businesses make good economic sense, just as they always have done. But still: I like the way you're thinking.

Nevertheless, even allowing for some exaggeration, I can't agree with you. The laws of economics don't go to sleep just because an activity is socially worthless or even harmful. The purveyors of high-cholesterol, obesity-promoting meals compete hard with each other. Polluting chemical plants compete with one another. Tobacco firms compete. And that's what matters: the simple act of competition forces profits down to a normal level. You can even see the same thing with the trade in illegal drugs. As Steven Levitt and Stephen Dubner showed in *Freakanomics*, most drug dealers live with their moms, simply because there are too many drug dealers competing for too little business.[7] Barriers to entry are low. Profits get forced down and down. It's competition that does this. The social value of the activity doesn't come into it.

But maybe your mind is moving along other lines. Perhaps you don't like conspiracy theories as a rule. Perhaps you think that the simplest explanation is always the likeliest one: Neil Armstrong really did walk on the moon, the CIA did not kill President Kennedy, Elvis is dead. I'm the same. I don't like conspiracy theories either. So here are two further propositions, either of which you might find attractive:

- ❑ Mitch Feierstein is an idiot or a liar, and he's gotten his figures wrong; or

- ❑ Mitch Feierstein has his figures quite correct, but there is some other perfectly innocent explanation of these data – we don't need to invoke a giant Ponzi scheme.

If you had doubts along these lines, congratulations. I don't want you to take things on trust. Taking too much on trust is a big part of what got us into this mess in the first place.

So let's go with your objections. You don't like my figures? Then please check them out. I've sourced my data on financial sector profits from the Bureau of Economic Affairs, the government agency charged with compiling these figures. The data are all available online. The notes at the end of this book tell you just where you can find them. There are a few little complications to deal with – changes in certain industrial categorizations, for the most part – but nothing major. Nothing that has direct bearing on the argument of this chapter. If you're even half-competent with a spreadsheet, you should be able to reproduce the data in this chapter yourself. It's basic arithmetic, not quantum mechanics.

Greta Krippner's figures are harder to reconstruct, but she too drew her data from impeccable government sources and has provided extensive details of her methodology. The fact is that if she'd messed up her figures, someone would have noticed. The same goes, in general, for all the data in this book. If you don't believe me, go check for yourself. Please.

As for the possibility of some other, more innocent explanation – well, if you think it's there, go find it. I'm not the first person to have noticed the scale of those financial profits. They've attracted widespread comment over the years. But so far as I know, no one has an explanation of why they're so large in relation to the broader economy. If you don't believe me, go online, browse the views of other commentators, and put me to the test. Bear in mind that the whole of economic theory since Adam Smith argues that competition drives returns on capital down to normal levels, which means that if you do find an 'innocent' explanation of Wall Street's profits that attracts you, it'll be you on one side of the fence and all of economic science on the other. So good luck with that.

In short, once you've done all the due diligence you can, I think you'll come back to my original two propositions. Either Wall Street is a modern miracle, the only industry in history that has learned how to levitate. Or those profits aren't really there at all. They're bogus. A con. A huge, expensive, Ponzi-ish con.

Of course, it's not much use providing the evidence of this con, if we can't demonstrate precisely how those bogus profits arise and what keeps them going. So that's where we'll turn next.

NINE

A house for Joe Schmoe

WHEN JOE SCHMOE – a GI with an honorable war record – returned from the Pacific, he found his girl waiting for him. To begin with, they went out on a couple of trial dates, getting reacquainted with each other. There was a little awkwardness at first, but they soon got over it. One thing led to another, until one day Joe proposed to his girl – I'm seeing her as a Betsy, all plump cheeks and flowered aprons. Betsy said yes. Joe found a good job as a production worker. He and Betsy got married (and everyone cried and said what a lovely couple they were). Now they needed a house. So Joe put on his best suit, went to his local bank, the First National Bank of Pumpernickel Creek, and asked for a mortgage.

The house Joe wanted to buy cost $1,000. He had $200 in savings. So he asked to borrow $800. The manager at First National (let's call him Jefferson Smith) wanted to check out the steadiness of Joe's job, the reliability of his income, and the soundness of the proposed collateral (the house). Having satisfied himself on those points – and recognizing that he was about to make a commitment that might endure for more than two decades – the bank manager approved the loan. Joe and Betsy bought their house. They raised three apple-cheeked and healthy children and naturally lived happily ever after. Joe's personal finances were almost as simple as his family history. He started out with an asset ($1,000 worth of house), a loan ($800), and equity in the house for the remaining $200. As time went by, he paid down the loan. His equity increased. And as the high quality of life in Pumpernickel Creek became more widely known, the value of the house went up too, thereby further enhancing Joe's equity and the family's prosperity.

The financial position for the bank was a little more complex, but only a little. Even in Pumpernickel Creek, money doesn't grow on trees. The $800 advanced by the bank had to come from somewhere. To some extent – let's say, to the tune of $150 – the money would have come from the bank's own capital resources: that is, money belonging to the bank itself, not owed on to anyone else. But that still leaves a gap of $650 to be filled, almost certainly with money which would have come from reinvesting customers' deposits. To keep the story simple, let's say that old Mrs Salzundpfeffer, one of the town's most respected inhabitants, chose to place exactly that amount of money on deposit at First National. So the bank's balance sheet looks like this: an asset of $800 (the mortgage which Joe Schmoe has to repay), a liability of $650 (the money which the bank will one day have to pay back to Mrs Salzundpfeffer), and equity of $150. Simple.

Equally simple is the way that everyone's motivations, risks, and incentives are aligned. If Joe wants to keep a roof over Betsy's head, he needs to keep up the payments on his mortgage. If the bank doesn't want to lose its shirt, it's going to take a good hard look at the quality of Joe's income and the value of his collateral. If those things are unsound, the bank will lose money. If Mrs Salzundpfeffer isn't going to lose her nest-egg, she'll be sure that First National has a deserved reputation for sound, conservative banking.

In this happy scenario, the logic extends to the income statement as much as the balance sheet. Joe doesn't want to pay too much for his mortgage; Mrs Salzundpfeffer wants a decent return on her savings. The bank can certainly make its turn in the middle, but never too much, because otherwise borrowers or depositors or both will go elsewhere.

This simple banking system can't avoid risk, because no banking system ever can. Maybe Joe Schmoe will be killed in an industrial accident. Maybe his house will blow away. Maybe these terrible things happen and a crucial insurance policy fails for some arcane reason. Maybe Joe isn't the straight-up guy we all thought him to be. Maybe Jefferson Smith is on the take. (Impossible!) Nevertheless, the system is as robust as you could want it to be. The bank is going to think hard about loan quality, because if those loans go bad, they injure the bank and no one else. No one is exposed to any credit risk from Joe Schmoe except the very people who looked hard into his credit history and decided that the risks were acceptable.

That system was a thoroughly sound one. Sure, it still needed plenty of government regulation around it, plus government deposit insurance to protect depositors from badly managed banks. What's more, with hindsight, we can see plenty of innovations that were able to help cut costs or improve risk management. Nevertheless, the basic model was sound. Risks and incentives were perfectly aligned.

Now let's jump six decades and take a look at how things worked for Joe's grandson, Joe Schmoe III. Unfortunately, somewhere down the line, the fine genes bequeathed by the original Joe and Betsy Schmoe have become seriously damaged. The new Joe has something of an alcohol problem. He's been in trouble with the law. He hasn't married his girlfriend, Joella, but has two kids with her nevertheless. They are living in a trailer park somewhere in California. The pair talk about getting themselves sorted out, but at the present moment they are twenty-first-century NINJAs: No Income, No Job, No Assets.

We're about to take a look at how the financial system of the last decade handled Joe and Joella's finances. We're going to take a look at the risks and the incentives in the system and see how they did – or did not – align. But before we proceed, a word of warning. If you've had any prior interest in these topics, you will already have read about the subprime mortgage problems which precipitated the first wave of the present credit crisis. So before we proceed, let me be clear: although I am using the mortgage market as the clearest possible illustration of how things can (and did) go wrong, my argument is general, not specific. I believe the problems we're about to look at – wildly escalating leverage, ballooning risks, disastrous incentives, lousy accounting, incompetent investors – are extremely widespread. They were, and are, not unique to the mortgage market. They are still highly prevalent in market after market today. What follows is a specific illustration of a general phenomenon. Until these general issues are addressed, we have a financial system which is more like a Ponzi scheme than a useful tool for the effective deployment of capital. What we have, in fact, is not a socially useful asset; it's a ticking time bomb.

OK. End of lecture. Back to Joe and Joella.

The happy couple are smoking weed with some buddies, when one of them happens to mention that he's bought his house – his trailer, that is. Joe and Joella are astonished. This guy (he calls himself Fat Boy) doesn't have a job or any income or any assets, so who would be dumb enough to lend him money? Fat Boy explains it. Property prices always rise. He's been lent 105% of the value of the trailer. The idea of that extra 5% is that he can invest in improving the property and/or setting a little aside for interest payments. In practice, Fat Boy laughs, that extra 5% is being inhaled right now and very sweet it tastes too. Joe and Joella ask about interest payments, and Fat Boy says that he's on something called a 'teaser rate,' which is very low. It'll start going up in a couple of years' time – but at that point, he says, he'll probably sell up, take the profits, invest in somewhere bigger. He sketches out the likely outline of his property empire, using the glowing tip of his joint to illustrate some of his larger ideas.

Maybe Fat Boy sounds like an idiot, but he's not the real idiot here. To understand the degree of insanity that afflicted our financial system just a few years back – and still afflicts it today – we've got to trace out what happens next stage by individual stage. So here goes.

Stage 1

Joe and Joella go to Fat Boy's bank and ask for a loan. To their silent amazement, they get it: 105% of the asset value. Super-low teaser rate of interest. And their trailer – or rather, their pre-manufactured housing unit, in Wall Street jargon – becomes theirs.

Stage 2

Joe and Joella's loan has been given to them by a recently formed unit of the First National Bank of Pumpernickel Creek: an internet-based home loan subsidiary called EZ Homes. EZ Homes did no real credit assessment of Joe and Joella, because it had no intention of holding on to the credit risk. EZ Homes, in fact, simply took a bundle of its recent home loans and sold the entire package. It did so by creating and selling an asset-backed security – effectively, a bond supported by the underlying mortgage assets and nothing else.

Please note that if this were the end of the financial chain (which it most certainly is not) you would already have a situation in which the end investor has done no or minimal due diligence on Joe and Joella. Boosters of the system liked to talk of risks being 'dispersed' by the securitization process, but that language would likely have puzzled our old-style bank manager. Risk is risk is risk is risk. If you make a loan, and know your borrower and check your collateral, you have a decent chance of getting your money back, plus a little extra by way of profit. If you don't know your borrower and haven't checked their financial capacity and haven't ascertained the strength of their collateral, then you haven't 'dispersed' anything at all except your common sense – and the likelihood of making any money for your ultimate investors.

Stage 3

In any case, however, things weren't as simple as a mere asset-backed securitization. An ambitious Wall Street bank – specifically, the Housing Issuance and Trading unit of Bear, Lehman, Lynch, Sachs, & Stanley – acquired a whole load of mortgage products and bundled them in a newly created structured investment vehicle or SIV. Such an SIV might have had a balance sheet looking a little like the one below. (These data are adapted – and simplified – from a genuine financing, in this case Goldman Sachs' controversial Timberwolf 1 issue.[1])

Assets ($m)	Liabilities ($m)
1,000+ mortgage products	9 AAA-rated floating rate notes (FRNs)
	8 AAA-rated FRNs
	100 AAA-rated FRNs
	200 AAA-rated FRNs
	100 AAA-rated FRNs
	100 AAA-rated FRNs
	305 AAA-rated FRNs
	107 AA-rated FRNs
	36 A-rated FRNs
	30 BBB-rated FRNs
	22 unrated income notes

Now, this might look a little confusing – actually, it *is* confusing – but the essence of it is simple enough. Those mortgage products provide a stream of cashflows (which come, let's remember, from Joe and Joella – and thousands of other borrowers – making payments to their primary banks). When the SIV receives those payments, it crunches some numbers. If all is well – that is, if the money coming in is sufficient to repay all those various noteholders – they will receive their payouts as expected. If all is not well – if there is a default (i.e. the incoming payments prove insufficient) – the noteholders are paid in order of seniority.

The AAA-rated noteholders come first. (There are so many tiers of them because of somewhat different details regarding maturity dates and the like.) Once the AAA-rated notes are made whole, the AA-rated noteholders get their turn, and so on down the chain.

Those ratings – the AAA, AA, A, and BBB – are external assessments of risk made by the ratings agencies. (More on them in the next couple of chapters.) The people at the top of the list are safest, because they have the first claim on any payments. The people at the bottom of the list are least safe, because they receive payment only in the event that everyone else has already been paid out. Needless to say, however, those taking the least risk also earn the lowest interest rate; those at the most risky, most speculative end of the deal are (in theory) well compensated for the risk they take. (I say 'in theory,' because when in practice these edifices of crappy assets collapsed, those at the bottom of the food chain often received nothing at all.) Structures of this sort are known as collateralized debt obligations, or CDOs.

When you finally understand the CDO structure and grasp the way that cash flows – and risks – cascade down the chain of bondholders, it's easy to get seduced by the logic of it all. Yet when you stand back and think about it, the logic is extraordinary. Joe and Joella do not look (or smell?) like investment grade borrowers. They have no credit history, no job, no income, no assets and – I don't want to be snobby about this, but – they live in a trailer park and have nothing to do all day but smoke marijuana with Fat Boy. Yet from that billion-dollar swamp of ultra-high-risk consumer lending, look what Wall Street managed to do: it created $980 million worth of investment grade assets. The 'AAA' rated assets were supposedly as safe as Treasury bonds issued by the US government. Even the 'BBB' rated assets were supposedly as safe as bonds issued by the governments of Russia, India, and Brazil. Even Fat Boy, as he sat there waving his joint to illustrate his path to Donald Trump style wealth, would have been disconcerted to learn that Wall Street rated around 80% of his loan as being at least as creditworthy as the US government itself. Lunacy.

Stage 4

It gets worse. The Housing Issuance and Trading unit at Bear, Lehman, Lynch, Sachs & Stanley (BLLSSHIT, for short) decided they liked stage 3 so much, they'd do it all over again. They'd create yet another structured investment vehicle – only this one wouldn't hold mortgage-backed securities on the asset side of its balance sheet, it would hold CDOs issued by structured investment vehicles created to hold mortgage-backed securities.

So what we've got now is Joe and Joella's crappy mortgage being packaged into a mortgage-backed security, then repackaged as a CDO, then re-repackaged as a 'CDO-squared.' And at every stage, the original crazy lending decision becomes less and less obvious to the ultimate end investor. That investor would have no way to check out the borrowing capacity of individual borrowers, no way to check the value of the ultimate collateral. The one over-ridingly crucial job of the fixed income investor is to check the credit quality of the bonds he or she is investing in – and the whole CDO-squared nonsense made that task impossi-ble to perform. Yet all the slick Wall Street salesmen needed to do to secure their sale was to point to the AAA rating bestowed on these bonds by the ratings agencies. A rock-solid rating, and an attractive yield: what could possibly go wrong?

Stage 5

You might think that all this is complex enough, crazy enough, tangled enough – but you'd be wrong. As it happens, there were Wall Streeters keen to see if they could create a 'CDO-cubed,' a CDO of a CDO of a CDO of a mortgage-backed security, backed by the full faith and credit of Joe and Joella – but as far as I know, the whole market blew up before people could be that stupid. Shame.

Nevertheless, there was room for one further twist in the screw before Armageddon arrived. As the mortgage market boomed to a peak of something over $10 trillion, there were investors starting to get anxious about the scale of their exposures. Some of these were motivated by ordinary credit-driven concerns. Others were bullish on the mortgage market but simply had to cap the total volume of their exposures. And so on. There was a huge variety of different motivations.

But there was one common solution for their needs: the credit default swap or CDS. Forget about the intricacies of the terminology. Credit default swaps operate exactly like regular insurance – in this case, insurance against credit risk and default. You pay your premium year after year. If the asset you've insured goes bad, then the insurance pays out. So if, for example, you bought a mortgage-backed security full of sub-prime mortgage assets, you might (when you came to your senses) decide to insure yourself against the possibility of default. It would have been a sensible thing to do. If you're dumb enough to buy a house in an earthquake zone in the first place, then at least have the sense to insure it properly.

So far, so sensible. The trouble, as ever, was Wall Street. Some smart guys on the Street noticed that the pattern of payouts on insurance schemes (a chain of small regular premiums followed by a potentially large one-off insurance payout) looked very like the pattern of payments on a CDO (a chain of small regular interest payments followed by a large final repayment of principal). Using a little financial magic it proved to be possible to turn those credit default swaps into a 'synthetic' CDO. In plain language, all those people taking out insurance against defaults were making bets on one side of the mortgage market, while the synthetic CDO enabled investors to bet on the other side of the market. In effect, that synthetic CDO created mortgage risk out of nowhere. That $10 trillion of mortgage risk was apparently not enough; Wall Street had to artificially create more from thin air. Many of these synthetic schemes were little more than Ponzi schemes, which pretended to offer AAA-quality assets and in practice were lethally weakened by the shoddiness of their underlying assets. The creators of those schemes made a fortune from creating them, lost heaps of money for their investors – and are still, for the most part, in business and thriving today. No one who created such a scheme has been jailed and almost nobody fined.

No doubt you've read this far with some mixed feelings. Relief to have gotten through it. Pleasure at having (mostly?) followed it. Anxiety that maybe you haven't quite. Some angry amazement that financial regulators were so dozy that they let all this happen without a murmur. But let's put all that to one side. This chapter has traced developments in the mortgage market as a means to an end. We're not so interested in risks that were specific to one financial market at one specific period in history – a market which more or less annihilated itself in 2008.

The crucial issue is this: the way Wall Street sees risk vs. the reality of those risks.

We'll look at the reality of the risks in the next chapter. But first, the Wall Street view. According to Wall Street, all these MBSs and CDOs and CDSs allowed the credit risk of Joe and Joella's mortgage to be ground so finely that it was spread like pollen across the entire financial system. Of course, if Joe and Joella failed to keep up with their payments, someone would have to absorb the loss, but in the Joe Schmoe / Jefferson Smith world, the hit was taken full in the face by one single institution, not even a large one. In the new financial system, the losses would be barely noticeable.

That was the first piece of good news – but there was more. In the old days, anyone who took credit risk was stuck with it. There simply wasn't anything they could do but absorb any hit when it came along. In the brave new world of the last decade, risk-takers could, if and when they chose, become risk-avoiders. Credit default swaps offered a way for people to exit bets they had taken and pass the risk to those whose confidence and whose balance sheets were up to the challenge.

Better still, the technology of financial derivatives allowed every separate element involved in a transaction to be separately priced and, if necessary, sold. Investors could gauge for themselves which risks were acceptable and which were not. Financial markets should be near-perfect mechanisms for evaluating and distributing those risks. In neoclassical economic theory, the dual process of self-interest and market pricing should ensure that risks weren't just widely distributed, but efficiently distributed too. Borrowers would be able to borrow cheaply (so more factories would get built). Lenders would be able to lend more securely (which would also tend to reduce overall economic costs). The result – in theory: everyone would get just a little bit richer. (Except for Wall Street, which would get very much richer.)

If these arguments had any merit, the basic arithmetic shouldn't have worried anyone much. In the first half of 2007, global banks made profits of approximately $425 billion. The banking system worldwide had core capital of almost $3,500 billion.[2] By mid-2008 the value of subprime mortgage securities had been written down by around $200 billion. The IMF reckoned there were subprime losses of a further $1,000 billion to deal with.[3]

Now, on Wall Street's logic, none of this should have been much of a problem. By mid-2008 subprime mortgage losses amounted to less than the profits earned in a single quarter. The losses to come would wipe out another year's worth of profits. The total losses wouldn't knock out even half of the banking system's hefty capital – and that's ignoring the system's capacity to rebuild capital by generating profits. Indeed, even that overstates things, because much of those subprime losses ended up outside the banking sector (as insurance companies and other investors got in on the act). So while a few badly managed or weakly capitalized banks might not have been able to ride out the crisis, the banking system as a whole should have emerged just fine. It would be a little like a fashion retailer screwing up its fall and winter ranges, taking a hit, fixing the problem, moving on. No one likes it when tough times come along, but those tough times are part of the price you pay for being in business at all. It shouldn't, ordinarily, be a big deal. That was the logic. The logic that everyone – almost everyone – believed for years.

And that logic failed catastrophically. When Lehman Brothers failed, its Chapter 11 (bankruptcy protection) filing reported this:[4]

Assets	$639 billion
Liabilities	$768 billion
Net value	*minus* $129 billion

Now, evidently you haven't had a good day at the office if, at the end of it, you have to report that you're insolvent to the tune of $129 billion. That's kind of an *oops!* moment, to put it mildly. On the other hand, that loss represented less than two months of banking profits. It represented a tiny 3.8% of the banking system's core capital . . . and bear in mind that it wasn't only banks that did business with Lehman. It was corporations and insurance firms and hedge funds and a host of others too. In other words, on Wall Street's logic, Lehman's bankruptcy should have been barely noticeable in the noise. A big deal if you stood close to the event; a mere pinprick if you were positioned further back.

Yet that pinprick triggered an unprecedented threat of collapse. In the US, and right across the world, governments and central banks stepped in to save the banking system. In the US, the UK, Ireland, and Iceland, you'd be hard pressed to find a single large bank which would not have gone bankrupt had governments not stepped in. In other markets – France, Germany, Spain, Italy, Japan – the consequences were possibly somewhat less catastrophic, but only because the American and British authorities had already thrown their bodies in front of the speeding train. Had it not been for the extraordinary vigor and generosity of American and British taxpayers, the major institutions in those other markets would have gone under too. (Of course, if you happened to be one of the taxpayers in question, you can't claim too much credit. I don't recall that you were ever given a choice.) And let's not be vague about what that collapse would have meant. It would have meant that when you went to your ATM, no cash would have come out of it. It would have meant that when nonfinancial firms tried to transmit cash in the ordinary course of their business, no cash would have been transmitted. The Lehman bankruptcy – that $129 billion pinprick – bankrupted capitalism. It was the day the world ended.

Wall Street claimed to have minimized and contained financial risks. In fact, those risks were aggregated, multiplied, and hidden. That was the case in 2008. It is still the case today. The next chapter starts to identify those risks. The chapter after that explains why Wall Street doesn't function the way ivory-tower economists think it must do.

After that, the theory stops and the grim accounting begins. We're only halfway through the credit crisis and the worst is yet to come.

TEN

How to hide a neutron bomb in ten easy steps

THE PREVIOUS CHAPTER talked about the evolution of financial markets from the simplicity of Joe Schmoe's mortgage to the horrendous complexity of Joe and Joella's. We saw how the Joe and Joella credit risk was ground up so fine that no single investor held more than a passing exposure to that fine couple. We saw how new ways to insure yourself against risk were created and deployed. We also saw that despite the proliferation of these 'risk minimization' technologies, when it came to the crunch they turned out to be risk *multiplication* technologies. Those financial neutron bombs are still scattered thickly across our financial system today. As a matter of fact, those bombs are so numerous and so dangerous, I can't even list them all. What follows is something like a top ten – or, in fact, a recipe for how to create a financial neutron bomb. It's a recipe that Wall Street has gleefully followed, with its normal high-energy zeal and creativity. Oh, and bear in mind that many of the most dangerous explosives sit in the gray land 'off balance sheet' – that is, not directly recorded in company accounts – which makes it almost impossible for third parties such as myself to quantify, or even fully describe, the risks involved. Needless to say, when those explosives detonate they have a curious habit of becoming 'on balance sheet' realities very fast and very destructively.

But we start with one risk – credit risk – that doesn't form part of that top ten, simply because credit risk is inherent in any financial system. Indeed, it's the point of the system; the reason why banks exist in the first place. So I don't have a problem with credit risk; it's what you do with it that counts.

And there was and is and always will be just one way to handle credit risk properly: by sitting down with all the data (and ideally eyeball to eyeball with the borrower) and figuring out whether the risk makes sense. The Joe Schmoe / Jefferson Smith banking system didn't eliminate credit risk; it just handled it properly. Called for evidence. Considered income flows. Weighed up the value of the collateral. Made an assessment of character. Produced a decision.

The slice'n'dice approach to credit risk – the way Wall Street operates today – means that everyone ends up exposed and no one ends up doing the analysis. In the mortgage market, no one ever really wondered whether Joe and Joella were good for the money they borrowed. The inevitable consequence was that some awful credit decisions were made.

That same lack of fundamental analysis is still true across huge acreages of the financial system today. When investors bought Greek sovereign debt, did they really do the math? Question the data? Consider economic fundamentals? Evaluate the politics? Figure out how a not very large, rich, or innovative European country could afford to run a railway system that racked up losses of more than $1 billion on sales of $253 million?[1] Or allow hairdressers to retire at fifty because they have a 'dangerous' occupation?[2] Or decide to back a system that mis-states its accounts, has gaping holes in pension provision, and routinely raids social security coffers for current spending?

Of course they didn't. No one could have made a sober analysis of the risks and decided to go ahead and invest. People who bought Greek debt did so because they didn't do their homework – and now they're reaping the rewards of their own idleness.

You can't eliminate credit risk from finance, and you shouldn't even try. What you can do is never take on a risk without thinking about it. That's not a fun game; it's not sexy, it's not innovative, and most of the time the result of all your hard work will be to confirm exactly what you guessed in the first place. Well, tough. If sexy is what you want, go into the movie business. If good credit decisions are what you want, you need to put in the hours.

Because credit risk lies at the heart of everything, many of the risks that follow trace back in some way to this one central issue. Nevertheless, as we'll see, the multiplying variety of risks means a massive increase in total risk.

Groupthink and reliance on authority

One of the major contributory factors in the mortgage crisis was the reliance of end investors on the credit ratings awarded by the major ratings agencies (Moody's, S&P, Fitch). Investors thought they didn't need to perform their own credit analysis, because someone else was doing it for them.

Sure enough, those ratings agencies called the mortgage market spectacularly wrong. Securities which were rated AAA turned out to be junk. Securities which carried a sub-investment-grade rating oftentimes turned out to be worthless. Now, to some extent, that's just human error. If smart people look at enough problems, there'll come a time when they call one wrong. The agencies do, I believe, do a decent job in trying to get things right, but in the end they're staffed by humans – and humans who, as we'll see in the next chapter, face an uphill struggle in making the right calls.

In particular, they tend to be slow in adjusting their opinions to a swift-changing reality. Their failures in the mortgage market are very well known, but you can take pretty much any credit crisis in history and find that the ratings agencies have been slow to catch up with reality. At the time of writing, Fitch has just downgraded Greek debt to CCC – that is, 'extremely speculative' and only one notch up from 'in default.' Fitch is damn right. And damn slow. Greek debt has been extremely speculative for a long while. Its debt to GDP ratio has been hovering at or above 100% for more than ten years. It has a history of falsifying its national accounts. Deficits have been high. Corruption is rife, tax avoidance ridiculous, politics dysfunctional, and the economy remarkably lacking in strong, competitive, export-oriented companies.

These longstanding features of Greek finances more or less define the notion of speculative sovereign borrower. What's more, in the years prior to the creation of the euro, markets knew perfectly well that Greek debt was speculative

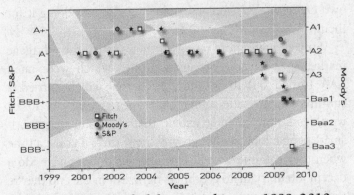

Figure 10.1: Greek debt rating history, 1999–2010

Source: 'Greek rating cut, but bail-out rate agreed,' *Financial Times*, April 9, 2010.

in the extreme. In 1994, the cost of borrowing money in drachmas for six months was over 25%. In the following years, it stayed in the mid-teens.[3] These huge rates tell us that investors knew perfectly well the Greek government could not be trusted to repay its loans without destroying value. Back then, the destruction happened via devaluation. Once Greece entered the eurozone, however, default was left as the only plausible option.

These things are obvious. However little you know about financial markets, you know that someone who can only borrow money at interest rates of between 16% and 30% is scarcely a trustworthy borrower. Yet, as you can see from figure 10.1, even *after* the credit crisis started to break in 2007–8, every single one of the major ratings agencies rated Greece at least A-, or 'upper medium grade.' How could that possibly be? The Greeks *lied* about their national accounts – deliberately falsified them – and on the kind of scale which would have brought about criminal prosecutions in any private sector company.[4] To me, no such borrower can be judged investment grade (that is, BBB or higher), at least until some years after the problem has been thoroughly exposed and addressed. Given that a country's credit standing rests on its capacity to levy taxes, I'd also suggest that a culture of outrageous tax avoidance – promoted in part by the authorities' blind acceptance of it – would tend to indicate that the country's *actual* revenue-generating capacity falls far short of its *theoretical* capacity for gathering taxes.

Once again, the conclusion is remarkably simple. Investors need to do their own homework. They need to avoid groupthink by practicing the habit of independent thought, evaluating risk for themselves. However hard and honestly the ratings agencies attempt to conduct their business – despite a biased and inappropriate set of incentives – they can't always be right. Very often, they'll prefer to opt for comfort rather than truth. They were wrong about the mortgage market. They are only now starting to catch up with problems in the sovereign debt market. The only protection for any investor is to start from the beginning every time, to do the homework, to think for themselves.

Liquidity risk

In the old days – the days of Joe Schmoe and Jefferson Smith – credit was, for the most part, not tradable. A loan was made, and the same two counterparties would then remain locked in a credit relationship which would last until the loan was repaid or the borrower declared bankruptcy. Since both parties knew they'd be tied together for the term of the loan, this arrangement forced discipline on both of them. Borrowers went to banks they trusted. Banks chose borrowers they deemed reliable. Simple good sense.

The development of a large and liquid corporate bond market in the late 1970s and 1980s brought many good things in its wake. Because borrowers could go straight to the ultimate investors, without needing an old-fashioned commercial bank to act as middleman, they could borrow more cheaply. That helped them make investments and develop their businesses. In a small way, we all benefited.

Investors benefited too. Previously, investors had, broadly speaking, three choices. They could buy equities on the stock market. They could acquire bonds issued by the government or a few very large banks and corporations. Or they could put their money on deposit in a bank. As the securities market opened up, they became able to build entire portfolios of corporate bonds. They no longer had to restrict themselves to blue-chip borrowers, the likes of General Electric and IBM. The creation of a market in sub-investment-grade debt – the junk bond market – meant all kinds of borrowers could now access investors directly, and vice versa.

As these markets developed, investors began to realize that this new form of credit relationship didn't have to be a lasting one. You could buy IBM bonds one day, wake up the next day and decide you wanted to invest in something else. So you sell IBM and buy whatever. A couple of phone calls and you're done. Investors no longer had to be the boring guys in finance. They could be traders too. They could be players.

And the very best thing, from an investor's perspective, about this new world? Risks were slashed. If you bought an AAA-rated bond issued by the well-known company American Widget Corp, you'd be aware that even a strong company carries some risk. If AWC ran into bad times – if competitors attacked its markets, prices tumbled, technology changed in adverse ways – then likely enough the ratings agencies would start to downgrade the bond. From AAA to AA+. From AA+ to AA, then maybe AA–. And at every stage, you'd have the option to bail out. If your investment fund wanted to concentrate only on the very strongest credits, you could simply have a rule that you'd sell up if a bond was downgraded below AA–.

Sure, you'd most likely take a hit as you made that sale. The price of a bond is inversely related to its yield, or interest rate. (That's a mathematical truism. If you don't understand why the rule exists, just trust me on it.[5]) Since less creditworthy borrowers have to pay higher interest rates than stronger borrowers, when a bond is downgraded, its price will fall. But you don't mind taking a hit. Losing a little money when you sell out of a bond is the price you pay to protect yourself against further weakness. In the old days, if a bank made a ten-year loan, it knew it was going to be on the hook for ten long and dangerous years. In the new world, if an investor bought a ten-year bond – or even (why not?) a thirty-year bond – they knew they weren't making a commitment that had to last as long as the bond. They could sell the bond whenever they wanted. Pass the risk on to someone else. This was the joy of the bond market – the joy of liquidity.

Don't get me wrong. Liquid bond markets have indeed brought huge benefits. They reduce the cost of finance. They make it easier for ordinary companies to do what they do. We all benefit. But you don't get innovations without risk; and in this case, the existence of liquid bond markets tempted banks and investors to believe that those markets would always be available. And virtually no market is always available. Why would it be? Markets exist when you have plenty of willing buyers on one side, plenty of willing sellers on the other. If circumstances alter, so that there are many more would-be sellers than would-be buyers, you no longer have a market. You have *Torschlusspanik* – a German word meaning literally 'door-closing-panic': a stampede for the exit, under conditions when the stampede is the very thing that's blocking up the exit.

Circumstances like this are anything but theoretical. When Lehman Brothers was starting to go under, it tried to exit the mortgage market positions that were causing it so much trouble. But as Lehman started selling assets, the market learned that it was selling. Because Lehman was such a significant player, that knowledge inevitably forced the price lower. Other investors figured they'd better sell before the price crashed completely. So the price fell lower. So Lehman was under still greater pressure to sell. So prices crashed until the market effectively locked up. These were firesale prices, only no one was buying.

Huge numbers of investors were caught in the crossfire. They'd bought shedloads of AAA-rated mortgage bonds containing subprime and other mortgages in the belief that (1) the credit agencies couldn't be *that* mistaken, and (2) if a problem arose they could always sell up and get out, suffering only a modest loss. Wrong! And wrong again! The consequences of those false beliefs were massive. They lay at the very heart of the first stage of the credit crisis, and inflicted losses of (depending on how you count them and whom you believe) between $1.5 and $3 trillion.

You can see the first shivers of *Torschlusspanik* in the sovereign debt market now. In mid-September 2011, the cost to Greece of borrowing money for two years rose to over 80% per annum, and market rumor placed some yields in excess of 100%. I know loan sharks who would be embarrassed to charge that much. Indeed, Greece could get a better rate than that by borrowing the cash on some ripoff store card deal. In effect, that 80% interest rate is simply a sign that funding is no longer available, that the country's debt market has lost all liquidity.[6] (As a rule of thumb, when interest rates rise to more than 7% or 8% payback becomes impossible, because you can never manage to pay back principal when you're spending so much on interest payments.) If you were one of the investors who figured that you didn't have to think about credit risk because you could always sell your bonds and move on, you'd have found that the modest hit you had been prepared for had turned suddenly into a knockout blow.

You'd think that maybe these experiences would have taught investors to think differently about the risks they take on, but nothing seems to teach investors anything. The incredible speed with which Wall Street returned to business as normal after the first credit crisis has seen credit and leverage returning to pre-Lehman levels. Each new problem is seen as a local matter. Oops! Bit of a screw-up in the mortgage market. Yikes! Got my fingers burned in Greece. But none of that is going to be a problem for my Spanish bonds (or my Italian bonds, or the bonds issued by banks who hold this stuff), because I can always sell out if things get sticky.

Risk quantification

So far, the risks we've spoken about would have been recognizable to the bankers of the Joe Schmoe / Jefferson Smith era. Back then folks didn't rely too much on ratings agencies and liquidity risk was much less prominent. Jefferson Smith would have been baffled by the idea of risk quantification. As far as he was concerned, the amount of money he had at risk was the amount he'd lent to Joe Schmoe minus the amount that Joe had repaid. The only risk to which Jefferson Smith was exposed was that some idiot in the office might not be able to do simple arithmetic.

The situation is utterly different today. For all that securities are designed to be tradable – a commoditized asset class using largely standardized legal language, conferring the same rights no matter which investor owns the security – they oftentimes don't trade much at all. Sometimes that doesn't matter too much. If you own an A-rated corporate bond, and you've done your homework and reckon that the A-rating is appropriate for the borrower in question, you can get a pretty good idea of the price your bond will trade at simply by looking at the prices at which other A-rated bonds are traded today. There'll be a margin of error, of course. Investors have different sentiments about different companies. There'll be things to think about in terms of liquidity, duration, currency, and so on. Nevertheless, if you're reasonably smart about these things, you should be able to do the math with a fair degree of confidence.

Those comments, however, apply only to bonds that come in plain vanilla, and it's increasingly rare for any large financial institution to stick to plain vanilla. In the heyday of the mortgage market many of the most complex securities hardly traded at all, and when they did the transaction prices weren't disclosed. (A major difference from the equity market, by the way. You can go online right now and check the buy-price and the sell-price on any major stock in the world. That publicly available information just doesn't exist for most parts of the bond market – a big reason why Wall Street finds it easy to rip off customers and investors.) Yet banks and others needed some way to value their portfolios – so instead of relying on actual prices paid in actual transactions for actual securities, they built mathematical models of how those securities *ought* to trade.

Now, if you ever wanted to illustrate how really, really smart people could be really, really stupid, those mathematical models would be a prime exhibit. They were wonders of the mathematician's art: a pleasure-garden filled with Gaussian copulae, stochastic probability projections, and Monte Carlo simulations. And they're bullshit. The only thing that matters is actual prices in actual situations. In any situation of market turbulence – the moments, in other words, when pricing really, really matters – you can bet your life that those models will fail. They'll fail because they're based on a whole heap of historical data, generated at a time when the market was not under stress, when pricing was not being generated in a live combat situation.

Fortunately, by now the worst excesses of the mortgage market have been obliterated. There are no more CDOs of CDOs, and I truly hope that there never will be again.* But the financial architecture we live with has become wildly Gothic all the same. Financial derivatives – Warren Buffett's

* Though rumor has it that banks are trying to recreate these now.

weapons of mass financial destruction' – are financial structures, typically involving options, that can massively multiply or mitigate asset exposures and/or pricing risks. The value of these products depends on several variables, such as changes in interest rates, currencies, credit, time value, and the like. In contrast to the relatively simple arithmetic needed to perform basic bond math, the valuation of derivatives is a dizzyingly complex and contested subject.

Nevertheless, usage of these potentially beneficial yet complex products has expanded to an extraordinary degree over the past three decades. In 'over-the-counter' derivatives (i.e. those that are privately negotiated) alone, there is some $600 trillion worth of notional principal outstanding (a term I'll define a little later) – that's over forty times the GDP of the United States.[7] Or forget the US. It's more than ten times the GDP of the entire world. And that's not all of them. As well as OTC derivatives, there are exchange-traded varieties available too, which add perhaps half as much again to the total stock. As a rough guide, then, the notional principal outstanding on the world's derivatives market is equal to at least fifteen times global GDP. If there's intelligent life on Mars, it's laughing at us.

And these comments assume that the officially collected totals for derivatives are correct. You'd hope they were right, of course: these derivatives have already helped blow up the financial system once, and may well do so again. But because derivatives are contingent liabilities – if you hold them, you *may* owe something or you may not – they live in the shadows off company balance sheets. Since shadows are a good place to hide stuff, and since plenty of firms have strong incentives to hide their most toxic obligations, you can never be quite sure what lurks in the darkness. Perhaps you think I'm exaggerating? Not so. Lehman Brothers was repeatedly criticized for its 'Repo 105' arrangements, which disguised $50 billion of debt under the cloak of phony sales.[8] The transactions weren't illegal but they were deliberately misleading. That's why they were conducted in the first place. Other firms may be doing similar things now, far away from the sight of the official stats. I don't know that they are doing so, but I don't know that they're not. What I do know is that the regulators lack the teeth and the resources to monitor these things effectively, and that financial institutions – particularly those under the greatest pressure to improve their results – have a strong incentive to indulge in precisely this type of arrangement. That's scary.

Having said all this, I should probably make a couple of disclaimers at this point. First, I've spent much of my career trading derivatives. I think they can be an incredibly helpful tool that can achieve some wonderful things. For example, I've pioneered the use of certain derivatives in the carbon-trading market. Those tools have assisted large corporations in the quest to make themselves carbon neutral. When one of their executives flies by jet around the world, those tools will ensure that someone somewhere replaces a coal-fired power plant with wind farms. I'm proud of that. There are plenty of other examples of honorable uses of derivatives. Low-income African farmers can now often use their mobile phones to check agricultural futures prices, and lock in a price today for a crop that won't be harvested for another three months. That gives the farmer a certainty he never had in the past; and that's a wonderful thing. Derivatives offer assistance in more mundane ways too. Airlines can protect themselves against a spike in oil prices, or a collapse in profits because of excessive snowfall. Multinational firms can protect themselves against currency swings. Homeowners can fix their mortgage payments. Heck, I once structured and provided the first protection to golf courses in the US for weather-related cancelations. OK, it's not the same as inventing penicillin, but in a modest way it made those golf courses more financially secure, and thus protected their employees and investors. There's no reason at all why derivatives shouldn't be used in ways that help people and firms meet their financial goals. That's why they exist.

Secondly, I should be clear about the meaning of the phrase 'notional principal outstanding.' Many derivatives contracts are based on some notional outstanding amount. So, for example, if you are paying a floating interest rate on some debt, and you'd prefer to pay a fixed interest rate instead, you and I could arrange a deal whereby we enter into an interest rate swap agreement. I'll pay you a floating rate – for example, three-month Libor. In exchange, you pay me an agreed fixed rate – for example, 4%. In effect, you've swapped your floating rate obligation for a fixed rate obligation. That achieves your objective.

Now, if you borrowed $100 million in the first place, and if our interest rate swap was for that full $100 million, then the notional principal outstanding is $100 million. That doesn't, however, mean that anything like that amount of cash is at stake. It isn't. In practice, the two sets of payments (my floating rate payment to you; your fixed rate payment to me) are set against each other. So if, for example, the floating rate chosen is 1% below the fixed rate we've agreed, you'll just pay the difference to me, according to our pre-agreed settlement terms. Under these circumstances, the amount of money changing hands in a given year is 1% of

$100 million, or just $1 million – a tiny fraction of that scary-looking notional principal outstanding. (The practical reality can be a lot more complex than this illustration suggests, of course.)

Nevertheless, and even taking these things into account, the purely speculative volume of derivatives contracts is extraordinarily huge. What's worse is that most people who get involved in this stuff don't understand it. Typically, a Wall Street banker comes along with a slick pitch and a credible story. The rewards seem huge and certain, the risks remote and improbable. The Wall Street banker never quotes you his fee for arranging the deal (because his fee is buried in the overall transaction structure), so while the banker will know to a penny how the contract has been priced and put together, the buyer likely doesn't have a clue. Plus, of course, the banker is a professional, high-end salesman, with huge incentives to get the deal done. Time after time, I've seen clients entering into ridiculous contracts which they don't understand – and paying an extortionate sum for the privilege. There are plenty of well-known examples of firms and organizations that have been all but destroyed by these contracts.

And buried right at the heart of this huge and dangerous mountain is *risk quantification*. Wall Street banks have the smartest, best-funded, best-resourced quantitative analysts ('quants') in the business, yet when it came to the first credit crisis, they simply didn't know the value of the stuff they carried on their balance sheets. They didn't know, that is, until the market ripped their bogus assumptions into a million small pieces, obliterating two leading firms (Bear Stearns and Lehman) and leaving all the other brokerages in fear of their lives – and on government life support. When the ground opened up in front of Citigroup, when the collapse in the mortgage market started to generate huge losses, the firm barely understood what had hit it. *Financial Times* journalist Gillian Tett, in her book *Fool's Gold*, reports one senior Citi manager saying bitterly: 'Perhaps there were a dozen people in the bank who really understood all this before – I doubt it was more.'[9] That Citi manager was wrong. There were *no* people in the bank who really understood it. By definition. If any of them had understood the true riskiness of these contracts, they'd never have entered into them. This was a huge bank. Taking huge risks. Incurring vast losses. And no one in the bank understood how it had happened.

At least Chuck Prince, Citi's CEO, had the grace to apologize profusely for his mismanagement of the firm when he appeared in front of the federal Financial Crisis Inquiry Commission. Robert Rubin – chairman of Citigroup, co-CEO of Goldman Sachs, former Treasury Secretary – refused to apologize, stating that the executive committee, which he chaired, 'wasn't a substantive part of the decision-making process.'[10] If it wasn't, it's not altogether clear what entitled him to draw more than $100 million in pay and benefits from the firm during his decade at the top. And Prince, for all his remorse, hasn't felt obliged to return any of his assets. On Planet Ponzi, grace goes only so far. It stops when it reaches the wallet.

And that's just Wall Street. That's the smart guys. The problem everywhere else is even more mountainous. If you want to know how a Ponzi scheme can stay alive so long, it's because you can pile up a hideous amount of losses in other people's balance sheets – and those people don't even know it's there.

Risk quantification. It sounds trivial. It sounds boring. It sounds like a case of just buying a bigger computer. But risk management kills firms. And there's only one way to avoid it: only play with stuff that you really, truly understand. And stick close to actual market pricing, because only then do you stay close to reality.

Long tail risk

There's a variant on risk quantification which carries its own separate hazards. Back in the 1990s, JP Morgan – then and now, one of the best-run banks on the market – invented a risk management technology which measured 'value at risk' or VAR. That is, it could tell you how much money you would stand to lose on your entire portfolio if interest rates rose a little, or if the yen fell a little, and so on. The technology was a terrific innovation, and became widespread across the market. But it had a limitation. It could only predict likely losses under likely scenarios. It was a way of measuring the losses you'd be exposed to 95 times out of 100, perhaps even 99 times out of 100.

Of course, that's information any decently managed financial institution needs – an essential part of the information that enables it to manage its ordinary risks as accurately as possible. Ninety-nine times out of a hundred, when you come into work, you won't find a tornado flying around your dealing room.

But ordinary risks are not the risks which are going to bury your firm – and the whole of Western capitalism – under a mountain of excessive debts and lousy assets. VAR technology was so dangerous because the technology was so good – 95% of the time. As it happened, JP Morgan was never suckered by its own creation. The firm remembered what it could do and what it could not do. Management wanted to build a 'fortress balance sheet' that would withstand the 1 in 10,000 chance, as well as the 95 in 100 one. So they did. When the first credit crisis hit, JP Morgan shipped some water, but not much. The safety of the firm was never jeopardized. The firm was profitable right through the financial crisis.[11]

Other institutions weren't so smart. They believed too much in the power of a technology – and way too little in the power of ordinary common sense, consistently applied. It was another example of too much reliance on computers, too little respect for the way markets can make suckers of us all.

Funding risk

As all these risks multiply, they generate new forms of danger – and dangers that are typically underestimated by those taking the risks.

The flipside of liquidity risk, for example (primarily a concern of investors) is funding risk (a concern of borrowers). This is the risk that the markets you rely on for your funding simply dry up, cease to operate, deny you funds at any reasonable price. The overconfident, overaggressive British bank Northern Rock failed in 2007 because it could no longer obtain funds. Historically, retail banks have always been careful to fund themselves largely by attracting customer deposits, because such deposits have historically proved a reliable and stable form of financing. Northern

Rock threw that tried-and-tested model out of the window, relying in very large part on short-term money market financing. That funding structure was insane in at least two respects. First, it generated a huge maturity mismatch between Northern Rock's long-term assets (primarily loans made to customers) and its very short-term funding. Secondly, it placed vastly excessive reliance on the continued willingness of commercial lenders to lend to it. It was simply asking for trouble – and in 2007 that's what it got. It took £26 billion of government loans to keep Northern Rock afloat, until the bank was effectively nationalized in 2008.[12]

That story was only the first in a chain of failures. The German bank IKB set up some off-balance-sheet investment vehicles that were funded exclusively in the commercial paper market (the main form of short-term borrowing). When those markets closed up, IKB was left with nowhere to turn. Dumb financing, maturity mismatches, disastrous outcomes.

Citigroup itself was felled by the same thing. When that manager spoke bitterly about how almost no one in the bank even knew about the thing that had eventually laid it low, the problem was only indirectly the collapse in the mortgage market. That collapse would have bankrupted some of Citi's off-balance-sheet vehicles, but Citi itself should have survived. It didn't, because it had guaranteed to provide those vehicles with funding, if normal sources of funding ever dried up. A simple guarantee to offer, but one that brought the company to its knees – and but for government support would have killed it.

One of the really astonishing aspects of these stories is how little those involved seem to have learned. The chairman of Northern Rock, Matt Ridley, was interrogated by British parliamentarians in the wake of the crisis – a crisis that had prompted the first bank run in Britain for 150 years. Instead of sounding apologetic or humble about his failures, Ridley sounded plaintive. He complained: 'The idea that all markets would close simultaneously was unforeseen by any major authority. We were hit by an unexpected and unpredictable concatenation of events.'[13]

Well, duh! Of course you don't expect the unexpected. That's why you take precautions and prudently manage your risks accordingly. The fact that Britain hadn't experienced a bank run for 150 years suggests that those precautions were hardly unknown to Ridley's predecessors. But in the era of the Ponzi scheme, why burden yourself with common sense, when you can just press the pedal to the metal and see how far you can travel before the engine blows? (In Ridley's case, the answer was around three years at a salary of £300,000 per year.[14] Those three years ended up adding around £100 billion to the British national debt.[15])

Counterparty risk

We ended the last chapter by noting a puzzling fact. The global financial system boasted core capital of a massive $3,500 billion and yet was laid low by a bankruptcy, Lehman's, to the tune of just $129 billion, of which a substantial portion – maybe half? – was owed to nonbank institutions. The risk minimization, hedging, and dispersal technologies of which Wall Street was so proud turned out to be risk maximization, multiplication, and concentration technologies. In this chapter so far we've addressed a good many of those risks – and of course, they all overlap and interact – but the white-hot core of the problem turned out to be counterparty risk.

That $129 billion which Lehman owed was a net figure: the value of its assets less the (rather larger) value of its debts. But the net figure was irrelevant. That wasn't what Lehman's creditors were thinking about. They were thinking: 'Am *I* going to get *my* money back?' And since there were $768 billion worth of creditors, there were a lot of worried people.

Even that $768 billion figure itself understates things. When Lehman (like any other institution) drew up its balance sheet, it noted down in the right-hand liabilities column only things that were actually owed. But Lehman sat in the middle of a massive network of derivative contracts – contracts that took the form, 'If X happens, you pay me Y.' Those obligations are called contingent liabilities, because they're only triggered if certain events happen. But that was hardly going to reassure all the thousands of creditors who had taken out various forms of derivatives insurance with Lehman. If Lehman had gone, their insurance had gone. Very significant financial assumptions now needed to be reconsidered.

What's more, although banks do need to report their contingent liabilities in a footnote to their financial statements (and trust me, that footnote tends to include some scarily huge numbers[16]), for management purposes they tend to focus on their net liabilities. So Lehman, for example, would have been in the middle of some interest rate bets which would pay out if interest rates rose and other bets which would pay out if interest rates fell. On a *net* basis, Lehman would have ensured that its exposure to movements in interest rates would have remained at tolerable levels. But that's to look at the world from Lehman's perspective. And on that fateful day in September 2008, Lehman no longer existed. Its creditors – gross, not net; contingent as well as actual – suddenly realized they had no idea if they'd ever get their money back.

The neutron bomb exploded outwards from there. If Lehman couldn't be trusted, then what about AIG? What about RBS? What about Merrill Lynch? What about Citi? The interbank market froze.* Everyone was suspicious of everyone else. No one knew how much those other parties had been injured by the succession of calamities (mortgage market problems, Lehman's failure, interbank funding constraints, massive excess leverage). So the 'strength' of Wall Street's risk management system – the way everyone was now connected to everyone else – turned into its biggest weakness. It was as though all the passengers on the *Titanic* were roped together, and the fattest guy had just fallen overboard.

Accounting risk

I hope that at least a few of you have read the foregoing pages with a gathering sense of puzzlement. Sure, you might be thinking, counterparty risk matters. You need to know who you're dealing with and whether they're good for the money. That's the kind of risk even Jefferson Smith could

---

* Just as it is freezing now. French and Italian banks are currently finding it all but impossible to issue commercial paper or certificates of deposit.

have understood. But since the kind of counterparties we're dealing with are generally large, sophisticated financial institutions, all of which produce detailed accounts on a quarterly basis, why wouldn't you just call up the latest set of accounts and take a look? If you like what you see, you've got a counterparty you can do business with. If you don't, then just say no. What's so hard about that?

Well, quite. I agree.

The Financial Accounting Standards Board (FASB) is the outfit which lays down the rules for generally accepted accounting practice in the US. The rules are intended to help accountants draw up accounts which will be:

❏ *objective* – accounts need to be based on objective evidence;

❏ *material* – accountants don't need to worry about items that are of no real consequence to the company or its stakeholders;

❏ *consistent* – accounts can't vary their rules from year to year;

❏ *conservative* – when accountants have a choice of two alternatives, they should opt for the one which is least likely to overstate assets or income.

There's nothing to argue with in those ambitions. And for the most part, FASB (and IASB, its international cousin) does an excellent job of developing rules that investors around the world can rely on implicitly. Trouble is, 'for the most part' isn't good enough, not remotely – and at the moment, with the support of FASB and IASB, international banks are preparing their accounts according to rules that more or less invite irresponsibility.

Here's the issue. In the old days, if a bank made a loan of $100, it figured on the bank's books as an asset worth $100. If the borrower ran into any kind of trouble, the bank's management would make a provision against expected losses. So if a bank thought it might stand to lose 20 cents on the dollar, it would take a $20 hit and report a loan value of $80. All sweet and simple – but it relied on the good faith and commercial sense of the managers in charge of making the loss provisions. Although the bank's auditors would need to approve the bank's valuations of its assets, they would recognize that they were not expert in credit evaluation, so – in the absence of gross error or evident manipulation – those auditors would likely agree with the bank's assessment. In any case, since bank loans weren't tradable, there was no other option available.

But that was banks. Wall Street brokerages were different. The assets that generally filled their balance sheets were securities: bonds, stocks, and so on. Since those things were openly traded, the rules applying to them were simpler, and tougher. If a brokerage bought a security for $100, but that security came to trade at just $80, the security would be valued at $80 on the broker's books. There was no room for argument. All the broker's financial assets would be assessed on their market value at each balance sheet date, a process called marking-to-market.' Simple. Smart. Tough. Objective.

As credit markets developed, however, loans too became tradable. Even when the loan itself wasn't traded there were traded derivatives – credit default swaps – which implied a price for each loan. So, in this new world, and taking account of FASB's stipulations about objectivity and conservatism, banks were told that they had to mark their loan portfolios to market. If that loan portfolio deteriorated in quality, perhaps because of a general economic slow-down, the market would dictate precisely what losses had been suffered and the balance sheet would reflect that new valuation. Simple. Smart. Tough. Objective.

But banker-kind cannot bear too much reality. In spring of 2009, when that reality was becoming too hot for banks to handle, they begged for, and were granted, a change in the rules. The new mark-to-market accounting was scrapped for banks, and in its place the older loan loss pro-visioning system was reinstated. The change meant reintroducing management discretion into the valuation of loan portfolios and removed the brutally objective measure-ment of the market.

If we lived in a world full of honor and sound judgment, the change wouldn't have made too much of a difference. The two approaches should, on balance, give more or less the same answers. But we do not live in that world. We live in a world where the easiest way for banks' management to avoid the consequences of lousy lending decisions is to ignore them completely.

For example, banks that have lent money to Greece typically hold some of those assets on their banking book, and some on their trading book. Same assets, same appalling credit situation, same losses. On the market at the moment, Greek debt is trading at 40 cents on the dollar. If my math is correct, that tells me that banks have made losses of at least 60 cents on the dollar. Hideous, huge, horrendous losses brought about by an astonishing degree of laziness and complacency when it came to judging the credit in the first place.

But are banks fessing up to those losses? Of course not! The debt held on their trading books – a tiny fraction of the whole – is valued at market prices. All the rest of it, the debt held on their banking books, is carried at something much closer to 100 cents on the dollar. But please don't take my word for these things. (To repeat: I don't want you to take my word for anything in this book; I invite you to check out any piece of data, any factual claim you like.) Here are the *Financial Times*'s comments on this very topic:

> Up until now, most banks have not written down the value of the bulk of their Greek sovereign bonds. Bonds can be held in two buckets on banks' balance sheets: trading books, which routinely mark the value of bonds to market, only hold a fraction of banks' sovereign bond investments; the balance is in so-called banking books, which are routinely held to maturity and are therefore not traditionally marked to market, ignoring plunges in bond values as a result.
>
> Of the €82.7bn in aggregate net exposure to Greek sovereign debt revealed in last week's European stress tests, just €3.9bn – or less than 5 per cent – is held in banks' trading books, according to an analysis by the *Financial Times*.
>
> Nearly €79bn, however, is held in institutions' banking book assets, which are not adjusted for swings in market value. A 21 per cent write-down or 'haircut' on Greek sovereign debt held in those portfolios would trigger losses of nearly €17bn across the 90 banks surveyed in this year's widely discredited tests.[17]

These comments come from Europe's most prestigious financial journal, and one whose language has a tendency to be somewhat dry and technical. But the composure of its style belies the gravity of what it is reporting. This whole article should really be printed in 48-point capitals and studded with exclamation points. *European banks have made losses of €17 billion and they are openly lying about them.* People even know that they're lying and yet nothing happens. Right now, the fraud police ought to be marching into management suites and snapping handcuffs on the occupants. And what do we have instead? A dry article in the *Financial Times* which implies a slightly eggy disapproval – and that's all. Nothing else – in the face of €17 billion of losses that have arisen in one tiny little corner of the financial world; €17 billion of losses created by a country with a GDP about the same as Maryland's.[18] Since, in fact, the latest EU restructuring plan seeks to impose losses on private creditors equal to 50% of those creditors' Greek assets, the destruction of value has been painfully real – no accounting fiction, but sober, painful fact.

But these problems aren't unique to Europe. Here's another example from the US, specifically the Bank of America. The BoA is, like many of its peers, in a bind. New rules are coming into force which will require it to hold a larger quantity of core capital. You can acquire that capital in one of two ways. You can earn good profits and retain a substantial proportion of them (i.e. you can't give too much of your profit to shareholders by way of dividend). Or you can issue new shares and raise fresh funds direct from the market. That's the good news. The bad news is that BoA's shareholders don't want to put their hands into their wallets for fresh capital and they don't want the BoA to restrict dividends while it concentrates on building up capital.

And there's another issue. BoA has made a hideous mess of its mortgage book and has huge losses to write off. But the more it acknowledges those losses, the more it reduces its capital. On the other hand, you can't *not* acknowledge those losses, because everyone knows they're there and people have started (not before time) to fret over them.

Pressure on every front. A circle that can't be squared.

Except it can. Because we live in a world where managements can simply manipulate their reported figures. A recent note from Bloomberg documents exactly how that process works.[19] Here's the four-step sequence that Bank of America followed:

1 Acknowledge a huge writedown on your mortgage book, driving that business $14.5 billion into the red. (Just pause a moment to contemplate that figure. Can you even imagine running a business so badly that it loses almost $15 billion? If you ran a business that badly, could you even imagine you would be in a job receiving lavish salary and bonuses and the respect of your peers? I'm guessing 'no.' Yet by one calculation, the bank has written off over $30 billion in this one business segment in the course of a calendar year and may need to write off tens of billions more.[20])

2 Deny any possibility that you will need to raise fresh capital from shareholders.

3 Identify an area where you can juggle your figures – let's say, the nonmortgage loan portfolio, which hasn't come under scrutiny the way the mortgage book has done.

4   Start juggling. In BoA's results, the provisions for future credit losses dropped 60%. In fact, in the quarter ending June 30, 2011, the bank undid provisions it had previously made, thereby magicking over $400 million of profit into the quarter that the previous year had seen a $600 million loss.

Now obviously, in a benign economic climate you would expect loan losses to come down. There's nothing in principle strange about seeing loss provisions rise and fall. But we are not in a benign economic climate. To pick just a few issues: (a) borrowers are currently experiencing bizarrely and unsustainably low interest rates; (b) the real economy is weak, joblessness high, and the outlook deteriorating; (c) the eurozone crisis is impairing countless European financial institutions, many of which do business with Bank of America; and (d) under any deficit reduction plan at all, the fiscal stimulus is about to be ripped away from the American economy and replaced with fiscal tightening of unprecedented severity, while (e) the scope for further economic support from the Fed is minimal. Under these circumstances, I personally would consider beefing up my loan loss provisions. I certainly wouldn't start undoing the ones I'd already made.

Although I've singled out the BoA in this discussion, I don't mean to imply that its standards are any different from those generally prevailing in the industry. The same basic point holds true for any number of other global banks. Instead of providing clear, objective measurements of value, our current accounting system does the exact opposite. It invites manipulation. It causes sane investors to stop trusting the balance sheets placed under their noses. Twenty years ago, Japan made a similar choice to eliminate truth from its banks' balance sheets and the result has been catastrophic. Western economies are currently following suit.

These issues are hugely significant. They matter because they go to the heart of this book's central claim. I'm claiming that we're living in the dying days of the biggest Ponzi scheme in history. If that's the case, I need to prove at least two things. First, that there has been a mountain of phony profits. Secondly, that there is an equal or larger mountain of buried losses.

We've already looked (in chapter 8) at the US financial system's totally disproportionate share of total profits. Given that the sector is a highly competitive one, economic theory has no way of explaining how those huge profits seem to arrive year after year after year. If the whole thing is just a Ponzi scheme, economic theory can breathe a sigh of relief.

But if the phony profits are hidden in plain view, where is the mountain of buried losses? The yawning gaps in the accounting rules laid down by FASB and IASB give you part of the answer. You tell banks they only have to fess up to losses if they feel like it . . . and what do you know, banks decide that their Greek debt is in tip-top shape and that their commercial loan portfolios have never been better. As for their mortgage books – why, they've cleared away all the embarrassments from the past and that book too is in the pink and feeling fine.

The simple fact is that we can no longer trust the balance sheets of banks. Or rather: we can trust every word they tell us about their mountainous debt obligations – those things are unfortunately only too real – but we have to stop trusting anything they tell us about their assets. The cold objective truth of the market is just too cold, too objective for most bankers today.

Oh, and finally, in case you're tempted to think that at least brokerages – firms that deal in securities rather than loans – have honest accounts, please recall my earlier comments on risk management. When market prices are scarce (as they often are), brokers end up marking their assets not to market, but to their *models* of the market. Yet as we saw in the collapse of the mortgage market, those models often bear absolutely no relation to reality – in effect, the big investment banks have been marking-to-magic: numbers plucked (with lots of mathematical fireworks) from thin air and presented to auditors. Auditors do not have the expertise to judge whether those models are accurate or not, so they'll ask a few questions, challenge a few details, then accept everything. That's not their fault. They don't have the knowledge or the authority to do otherwise – and, of course, final responsibility for any set of accounts lies with the management who sign them, not the auditors who verify them.

Either way, the result is the same – some impressive-looking numbers, and losses multiplying like termites out of sight.

Legal risk

Let's move on: from accountants to lawyers.

In the old days, a bond was a physical piece of paper. If a company – General Motors, let's say – wanted to raise $100 million, it might issue 10,000 bonds with a face value of $10,000 each. Those old bonds had coupons down the side which investors would physically cut out and present for payment each time an interest payment was due. These days, those fancily printed bits of paper have largely given way to electronics, but those old-fashioned certificates were a nice reminder that bonds are little more than fancy IOUs, the most ancient form of borrowing you can imagine.

At the same time, the physical piece of paper only ever mattered because it represented something: a contract between borrower and lender. The things that the borrower could and couldn't do. The things that the lender could and couldn't expect. Naturally enough, judges in the US, Britain, and elsewhere long ago evolved a sophisticated case law to handle any disputes. What happened if the bond issuer went bankrupt – the order in which creditors were paid out, how collateral was allocated – all these things and more were worked out in such a way that ordinary borrowing and lending became a smoothly operating machine.

In the last ten or fifteen years, things have become vastly more complicated. Most of the financial innovation in that period has been driven, in the first instance, by mathematical possibility – the kind of thing that looks smart on a spreadsheet. But those spreadsheets are meaningless unless they turn into enforceable contracts and the contracts which emerge are often insanely complicated.

Take, for example, the CDO-squared, a CDO backed by CDOs. Bearing in mind that many SIVs were created with multiple different tiers of debt, the legal language was forced to become ludicrously complex. If you don't believe me, take a look for yourself. Here is just one sentence taken from a 300-page 2007-vintage prospectus for a CDO-squared:

Unless notified by a Majority of any Class of
Secured Notes or Composite Notes or a Majority-
in-Interest of Subordinated Noteholders that
such Class of Secured Notes, Composite Notes or
the Subordinated Notes could be materially and
adversely affected (or in the case of the Class A-1
Notes, unless notified by a Majority of the Class A-
1 Notes that such Class of Notes could be
adversely affected), or by each applicable Short
Synthetic Counterparty that it would be materially
and adversely affected, or by the TRS Counterparty that it would be materially and adversely
affected, the Trustee may rely in good faith with
the written advice of counsel or an officer's
certificate of the Issuer or the Collateral Manager
delivered to the Trustee as to whether or not such
Class of Secured Notes or Composite Notes, the
Subordinated Notes, each applicable Short Synthetic Counterparty or the TRS Counterparty (or
with respect to any Short Synthetic Counterparty
or the TRS Counterparty, an opinion of counsel
only) would be materially and adversely affected
(or in the case of the Class A-1 Notes, could be
adversely affected) by such change (after giving
notice of such change to the holders of the
Secured Notes, the Composite Notes and the
Subordinated Notes and to each applicable Short
Synthetic Counterparty and the TRS Counterparty).[21]

These things weren't deliberately designed to confuse
and bamboozle – but contracts, remember, are essentially

tools for the battlefield. They're there to tell you what needs to happen if things go wrong. When Lehman blew up, all of a sudden the scale of the likely battlefield appeared in view for the first time. Lehman stood at the center of thousand upon thousand of these contracts. Each one was meticulously written. The intricate legal clockwork at the heart of each offering made perfect logical sense. But the idea of testing all this stuff in a bankruptcy court . . . ! For all the theoretical perfection of the clockwork, when it actually came to the crunch creditors realized they had no idea what the hell was going to happen, or when. In place of the old certainties there was only a radical uncertainty, a realization that they didn't actually know anything at all. The Lehman bankruptcy is estimated to have cost – so far – a staggering $2.4 billion in legal, advisory, and other fees, with huge issues remaining unsettled. Two years and billions of dollars later, the uncertainty remains.[22]

Lehman is now history. But the simultaneously minutely specified and impenetrably unclear web of legal obligation is simply accumulating, year by year. Wall Street firms continue to sell complex derivatives and weirdly challenging structured products. Each time, the spreadsheets make sense. Each time, the legalities are carefully, painfully executed. And the next time there is a major bankruptcy on Wall Street or in the City of London, it'll be the exact same thing. Every little detail will make sense when you look at it up close – but when you climb to the nearest mountaintop and look down at the lines of battle below, you'll realize that once again you know nothing at all about how the conflict will play out. That's Wall Street in a nutshell: very smart guys who do very stupid things.

Settlement risk

Finally, we have two arcane and tedious-sounding risks to deal with. Tedious, that is, until you remember that the global financial collapse of 2008 came about because of things so tedious you never read a word about them until all of a sudden they saddled you with debt, halted your pay rise, and threatened your job.

First up, settlement risk. If your job required you to drive a Ferrari fast round twisting mountain switchbacks, you'd probably take care with the boring things before you set out. Brake checks. Wheel joints. Tire treads. Bearings.

Boring, sure. Life-saving, definitely.

Wall Street isn't like that. Those guys drive Ferraris all right, but their garage services are in a mess. When securities are traded, they are, most of the time, traded by telephone. A trader at a brokerage calls up some counter-party, pitches a deal, agrees a price, agrees a trade. In the old days, traders would physically scribble a note of that trade on a piece of paper and fling it at the backroom boys to deal with. These days, the note is normally electronic, but the principle is the same. The trader agrees a deal and moves on to the next thing; the back office staff have to execute the trade. Specifically, a security needs to be delivered to the buyer, funds have to be remitted to the seller. The normal settlement lag, the time between delivery of the security and remission of funds, is between one and three days.

That process is unbelievably simple. It's in principle no more complicated than you buying a pound of tomatoes. The seller hands you the tomatoes. You hand the seller a dollar, or a dollar fifty. That's it. That's all there is to any trade.

And Wall Street *regularly* screws up. According to *The Economist*, in 2010 America's primary dealers (a group that comprises about two dozen large banks and brokerages) generated an average of $128 billion worth of failed trades *per day*.[23] That's roughly 50% more than their combined net capital at risk. And that's only the average. In fall 2008, the daily value of failed trades spiked to over $500 billion. That's half a *trillion* dollars' worth of failed trades. Per day. In the US markets alone. Including only the primary dealers, the guys who ought to know best.

The same article quotes a report put out by the Kauffman Foundation, an outfit aimed at promoting entrepreneurship, commenting: 'Every fail introduces a cumulative and potentially compounding liquidity risk into the orderly process of settling the $7.5 trillion of security transactions completed each day.' That's precisely right. Mistakes of this sort don't cause much harm when markets are orderly and the interbank market feels confident. But what happens when times turn sour? Let's say a firm runs into trouble. If it's already short of liquidity, a few failed trades could amplify those problems, thereby aggravating the underlying problems and advertising its plight across the financial system. The initial problem doesn't even have to be huge for the compounding effect to cause rapid, un-predictable, and almost random destruction. Those liquidity issues have killed firms before now and will do so again.

Once again, we start out with an issue that sounds dry and technical and emerge with a fact that ought to send sane people screaming for the hilltops. Maybe those folk who fill their cellars with bottled water and shotgun shells aren't so crazy after all. At least they're thinking about the risks that might lie ahead. Wall Street appears to have lost that habit altogether.

Market vulnerability

On May 6, 2010, the US financial world faced meltdown. Starting at 2.42 p.m., the Dow Jones stock market index dropped 600 points in five minutes. Given that it had already fallen by 300 points that day, by 2.47 p.m. the market had dropped almost 1,000 points since opening that morning – the biggest intraday point decline in the history of the Dow Jones. And then the slide stopped. Prices rallied. By 3.07 p.m. the market was back pretty much where it had been twenty-five minutes earlier.

What had happened? That sickening lurch was not triggered by some major world event. In fact, for a long time no one really knew what had set it off. There was a cute theory around for a while that some trader with a 'fat finger' had accidentally added a zero or two to a sell order for Procter & Gamble shares, and everything else had followed from there. A cute theory, but completely false. Procter & Gamble shares did not, in fact, lead the fall, nor was their decline particularly pronounced.

Fortunately, there followed a detailed investigation by the Securities and Exchange Commission (SEC) and the Commodities Futures Trading Commission (CFTC). Their report makes shocking reading. (The document, available online, is entitled *Findings Regarding the Market Events of May 6, 2010*.) For one thing, to state what happened to the Dow Jones index is, in effect, to state what happened to the *average* major stock. Startling as those average movements were, they were dwarfed by some of the more extreme movements that took place. In the words of the report:

> Over 20,000 trades across more than 300 securities were executed at prices more than 60% away from their values just moments before. Moreover, many of these trades were executed at prices of a penny or less, or as high as $100,000, before prices of those securities returned to their 'pre-crash' levels.

If that snippet doesn't make your jaw drop, you've got a problem with your reflexes. Twenty thousand trades made at prices that were 60% or more awry? Just imagine the stunning amounts of value being destroyed in those few minutes. Commenting on these things, the *Wall Street Journal* observed that the report 'portrayed a market so fragmented and fragile that a single large trade could send stocks into a sudden spiral.'[24]

So what *did* happen? The detailed answer is complex – you'd need to read the *Findings* report to get the full story – but the key ingredients were:

❏ market nervousness, causing an ordinary, orderly decline in the stock market;

❏ an increase in volatility (a measure of price variability) – again, of the sort which is common enough when market conditions are uncertain;

❑ a sharp decrease in the liquidity of certain stock market based derivatives contracts;

❑ a large sell order placed in that derivatives market, via a computer-based selling algorithm, followed by

❑ further computer-based trading that effectively sucked the liquidity out of (a) the relevant derivatives market and (b) the markets in the underlying stocks.

Although there have been a few regulatory changes since the report was published, there has been almost no fundamental change. Market nervousness is likely to increase over the coming months and years. Volatility will increase. Liquidity will prove to be exceptionally fragile, just as it was in the dark days of 2008. And of course, derivatives markets are still vastly powerful, as is program-based trading.

Indeed, putting those regulatory tweaks to one side, I'd argue that the fundamental position has grown worse, not better, since 2010. I don't want to get too technical, but exchange traded funds – effectively, mutual funds that boast a stock market quotation – are, in many ways, following the trajectory of the mortgage market. A fundamentally good, useful, and value-creating idea is being gradually transformed – via ceaseless 'financial innovation' – into a darkly menacing shadow extending over an ever larger section of the financial system.[25] That shadow is spreading extremely fast: today the total asset value of ETFs runs to $1.5 trillion, up almost 50% in eighteen months. What's more, the quality and fundamental liquidity of ETFs are declining all the time. Our weak-willed regulators know these things but aren't taking the forceful steps that would be needed to control them.*

In short, if that 'flash crash' could happen in 2010, it could happen again now: the markets of 2011 and 2012 remain highly vulnerable. As a matter of fact, the same thing already has happened again, and worse. In November 2010, the sugar market saw a 20% collapse in prices over two days. Cotton prices are also exceptionally volatile.[26] The same has been true of cocoa futures.[27] By good fortune, none of these flash crashes have yet caused much damage, but poorly maintained levees didn't do much harm to New Orleans until 2005. The mortgage market looked to be working fine, until it came close to destroying the international financial system.

In 2010 we were fortunate that the flash crash happened when the markets were still being buoyed up by ultra-low interest rates, by quantitative easing, by massive fiscal stimulus, and by a broad sense of returning security in the financial markets. Those props (disastrous as they're proving in the longer run) were enough to stop the meltdown. But just suppose the next crash happens when another major financial institution is on the brink. When nerves are shredded. When panic is only half a rumor away. Under these circumstances, a flash crash could easily precipitate

---

* And, what do you know, not long after I wrote this paragraph an alleged $2 billion fraud was uncovered on the ETF trading desk of Swiss bank UBS. Speaking as a financial expert, I'd say that $2 billion is quite a lot of money. Can you imagine operating a bank with risk management systems so slipshod that you can simply lose $2 billion? Do you not think that somebody might have noticed after, let's say, the first few hundred million went missing? It's astonishing how much money Wall Street handles – and how chaotic its control systems continue to be.

failure on a Lehman-like scale. And, with some minor exceptions, all the circumstances which allowed the market to fail in 2010 are still in place today, some of them to an even greater extent. Disaster lies just round the corner.

It's extraordinary that regulators do not pursue these matters more aggressively. Take the relatively simple matter of the $128 billion worth of failed trades each day. If the regulators simply fined both parties to a failed trade 0.5% of the transaction value, irrespective of fault, the failures would vanish, almost overnight. Why on earth are regulators not imposing such sanctions with all possible haste? It would be an unbelievably simple fix and would completely cure a potentially lethal problem. Yet it's not being done.

Even more stunning than the lethargy of regulators, however, is the complacent inertia of market participants themselves. At least the regulators will still be in a job if things go disastrously wrong. The same cannot be said for many bankers. Why are they so ready to place their jobs, their banks, and the very financial system itself at risk? That sad tale is the story of the next chapter.

ELEVEN

Collecting nickels in front of steamrollers

THE PREVIOUS CHAPTER looked at the monumental risks that have built up in a system dedicated to the management, dispersal, and efficient pricing of risk. There's quite a paradox here. Financial markets are often said to come as close as is possible to the economists' ideal of a competitive, well-informed, frictionless market. If neoclassical economic theory made any kind of sense, financial markets should be its showcase: the best possible example of markets in action.

Unfortunately, markets don't follow theory; they prefer reality. And reality is messy, full of compromise and skewed, absent, or contradictory incentives. As long as those incentives are so badly flawed as they are now, the system will always create risks that threaten to destroy the entire capitalist system. In this chapter as in the previous one, I'll limit myself to identifying the half-dozen most outrageous incentivization issues. There are many more, but we have to stop somewhere.

I should make it clear that I don't exempt my own industry from these problems. As we'll see, hedge fund managers, like myself, are incentivized both excessively (on average, we're paid too much) and wrongly (we're paid for the wrong things). I personally benefit from these misalignments. Some readers will want to criticize me for this. You may think that I should either refuse my current levels of compensation or just take the money and accept the system.

I don't believe either criticism is appropriate. In the first place, almost no one turns down money which is freely and legally offered. Why would they? More to the point, though, it's not as though individual choices are the issue. I personally strive to behave in an ethical and honorable manner. That involves making money for my investors – because that's the task they give me – but it also involves staying a long way away from investments that I see as little better than Ponzi schemes. (I stayed a long way away from mortgage products and routinely turn down investments which I regard as their contemporary successors.) But so what? A system can be profoundly flawed even if most of its participants behave with honor. What's required is a system that encourages and enforces good behavior. The current setup does the opposite.

As for the idea that I should keep silent about the flaws in the system just because I'm a beneficiary – I think that's crazy. It's those of us who are active within the system who are best placed to diagnose its faults. Indeed, I wish that far more financial insiders would speak up about the faults they know to exist. There were plenty of insiders who grew anxious about the mortgage market collapse before it tipped over into disaster, yet those anxieties were seldom heard outside a narrow, technocratic circle. The topics addressed in this book affect all of us. Literally everybody on the planet. If financial catastrophe hits the world again – and hits it at a time when governments are already at the limits of their financial capacity – the consequences will be profound and universal. The world faces few issues that are more urgent or more pressing. We insiders have a duty to speak up, to attract attention, to solicit change.

That's the preamble. Now for the problems.

The market

Any market has two halves: buyers and sellers. On Wall Street, the sellers are typically large firms – Goldman Sachs, Morgan Stanley, JP Morgan, Barclays, Deutsche, and so on. They're selling securities to investors (the buy-side), a group which includes pension funds, hedge funds, insurance companies, high net worth individuals, and plenty of others besides. Naturally, because sell-side firms are also traders, they often buy securities as well as selling them. Nevertheless, it's conceptually useful to look at the specific incentives faced by sell-side salespeople and traders, because those incentives lay the foundation for much of what's wrong with the system.

Before we look at the sell-side, however, it's worth starting with the basics: the kill-or-be-killed nature of the market itself. I've said before that the equity market is very transparent. You can check equity prices on your computer screen right now. If you call a broker to buy or sell some equities, that broker will be looking at the exact same prices as you are. If he rips you off, you'll know about it, and he'll know that you know. That doesn't make cheating impossible, but it does make it a whole lot harder. Add to that the fact that the equity market is highly regulated and attracts much more media attention than any other, and it forms a fairly safe playground for investors.

The bond market isn't like that. Michael Lewis describes it in *The Big Short*, his excellent book on the mortgage market, in this way:

> Bond salesmen could say and do anything without fear that they'd be reported to some authority. Bond traders could exploit inside information without worrying that they would be caught. Bond technicians could dream up ever more complicated securities without worrying too much about government regulation – one reason why so many derivatives had been derived, one way or another, from bonds. The bigger, more liquid end of the bond market – the market for US Treasury bonds, for example – traded on screens, but in many cases the only way to determine if the price some bond trader had given you was even close to fair was to call around and hope to find some other bond trader making a market in that particular obscure security. The opacity and complexity of the bond market was, for big Wall Street firms, a huge advantage. The bond market customer lived in perpetual fear of what he didn't know. If Wall Street bond departments were increasingly the source of Wall Street profits, it was in part because of this: In the bond market it was still possible to make huge sums of money from the fear, and the ignorance of customers.[1]

Just pause there for a moment. Those neoclassical ivory-tower economists who believe that Wall Street has to work perfectly because it's a market haven't understood one of the Street's most essential aspects. Markets need a number of things to work, of which one of the most basic requirements is transparency, equality of information. Take, for example, the used-car market. Sellers generally know exactly what state a given vehicle is in. Buyers are largely ignorant. It's easy for sellers to rip off buyers; hard and expensive for buyers to protect themselves. That's something that has been understood by economists for decades – it's been one of the hottest topics in the subject – yet they've almost universally failed to apply the same logic to the financial markets. So let me be clear: most bond markets are exceptionally one-sided. So are most derivatives markets. The idea that these things somehow function with unique excellence is the precise reverse of the truth. To quote Michael Lewis again: 'An investor who went from the stock market to the bond market was like a small, furry animal raised on an island without predators removed to a pit full of pythons.'[2]

So let's look at the pythons.

The sell-side

Willie Sutton was one of America's best-known bank robbers. When asked by a journalist why he robbed banks, Sutton replied simply: 'Because that's where the money is.'

A good answer, but wrong. Yes, banks are where the money is, but you need to be an idiot to rob them. If you want to get rich, you need to work in one, ideally on Wall Street or in the City of London. If you head for one of the right banks and get the right sort of job (whatever you do, avoid the back office), you'll make plenty of dough, no matter what niche you end up in. But if you want to get ridiculously wealthy, ridiculously young, then the bond market – or the derivatives market – is the place to go. Greg Lippmann, for example, reputedly made an annual bonus of between $4 million and $6 million in the years leading up to the mortgage crash. As his bets against that crash started paying off, he was supposedly offered a $50 million bonus.[3] That kind of money was insufficient to retain him, however, and he walked out on Deutsche Bank, his employer, taking several of his team with him. Such stories are exceptional, of course – most traders are not offered $50 million bonuses – but they're also indicative. No other industry generates even exceptions like these.

You only get these bonuses in one way: by being seen to make money for your employer. And you make money for your employer by taking an item worth $100 and selling it to someone for $101. If you sell it for what it's worth, you'll never make enough money to convince your employer that you're worth retaining. Fortunately, the bias in the market makes it relatively easy to make such sales. Buyers don't find it easy to check whether the thing you're selling them is worth $100 or $101. Plus you're probably smarter than they are, and better resourced, and more motivated, and harder-working. Plus you have a huge expense account, which means you can make your pitch over a fancy meal or an upmarket sports event.

You're also helped by accounting rules which hide reality – in the form of genuine information about prices – from buyers. When market prices do emerge to suggest that their new $101 acquisition is worth only $100, the sell-side guy will be on hand to say that these prices are bullshit, that any softness in prices is only temporary, that the buyer was a smart guy all along.

In a way, none of this is surprising. Anyone selling any kind of product has an incentive to sell as many of it as possible, no matter whether they're suitable for the customer or not, and at as high a price as possible, no matter whether that price is fair value or not. What makes the bond and derivatives markets different is that those sell-side incentives are huge, the salesmen superb, and true price discovery difficult – and current accounting standards keep price reality hidden from view long after the sale has been concluded. Those lopsided conditions themselves would likely cause problems no matter how appropriate the incentives elsewhere in the system – but unfortunately those other incentives are just as skewed as well.

The buy-side

On the buy-side, investment managers are typically compensated with an annual fee skimmed off the value of assets under management. For hedge funds, that might be set at 2% of asset value. For funds that are less actively managed, it might be 1% or even less. And it all looks logical. Fund managers go into their offices each and every day, and work hard to create value. The annual management fee is intended to compensate them for their ordinary, regular, day-to-day effort and for the expenses they incur along the way.

Yet the arrangement can also create its own perverse incentives. There are, for example, plenty of highly successful fund managers who owe their success to their sales ability. The more funds a group has under management, the more money it makes – and the bigger the fund manager's fee. Obviously it would be nice if those funds were well invested, beat benchmarks, and made money – but they still pay nicely even if they don't. There are managers who are wonderful at putting together the glossy brochures, at offering suites of fine-sounding services, at glad-handing investors and collecting money . . . but who have a poor track record at actually managing the funds they deploy.

What's more, the more money you collect, the more the pressure is on you to get it invested. That pressure can lead to ill-judged investment decisions. I recall one promoter who pitched a construction project to me. The idea was to build some high-spec apartment blocks in Europe. Each unit was projected to sell for close to €200,000. The rate of return was estimated to be in excess of 25%. What's more, the project had everything you'd expect: architect's drawings, planning consents, detailed spreadsheets, careful costings – it was a very professionally designed package. Very investable, in the jargon.

Now, I'm an investment manager. If I'd chosen to plough my investors' funds into that project, I'd have been able to get invested quickly, predict strong returns, seek more capital for more investments. As a result, I'd have made money – those annual management fees would have seen to that. Unfortunately, this project had a serious flaw. Although €200,000 sounds like a fair price for a luxury apartment, the project was located in a country in eastern Europe where the average wage was, at the time, just €9,000 a year – and that at a time when the economy was faltering, credit was deteriorating, and there were serious concerns over the value of real estate. The projected selling price was effectively an imaginary number, a fiction. The apartments would never sell for that price and those tempting 25% returns would never be achieved. I suspect the promoter knew as much when he put the package together – and he didn't care, because he knew he'd find investors to back it anyway. (You won't be surprised to learn that I wasn't one of them.)

There's another pressure on fund managers – especially the poor or mediocre ones. Let's take the example of a traditional fund manager whose task is to invest in the US stock market. Most likely, his performance will be compared with the S&P 500, a benchmark reflecting the stock market performance of the country's 500 largest corporations. One obvious strategy for that investment manager is simply to buy a little piece of every stock in the S&P 500, thereby perfectly matching the index. It's tempting to think that if a fund manager does that and nothing else, he can't fail to match the benchmark – since, after all, he's effectively buying that benchmark.

Unfortunately, that logic is dead wrong. Because of his fees and expenses, a manager who adopts that strategy will always fall short of the index performance. That shortfall might only be a percentage point or two, but the shortfall compounds over time. Invest $100 at 5% for twenty years and it will return $265. The same amount invested at 6% over the same period will be worth $320. A 7% investment return will yield $387. Differences of this magnitude simply can't and shouldn't be ignored. A capable investment manager should have strategies for dealing with this challenge. If you know what you're doing, you should be able to trade options around your equity positions, thereby earning back your fees and expenses, and perhaps even a little more.

But not everyone has the ability to do that. The investment management world has plenty of sophisticated managers, but also far too many mediocre ones. Those mediocre ones are always struggling to catch up with their benchmarks – and consequently also tempted to 'chase yield' wherever it can be found. There are a million ways to chase yield, many of which can be extraordinarily destructive. For example: you borrow some money (at a low interest rate) in yen, and invest the cash (at a high interest rate) in Aussie dollars. Or you switch out of (low-yielding) US Treasuries and buy into (higher yielding) AAA-rated mortgage market securities, founded in part on subprime debt. Or you get out of (low-yielding) German bonds in order to enjoy the higher rates available on Greek, Italian, or Portuguese ones. Or you decide to insure some AAA-rated securities – maybe even those CDOs – and collect some insurance premiums along the way.

There are countless other recipes that have been fashionable at one time or another, and they all work. That is, in a typical year, these investment strategies will add modestly, but significantly, to profits. They can transform an ordinary (sub-benchmark) manager into one who equals or modestly exceeds the benchmark. You can see why they catch on.[4]

They all work; and they're all lethal. They're shockingly dangerous. There are no free lunches in the financial markets. These strategies may show a modest profit in most years – but in others they will bring huge losses. Collectively they have been nicknamed a way of 'picking up nickels in front of steamrollers.' For a little while, you get to fill your pocket with nickels. But one day you'll get unlucky and that bad luck will destroy you. It was a steamroller which blatted AIG out of existence. It was a steamroller that wrought vast damage to institutional balance sheets in 2008–9. It's a steamroller that's back right now, crushing bank balance sheets across Europe.

No organization's investment fund, no individual, should ever want their investment manager to be fooling around anywhere close to steamrollers – but the remorseless logic of the industry inevitably creates an eternal search for easy nickels. So wherever there's a trail of nickels glinting in the sunshine, there's a rush of investors scrabbling to pick them up – and a steamroller grinding away in the nearby shadows.

Incentive fees

In addition to those regular annual management fees, investment managers are sometimes also incentivized with performance fees. When well designed, those performance fees can do a lot to align the fund manager's incentives with those of his clients. They can encourage thoughtful, active, value-creating investment strategies. And on average, the performance of the hedge fund industry over time has been creditable. Up until 2008, hedge funds exhibited less volatility than the broader market. They made money in good times, and either made money or preserved it when markets were falling. In 2008 some of that gloss was removed when the industry lost money in calamitous markets – but it still lost less than the market overall.[5] (And of course, some fund managers saw the collapse coming and made money out of it. I was one of them.)

The overall, average result, however, conceals the danger lurking at the fringes. Poorly designed performance fees, or even well-designed fee structures applied by idiots, can cause immense harm by encouraging high-risk, high-reward strategies which may be directly contrary to investors' interests. The poster-child for irresponsible risk-taking was Long-Term Capital Management, which failed in 1998 under a senior management too impressed by its own academic excellence. Unfortunately, the real world is no respecter of academic reputations. The firm took on too much debt and bet the proceeds with too little thought for what might happen if things didn't turn out as expected. When the Asian financial crisis was followed by a Russian one, LTCM found that its 'safe' bets had turned sour on a colossal scale. Given the scale of leverage at the firm – its capital represented just 3% of assets – there was no return from that misjudgment. A bailout, organized by the New York Fed, saw the firm's creditors take control. The $1.9 billion which the firm's principals had invested in it was wiped out.[6]

The story contains another moral. The Fed organized a bailout of the fund because it was deemed too big to fail, because it was seen as being of systemic importance. That was a crazy decision. Lenders who make bad credit decisions should lose money. That's the only mechanism which will force them to improve their decisionmaking. The Fed chose to send precisely the opposite message: lenders who lend money to large, well-connected Wall Street firms will never lose money, because the government will protect them. It's no coincidence that the bailout of LTCM inaugurated a decade in which credit standards sank to all-time lows. More remarkable still, the authorities haven't even now understood their error. The bankruptcy of Lehman Brothers was a one-off. Everyone else got bailed out. Bear Stearns, AIG, General Motors, Citigroup, Goldman Sachs, Morgan Stanley – virtually everyone on Wall Street and plenty of firms in the world beyond. As long as creditors believe they're going to be bailed out in the event of disaster, their incentives are crazily upside down. Make money – and you win. Lose money – and the government pays. That era is coming to an end as governments run out of money, out of borrowing capacity, out of financial and moral creditworthiness. It can't end too soon.

Ratings agencies

In the chaos of the bond markets, you'd hope that it would at least be possible to rely on the calm good sense of the ratings agencies. After all, they're independent, they're among the few players who don't have a dog in the fight. Naturally, they won't get every judgment correct, because no human on earth ever will, but at least they try.

And that is, to an extent, true. Ratings agencies do OK. Perhaps, given the circumstances, they do very well. On the other hand, there are at least two major reasons for doubting the credibility of any ratings agency on any issue. For one thing, the agencies are paid by the people issuing the security, not the people benefiting from the credit analysis. That's precisely the wrong way round. For example, if you're out to buy a used car and you are not yourself expert in judging the mechanical condition of the car you're about to purchase, you might well want to make use of an independent auto expert. But if so, wouldn't you want to be the one paying the expert? If the expert is being paid by the used-car salesman – which is how it works in the securities market – do you really think you're going to be told the full truth about the vehicle?[7]

These are not theoretical concerns. William Harrington, a former senior vice president at Moody's, exposed the dangerous reality of the conflict of interest in a filing presented to the SEC. In the words of the British *Guardian* newspaper:

> Harrington claims that Moody's uses a long-standing culture of 'intimidation and harassment' to persuade its analysts to ensure ratings match those wanted by the company's clients. He says Moody's compliance department 'actively harasses analysts viewed as "troublesome"' and said management 'rewarded lenient voting'.
>
> 'The goal of management is to mold analysts into pliable corporate citizens who cast their committee votes in line with the unchanging corporate credo of maximizing earnings of the largely captive franchise,' he said.[8]

That is, if true, terrifying.

Secondly, the guys at the ratings agencies are paid way less than their counterparts on Wall Street, have far fewer resources available to them, and do not participate directly in the markets themselves. Conversely, when some bunch of super-smart, super-well-paid, and massively bonus-driven Wall Streeters come to issue a security, their task is to play the system in order to achieve the highest possible rating. The contest is wholly, and structurally, unequal. You could change the top management of any ratings agency or shake up their recruitment and training policies and you'd still have the exact same mismatch, the exact same problem.

I have direct experience of these issues myself. I'm a recognized international expert on the energy and carbon markets. It's that expertise which, over the past few years, I've successfully put to work on behalf of my investors. At one point, I received a call from a ratings agency asking if they could pick my brains on the way these markets worked. I was happy enough to say yes, and before too long I had three guys from the agency sitting in my office. But what the heck was I to say to them? I had three options. The first was to stick with generalities, to offer a few helpful pointers, a little friendly advice, but to stay clear of anything genuinely useful. Option two was to tell the full truth, as I saw it. Telling the truth would have involved explaining how my firm evaluated credit and other risks, and setting out our detailed pricing model. The third option was the sneaky one. I could tell my visitors what I wanted them to believe. If I could give them a misleading picture of risks and pricing, they would influence the market in a way that would create some fabulous buying opportunities for me.

The last of those options is unquestionably the one that would have made me the most money. Unfortunately, my ethics prevent me from telling outright lies in the pursuit of profit, so option three was not available. Option two might look attractive, except that my edge in the market arises from my slowly acquired authority and expertise. To give that knowledge away for free would be doing myself no favors and would have been directly contrary to the interests of my investors, whom I am paid to look after. So I handed out the coffee, offered a few banalities, and explained why I was not in a position to say anything useful. That was a useless outcome for the agency and a pointless one for me, but at least I wasn't lying and they went away no worse informed than they arrived. I'm certain, however, that most investment banks would have seen such a meeting as a wonderful opportunity to rig the system in their favor – and indeed, you'd have good grounds for arguing that in so doing those banks would simply have been working hard on behalf of their shareholders.

Finally, the ratings agencies are placed in an impossible situation by the regulators. Because the ratings given to certain securities can affect how those securities are treated by regulators and central banks, a change in an agency's opinion about a particular bond can cause dramatic sell-offs as investors rush for the exit. Naturally, it was never the regulators' intention to cause such herdlike shifts of behavior, yet that's often precisely what happens.[9]

You see this effect time and time again in the crisis in the euro bond markets. Take, for example, the genuinely bizarre discussion of when precisely Greek government bonds would be ineligible for use as collateral at the European Central Bank.[10] Because a number of European banks were seeing their liquidity and solvency come under pressure, the ECB wanted to make it as easy as possible for them to get access to cheap funds. It therefore offered a facility whereby banks would post collateral – typically, eurozone sovereign bonds – and it would lend money in exchange.

As you'd expect, I have a fundamental disagreement with the Ponzi-ish logic at work here. If a bank is experiencing financial distress because it's mismanaged its business, either it should be left to go bust or it should find a way to repair its finances by raising capital and starting again. That's what would happen in any other industry, and that's what has to happen if mismanagement is not to be rewarded and encouraged. But let's put those heretical thoughts to one side, and agree that the best way to help a weak bank is to extend easy credit on the back of unsound collateral. The ECB, however, could bend its rules only so far. It was able to accept collateral of doubtful worth and minimal saleability, but it was not permitted to accept securities that were actually in default . . . and it was left to the ratings agencies to state whether a given security was in default or not. All of a sudden, the fate of financial markets hung on whether or not an independent agency would or would not declare default. Even though the entire world knew that Greece was effectively in default, what came to matter was what the three major agencies would say on the subject. They were subject to strong – and wholly inappropriate – political pressure. Markets which were already febrile were ready to charge off a cliff if the ratings agencies declared default.

The agencies should not be exposed to these pressures, and there are indeed discussions afoot about ways to decouple the decisions of the ratings agencies from the decisionmaking processes of the central banks and other major official bodies active in the financial markets. But these discussions have borne no fruit yet, and may indeed never do so.[11] In the meantime, the agencies are left to do their impossible job, burdened with inadequate resources, excessive expectations, inappropriate incentives, and political opprobrium. But they've no right to complain. Truthtellers on Planet Ponzi were never likely to be popular.

The regulators

As I write, the SEC is conducting a major investigation into a highly controversial mortgage security sale led by Goldman Sachs. The joint chief counsel for the SEC is a former partner of Linklaters, Adam Glass. When he was at Linklaters, Glass advised Paulson & Company, a major hedge fund firm. The most notorious incident in that firm's record is its role in constructing the controversial mortgage security created by Goldman Sachs. So, to summarize, at the head of the SEC's legal staff is a man closely associated with the very transactions that the SEC is now investigating (though he is not himself on the investigation team).[12]

Suspiciously minded readers will instantly want to draw the obvious conclusion: there's a huge conspiracy here; rich people are bound to protect their own interests; no major fraudster will ever be brought to justice. I don't agree. For one thing, some very important fraudsters have been brought to justice recently – Bernie Madoff, Raj Rajaratnam – and sentenced to some swingeing jail time.[13] For another thing, Glass isn't accused of having done anything wrong, either when he was at Linklaters or now at the SEC. And for yet another thing, Glass has done something that few of us would ever do. He gave up a partnership at Linklaters (average salary: $2.3 million) to work for the government (maximum salary: $233,000). That makes him, in my eyes, a man of honor.

What, in fact, the Glass story draws attention to is the almost impossible position in which we place our regulators. Their salaries are so low in comparison with their private sector counterparts that they have an almost irresistible temptation to serve their two or three years at the SEC, then return to the lavish remuneration available outside. And when they do return to the private sector, they have a wonderful new skill to offer: insight into the workings of the principal financial regulator. According to a study conducted by the Project on Government Oversight:

- ❏ Between 2006 and 2010, 219 former SEC employees filed 789 post-employment statements indicating their intent to represent an outside client before the Commission

- ❏ Some former SEC employees filed statements within days of leaving the Commission, with one employee filing within 2 days of leaving

- ❏ Some former SEC employees filed numerous statements during this time period, with one former employee filing 20 statements[14]

To put it bluntly, the SEC is seen by many of its employees as a training ground which will qualify them for lucrative private sector work in the future. The SEC is, in effect, training its employees to play the system. Even when it works the other way – that is, when private sector employees choose to become regulators – you are almost inevitably recruiting people strongly in sympathy with the goals and methods of the private sector. Those aren't necessarily the folks best placed to get tough if they have to.

Although I've singled out the SEC in these paragraphs, I do so only to illustrate a broader issue. All the financial regulators in every major market suffer from these problems. Sometimes they are so blatant as to take your breath away.

The chair of the Commodities Futures Trading Commission under President George H. W. Bush was Wendy Gramm. A few days before leaving office, she granted an order allowing Enron to trade certain derivatives without CFTC supevision. A few weeks after that, she was given a seat on Enron's board – and we all know how successful that board went on to be.

These conflicts of interest are so gross as to seem almost criminal, yet it's wrong to focus on individual malfeasance when the problem is systemic. Bluntly put, our regulators face impossible odds. We saw, in an earlier chapter, the extraordinary extent and effectiveness of corporate lobbying in Washington. Government regulators – however idealistic, capable, and tough they may be – are fighting an enemy with infinitely greater resources and infinitely more at stake than themselves. Arthur Levitt, a former chairman of the SEC, recalled in his wise and hard-hitting book *Take on the Street*:

> During my seven and a half years in Washington . . . nothing astonished me more than witnessing the powerful special interest groups in full swing when they thought a proposed rule or a piece of legislation might hurt them, giving nary a thought to how the proposal might help the investing public. With laserlike precision, groups representing Wall Street firms, mutual fund companies, accounting firms, or corporate managers would quickly set about to defeat even minor threats. Individual investors, with no organized labor or trade association to represent their views in Washington, never knew what hit them.[15]

That last phrase is particularly telling: 'never knew what hit them.' It's precisely right. Individual investors aren't even aware of the battles that they're losing, of what's at stake, of the cumulative damage being done.

As for the regulators, Congress and Wall Street can conspire to render them toothless simply by depriving them of the funds needed to do their job. The Commodities Futures Trading Commission has, for example, recently halted a technology program designed to identify patterns of suspicious trading because of budget restrictions forcing cuts in its $11 million technology budget.[16] Worse still, the panel set up to dissect the causes of the financial crisis – the Financial Crisis Inquiry Commission – has been given a budget of just $8 million.[17] That compares with $38 million spent by a federal bankruptcy trustee looking at the Lehman collapse.[18] It compares with $30 million spent investigating the Monica Lewinsky 'scandal.'[19] It compares with at least $130 million spent investigating the accident to the space shuttle Columbia.[20]

Forgive my heartlessness, but when space shuttles explode they do not threaten the entire fabric of Western capitalism. When the financial system explodes, it does. And forgive my political naivety, but when an American president stains an intern's dress, he causes damage that can be remedied by an ordinary dry-cleaner for about $15. When the American financial system sprays toxic waste over the entire economy, the damage totals so many trillions of dollars it's hard to know quite how to count them. The IMF estimated the fiscal impact of the crisis of 2007–8 on the US at 35% of GDP, or about $4.5 trillion.[21] The crisis caused a similar degree of destruction to government finances in Italy, Japan, Spain, and France. It caused a whole lot more in the

UK. It caused a lot, but slightly less, in Germany. And that's only the fiscal impact. The cost in lost output is so large it pretty much burns the calculator up to start figuring it out. But if you reckon the cost of lost output at a permanent 5% of global GDP, the present value of that loss soars to easily more than $100 trillion, even on quite conservative assumptions about discount rates and the like. A Bank of England paper guesstimated the cost of lost output at between $60 trillion and $200 trillion.[22] And yet the committee set up to investigate these things was given about one-quarter of the budget of the Monica Lewinsky one. It's beyond outrageous. The solution is as plain as sunshine. We need to give the regulators real cash and real teeth. One of the eye-watering aspects of the current crisis is encapsulated in a few simple statistics:[23]

Number of bankers in jail in the US	0
Number of bankers in jail in the UK	0
Number of bankers in jail elsewhere in Europe	0
Number of bankers in jail in Japan	0
Total number of bankers in jail	**0**

These data don't include the imprisonment of Bernie Madoff, because his fraud had no direct connection with the financial crisis (except inasmuch as the failure to catch and jail him earlier reveals extensive flaws in Wall Street's culture and supervision). And the simple truth – so howlingly obvious it should hardly need spelling out – is that very many more bankers should have been jailed for their role in the catastrophe. Don't take my word for it. Former chairman of the Federal Reserve Alan Greenspan is on the record as saying:

There are two fundamental reforms that we need.
[One], to get adequate levels of capital [in the
banking system] and two, to get far higher levels of
enforcement of fraud statutes – the existing ones,
I'm not even talking about new ones. Things were
being done which were certainly illegal and clearly
criminal in certain cases . . . Fraud creates very
considerable instability in competitive markets. If
you cannot trust your counterparties, it won't
work. And indeed we saw that it didn't.[24]

I'm not about to start listing those firms and individuals
who committed criminal acts. I don't fancy spending the rest
of my life being sued for libel. In any case, I don't personally
know enough of the detail to be sure which transactions
may have constituted criminal fraud and which were merely
pushing – but legally pushing – the boundaries of acceptable market practice. On the other hand, you only need to
look at the torrent of lawsuits and out-of-court settlements
being conducted between banks, regulators, and other
governmental or quasi-governmental agencies to realize that
the boundaries of acceptable practice were given a real pasting. For example, recent news stories have reported:

❏ *Settlement for mishandled foreclosures*: 'The 14 largest
U.S. mortgage servicers must pay back homeowners
for losses from foreclosures or loans that were mishandled in the wake of the housing collapse,
the first of a set of sanctions regulators are seeking
against the companies.'[25]

❏ *Lawsuits filed by FHFA*: 'Bank of America Corp. and

JP Morgan Chase & Co. (JPM) were among 17 banks sued by the U.S. to recoup $196 billion spent on mortgage-backed securities bought by Fannie Mae and Freddie Mac.'[26]

❏ *Mortgage-bond fraud settlement*: 'U.S. securities regulators are expected to reach a settlement with major banks as soon as this week over mortgage-bond fraud, which contributed to the financial crisis.'[27]

❏ *Fraudulent lending charges against BoA*: 'Nevada's attorney general on Tuesday accused the bank of repeatedly violating its $8.4 billion agreement with that state and others to address fraudulent lending charges involving its Countrywide unit, which it bought in 2008.' Bank of America is contesting the charges.[28]

❏ *Goldman Sachs settlement with SEC*: 'Goldman Sachs agreed on Thursday to pay a lower-than-expected $550m fine to settle US regulators' accusations that it misled investors in a mortgage-backed security – a move that ends the highest profile regulatory case since the crisis.'[29]

❏ *Morgan Stanley sued by Allstate*: 'Morgan Stanley (MS) was sued for fraud by Allstate Insurance Co. over residential mortgage-backed securities in which the insurer invested, according to a complaint filed in New York.'[30]

❏ *Madoff trustee sues JP Morgan*: '"The bankruptcy code allows the trustee to stand in the shoes of a judgment creditor and assert common-law claims against JPMC," [Trustee Irving Picard] said in a court filing yesterday. JP Morgan, as Madoff's primary banker, was central to the fraud and "complicit" in it, he said.'[31]

Let me repeat, I am categorically *not* alleging that all, or even any, of these suits and claims and settlements revolve around criminality. Nor am I suggesting that any of the fine (and litigious) firms named above have a systemic problem with criminality. What I do say, however, is that the sheer volume of legal activity indicates something crucially significant about the culture that has come into being on Wall Street. Like Alan Greenspan, I consider it inconceivable that the credit crisis of 2008–9 arose without there being extensive deception and criminality. Naturally it's important that federal regulators, and authorities such as the FHFA, do all they can to recover money where they believe they have the legal scope to do so. But it is also important to launch criminal investigations into individuals wherever charges could credibly stick. It's important to prosecute those charges in court, to push for the severest possible sentences, and not to be distracted by the possibility of securing some multimillion or multibillion out-of-court settlement instead.

Toward the end of this book I'll suggest some possible solutions to some of the problems enumerated in this chapter; but for now, just take a note of the fundamental issue at stake. To be effective, financial regulators need to have guts, teeth, brains, and independence. They need to be able to kick ass, inflict losses, and override vested interests, and to do all these things despite the fact that those vested interests will be prepared to spend tens or hundreds of millions in lobbying against any adverse change in their conditions of business. And we want them to do these things for one-tenth of the remuneration that they could get elsewhere. What's remarkable, in fact, is how well these guys do, given the circumstances. But they're fighting their way uphill with the wind in their faces. And they mostly lose.

This survey of biased, asymmetric, and inappropriate incentives should really end with a study of politicians: the breed who ought to be in charge of sorting through all this muddle and instead have played such a huge part in creating it. For the past three decades, the record of government in the United States in particular has been atrocious. This current administration, like those that preceded it, has utterly failed to deliver long-awaited and essential change. The only fools worse than the fools in the White House are the ones in Congress. The only idiots worse than the idiots in the Senate are the ones in the House. And the only idiots worse than either are the rest of us, the dummies who choose to put up with them all.

We'll get to all that, but not yet. We've studied how the theoretical perfection of the financial markets is a mirage; a mirage concealing a minefield. We've labeled some of the mines – the buried risks, the dangerous incentives – but that's not the same as establishing the likely cost as they detonate. That's our next task. We need to survey the housing market, the bond and equity markets. We need to test the solidity of bank balance sheets, consider the weight of accumulated household debt, review the situation in Europe and Japan, see if we can feel our way to some kind of likely damage appraisal.

Only once we've done all that will our rap sheet be complete. We'll talk about politicians all right, but only at the end of the book, once we have a proper understanding of the swamp they've led us into. Next up: the roof over your head.

TWELVE

I'm short your house

O N APRIL 13, 2011, a Senate committee released a 635-page report on the financial crisis. Senator Carl Levin, the committee chairman, commented that

> the report discloses how financial firms deliberately took advantage of their clients and investors, how credit rating agencies assigned AAA ratings to high risk securities, and how regulators sat on their hands instead of reining in the unsafe and unsound practices all around them. Rampant conflicts of interest are the threads that run through every chapter of this sordid story.[1]

Along with the report, some 5,800 pages of previously unseen documents were released, providing detailed support for Levin's claims. Included in those 5,800 pages was the following email, written by Greg Lippmann, a trader at Deutsche Bank, to Michelle Borre, an investor at OppenheimerFunds, Inc. I present the email here just as it was written: all caps, muddled spacing, and punctuation that your English teacher wouldn't have liked.

A CLIENT THAT DID THE SAME TRADE AS U
WITH US SENT ME A TSHIRT "IM SHORT
YOUR HOUSE" . . . I JUST BOUGHT 20 OF EM
TO GIVE TO CLIENT S THAT DO THE TRADE
WITH US.DO U WANT 1 OR 2 ?[2]

It's an interesting message. Let's start by looking at its most obvious feature: its lack of even the most rudimentary effort at presentation. The transaction referred to involved a vast sum of money. Michelle Borre was not an in-house colleague, but an external client. Deutsche and Oppenheimer are both leading institutions whose standards were and are, presumably, as high as those of any of their peers. Yet the message has a kind of teenage quality to it. It calls to mind high-schoolers 'starting a rock band' in their garage, kids getting drunk or smoking weed for the first time. A culture which permits and encourages messages of that kind is a culture that has left ordinary professional standards a long way behind it. And those standards matter. They're not the same as ethics, but they're related.

(And, to digress for a moment, one could say something similar about the financial markets' relationship with drugs. The British *Guardian* newspaper quoted one former addict:

'It is absolutely rife in the City,' Daniel [not his real name] says. 'The cocaine dealers have not gone out of business because I've stopped. I could take you five minutes from here to 15 or 20 bars where you would be guaranteed to be able to buy cocaine.'

Daniel claims there are bars in the City where regular customers order bottles of wine that are not advertised. In fact, these vintages aren't on sale, but are a code for ordering cocaine from bar staff.

'It is all put on the expense account as a £60 bottle of wine, but what the waiters are selling is a wrap of cocaine,' said Daniel. 'These bars are run by criminal syndicates where the food and drink is incidental. They are fronts for drugs.'[3]

According to the same report, addiction problems have increased since financial markets became more turbulent. I'm not sympathetic, however. Why should drug laws be enforced vigorously in the South Bronx and Tottenham, but not on Wall Street and in the City of London? It's yet another case of double standards.)

Turning to the text itself, the slogan 'I'm short your house' is Wall Street jargon meaning that I've taken a bet which will pay off if the value of your house falls. The greater the loss of value, the more money I make. That's the joke at the heart of the email. And it's a nasty one. The humor is spiteful. Nor was it a one-off aberration. A little later in the same package of documents, there's an email from Lippmann describing a customer as 'a CDO guy puking up a pig [that] he bought.' Nice.

Naturally, we all say things like this from time to time, but mostly we try to act with a little courtesy and consideration; a little dignity. We certainly try to act that way if we're dealing with major clients in the course of important business. Wall Street, however, comes to disregard such niceties, because every transaction, every bet, comes down to a simple play of numbers, a spin of the roulette wheel. The fact that houses, mortgages, personal debts are at stake

– or, indeed, that companies, jobs, wages, and investments may be – shrinks to almost nothing. It all boils down to a lame, slightly spiteful joke.

Yet having said all that, Greg Lippmann and his colleagues called this right. There *was* a housing bubble. Lippmann and others saw it coming and made a ton of money by placing the right bets at the right time. If that strikes you as an utterly unhelpful response to the mass insanity of a housing bubble, I'm afraid to say I disagree. The bigger bubbles become, the more damage they do. Short-sellers help prick those bubbles. Funnily enough, one of the things the world needed most in the years running up to 2008 was more people like Greg Lippmann. They couldn't singlehandedly have stopped the bubble expanding, but they'd have moderated its extent and its ultimate destructive impact.

So you'll forgive me, I hope, if I confess that I too am negative on the housing market. I'm not, right this moment, short your house but – well, I'm in that general camp. Sorry.

The facts are these. In my opinion, one of the best indices of US house prices is the national Case–Shiller index. If you take January 1, 1995 as representing 100, the index rose to 114.5 by January 2000. From that point, house prices began to climb and climb. The index grew nonstop until the start of 2006, at which point it stood at 183.9, having almost doubled over little more than ten years. Bear in mind that the index is so constructed as to track like-for-like sales. So it doesn't climb because houses are getting larger or better; it climbs as a result of inflation, pure and simple.[4]

And from early 2006, the index collapsed. It fell in every quarter until spring 2009, when it stood at 118.3, or approximately where it had been at the start of the decade. After a flickering, uncertain recovery, prices dropped again and are still falling as I write. The index currently stands at 110.1 – that is, close to its long-term norm. In relation to 'owner's equivalent rent,' prices are also in line with historic norms for the first time in years.[5] These facts are of comfort to many. They would seem to prove that house prices have, after their lengthy high-altitude mountaineering trip, finally returned to base camp. They've normalized.

Which is my point. House prices have more or less normalized at a time when every single feature of the domestic economy is calling for them to be well *below* the norm. Unemployment is higher than it's been for almost thirty years – and thirty years ago, the spike in joblessness was fierce, but brief. Today, the jobless figures are high and settling there, a new and frightening combination.[6] Soon the various elements of the government's emergency response to the credit crisis are going to start dropping away. Although our politicians have not shown vision, leadership, or muscle in bringing the deficit under control, the bond markets will bring their own brutal discipline to bear. The wall of government money which is keeping economic activity as high as it is will have to crumble eventually. When it does, spending will fall, unemployment will rise, and house prices will come under pressure again.

Meantime, the crisis in the housing market itself shows no signs of abating. Although, at the time of writing, house prices are somewhat stable or trending only a little downward, the FHFA reports that around 30% of all house transactions are arising from distressed sales of some sort. That is a stunning statistic. In a way, it says as much as our unemployment statistics do about the crisis that is gripping

America. Just think for a moment of the trauma of re-possession, what it would feel like. Right now, almost one-third of all home sales feel something like that. That's how bubbles feel as they pop.[7] The 2,000,000 construction workers who lost their jobs were among those injured by the popping.[8] Meanwhile, despite a collapse in the number of new houses being built,[9] the stock of homes available for sale is still well above its historical average.[10] In America, in 2010, some 23.1% of homes were in negative equity,[11] and more than a quarter are currently in negative equity or near-negative equity.[12] Every tick downwards in house prices will drag ever greater tranches of the US population into that frightening and unwanted position. Perhaps most scary of all, there are between 1.5 and 2 million homes not yet on the market but where the mortgages are delinquent or fore-closure proceedings have taken place. Those homes will, one day, need to be sold.[13] When that great dam of selling activity finally bursts, the effect on house prices will be catastrophic.

Finally, all this – the negative equity, the distressed sales, the unsold homes, the falling prices – is happening while the Fed desperately attempts to keep the great American Ponzi scheme alive for as long as possible. Interest rates are at historic lows. Mortgage rates have tracked them down. In our inflationary times, this monetary laxity cannot be maintained for ever. Interest rates will have to rise. When they do, the results will be grim. At present, the collapse in the housing market has been initiated by a collapse in the subprime market. Subprime mortgages have turned delin-quent in huge numbers. Prime mortgages have remained relatively unaffected.[14]

I'm not certain that it will happen – no one can predict

the future with perfect accuracy – but the likelihood is that gathering economic pressures will start to place the prime housing market under pressure. Delinquencies will rise. Distressed sales will rise. Prices will fall. Negative equity will become even more common. As interest rates increase from their historic lows and as 'teaser rate' mortgages click through to their full-price level, things will only get worse. In more and more households across the country, wives and husbands will look at each other across the dinner table, asking why the heck they're struggling to pay the mortgage when the loan is worth tens of thousands more than the house. Housing markets are volatile. We've known that for eons, but on Planet Ponzi that knowledge came to be translated into the notion that prices were volatile in one direction only: upwards. And that's not true. Volatility means prices can surge crazily upwards and lurch sickeningly downwards. We've ridden the first of those curves for a decade or so. The full depths of the descent may only now be opening before us.

(And, of course, those depths are likely to add a crashing extra burden to the federal government's debt. In 2011, some 96.5% of all new US mortgages were guaranteed by Uncle Sam, up from an already staggering 90% a couple of years earlier. So when those mortgages go bad, Uncle Sam is going to find himself picking up the lion's share of the tab.)

The same goes for commercial real estate. Prices have plummeted, but the crisis here has felt somewhat static, in large part because when financial distress affects commercial real estate, you don't get hard-luck stories of families being forced out on to the street. But the situation is dire all the same. As long ago as January 2010, Richard Parkus, the head of commercial real estate research at Deutsche Bank,

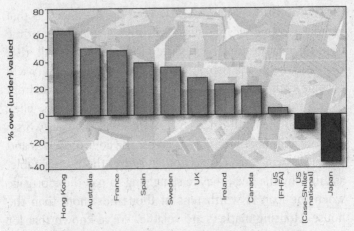

Figure 12.1: The coming house price crash

Source: 'Rooms with a view,' *The Economist*, July 7, 2011.

commented: 'It's a train wreck in slow motion. Because it's in slow motion, people get this sense that it's really not happening. It is happening.'[15] Parkus is absolutely right. Bear in mind that commercial mortgages generally refinance every three to ten years. That means that loans made during the boom are coming up for refinancing now. Since prices have fallen and – at last! – lending standards have risen, there will be countless borrowers unable to roll over their debt. That means more bankruptcies, and yet another source of fear and uncertainty for the economy at large.

These are hardly comforting thoughts, so permit me to cheer you up with a little splash of *Schadenfreude*. The American housing market looks dire, but it's in much, much better shape than most of its foreign counterparts. According to data compiled by *The Economist*, the US market has already adjusted far more than most. Figure 12.1

presents *The Economist*'s estimates of over- or undervaluation for some selected international housing markets, using long-term ratios of house prices to rent by way of a valuation benchmark. Housing markets in Europe, Hong Kong, and Australasia are still gripped by overvaluation on a massive scale. Canada's housing bubble has been kept inflated by the strong performance of its economy.

The three final bars in the chart hold up a mirror to the possible future for those markets. The two different estimates for the US market arise because of the lack of a single agreed measure for US house prices. A reasonable guess would place the truth at somewhere between the FHFA measure and the Case–Shiller one. Yet, in a way, the crucial entry is the very last one. It explains why I'm not comforted by the idea that the US market has 'normalized.' It reminds us that volatility cuts in two directions. Two decades on from the collapse of its own bubble, the Japanese property market is more than 35% below its own 'normal' value. My own guess is that the US market will need to touch those levels before it will truly shake off the effects of the last decade.

I'm not alone in thinking so. Robert Shiller himself said that a further fall of 10–25% 'wouldn't surprise me at all,' commenting that, 'in real terms, there has never been a bust of this proportion.'[16] He's right. We're in new territory, desolate and hostile. We'll talk about the implications for the banks in another chapter. Needless to say, those implications aren't going to be pretty. And the greater the pressure on the banks, the more they'll seek to conserve their liquidity position by refusing mortgage request applications. Which means the housing market will come under yet greater pressure. Which means . . .

Well, you get the picture. If you own a house, it's probably not the picture you wanted to see, but truth isn't about what you want or hope, it's about what is. The desire to see things some other way is at the heart of the thinking that gave us Planet Ponzi, that gave us all these insane housing markets worldwide. What we're experiencing now and what we're about to experience is the slow elimination by fire of that way of seeing the world. If that's not what you signed up for when you started this chapter, remember I did try to warn you. I'm not short your house, but still . . .

Sorry.

THIRTEEN

A brief flash of reality

ONE OF THE MOST important papers in the history of the social sciences reported the results of a strange little experiment conducted by researchers Amos Tversky and Daniel Kahneman. It's a paper which, ideally, every investor and every regulator should read. Everyone with an interest in the financial markets, in fact – a group which includes all those who have money and all those who would like to.

The study was simple and emphatic. It took a group of subjects and asked them various questions – for example, the percentage of African countries among the United Nations member states. Since, naturally, people often didn't know the answers, they were obliged to guess. But the questions weren't presented in an altogether open way. The process worked a little like a game show. The experimenter would spin a 'wheel of fortune' in the subject's presence. If, let's say, the number 10% came up, the subject would be asked to guess whether the percentage of African nations in the UN was more or less than that 10%. They were then asked to supply their own guess as to the correct figure. If the number 65% came up instead, it worked the same way.

People had to guess if the percentage was more or less than 65%, then make their own guess.[1]

If humans were genuinely rational, the spinning wheel would make no difference to the guesses people made. Why should it? Not only could it have nothing to tell anyone about the correct answer, but its essential randomness was completely visible to the subjects of the experiment. They could see the wheel being spun. But you've already guessed the punchline. People's guesses were hugely biased by the spin of the wheel. Those given the number 10% by the wheel guessed that the correct number was 25%. Those given the number 65% guessed 45%. Even when subjects were given a reward for giving (approximately) correct answers, the bias persisted. The spin of a wheel had them hooked. The name given by Tversky and Kahneman to this weird little phenomenon was 'anchoring bias.' People found themselves transfixed by the anchoring they were given by the questioning, even when they knew the anchor was random.

A second well-studied phenomenon is our so-called 'optimism bias.' That bias produces precisely the effects you'd guess. We humans expect to live longer than average, to be healthier, to have a lower chance of divorce, to be more successful.[2] There are paunchy middle-aged men who honestly think they'd stand a chance with Angelina Jolie. There are plump middle-aged women who honestly think that Brad Pitt would be entranced, if only he'd just get to know them. These things are so well documented by now that the British Treasury, for example, sets out guidelines for how project appraisers need to adjust their cost and timing estimates to overcome their own involuntary optimism.[3]

These things matter because they affect us all, and those who live on Planet Ponzi most of all. Take a look at figure

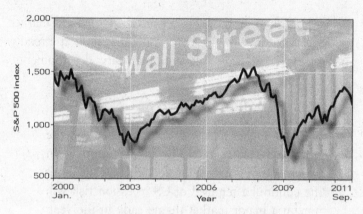

Figure 13.1: The return to 1500
Source: S&P.

13.1, which graphs the S&P 500 stock market index from January 2000 to date. On August 26, 2011 – the day I'm writing this page – the S&P opened at a level of 1159. How long do you guess it will take the index to recover the 1500 level that it first achieved in the early part of 2000? It would be good if you paused to answer that question before reading on. Take a look at the numbers. Have a think. *How long before we get back to 1500*?

If you're like most of us, your train of thought will have run something like this: 'Well, I can see we're due a little downturn – that's the argument of this book after all and I can see it makes sense – but *then again we were at 1500 around twelve years ago*. That's a heck of a long time to be treading water and the economy does grow, after all. So let's say, we'll have another bad year or two, then climb back to 1500 and start to make progress from there.'

You were thinking something like that, right? And if you were, you're in good company. In December 2010, Goldman

Sachs published its thoughts on the economic and market outlook for the coming year. The firm took a broadly positive view of economic and monetary developments, commenting:

> Growth is likely to accelerate, but there is plenty of spare capacity to keep policymakers on the sidelines. This is typically an environment in which equities and credit do well, and we think the continued removal of US recession risk will remain a major market theme early in the year. Indeed, our strategists are fairly optimistic. Our Portfolio Strategy team's end-2011 index targets envisage 14%–29% returns across the major equity markets.

Specifically, the firm estimated that the S&P 500 would end the year at 1450.[4]

We know already that that happy outcome is not looking probable now. We know now that 'removal of US recession risk' is not a phrase that would seem particularly wise even six months after it was written. The people who wrote that Goldman Sachs report were extremely smart people with a deep knowledge of the financial markets. Nevertheless, they – and nearly all their fellow commentators on Wall Street and in the media – look at the markets with a *buyer's* eye. The assumption common to almost all of us is that the equity markets will make money over the long run, that setbacks are temporary, that growth is the natural order of things. Given that the most influential commentators on these markets are firms like Goldman – which make money by selling the securities they're commenting on, which profit by encouraging investors to trade – our natural biases are liable to run rampant. We're hardwired to look at financial data with an optimistic bias, then strongly encouraged to do so by firms whose job is to sell us the underlying securities.

So let's seek to overcome those biases. Let's recall that only once in the past decade has the world come close to recognizing the reality of Planet Ponzi. In the winter of 2008–9, investors took a cold, hard look at the world that was collapsing around them and they saw it for what it was: insolvent banks, overleveraged corporations, wasteful governments, unrelenting competition from the emerging markets. That winter, markets were lit by a brief flash of reality – and, for the first time in a decade, they got things right. In March 2009, the S&P index traded at 683 points, well under half that fantasy 1500 level I used to 'anchor' your response a few moments ago. Less than half the level that Goldman Sachs was projecting for 2011. In March 2009, markets were frightened, but they were sane. They priced the world as they saw it, not as they wanted it to be.

That moment of reality did not endure for long. The sheer weight of government and monetary interventions eventually persuaded markets to close their eyes again and dream. In March 2009, the MSCI index of world equities – an index which includes all markets, developed and emerging – touched 175 points. Little more than two years later, that index had more than doubled, reaching over 350. No sane individual could believe that the value of the world economy had doubled in the space of two terrifying and depressing years. On the contrary, and as we've already seen, that torrent of government and monetary interventions has simply compounded the original problem. The credit crisis arose because of weak lending, excessive debt, inflated expectations, and overgenerous monetary policy. Worldwide, governments have chosen to respond by running huge deficits, bailing out failed investors and lousy investments, adding to the pile of debt, and printing money. You might just as well seek to fight a fire by hosing it with gasoline. It's no coincidence that the developed world's most successful governments – currently Canada, Sweden, and Germany – have consistently resisted these temptations. If anything, the world economy (or at least the American, European, and Japanese parts of it) has *lost* value over the past two years. At the very least, the hole we're in has just got a few trillion dollars deeper.

But let's return to the question of where equity markets ought to be. Robert Shiller, the un-Ponzi-ish economist who produced the housing index reviewed in the previous chapter, has produced a wonderful tool for examining fundamental value in the equity markets. We'll look at that in a moment, but first a brief refresher on equity valuation. When you buy stock in a company, you become a part-owner of the firm, entitled to a share of its profits. Some firms will return a large proportion of those profits to shareholders by way of dividends (or share buybacks). Other firms, particularly those needing capital to fund investment activity, will retain all or most of their profits. Because shareholders benefit either way – they get either dividends in their pockets today or a promise of expanded profits tomorrow – it is profits or earnings which form the basis of equity valuation. Naturally, a firm is worth substantially more than its current year profits, as it'll expect to generate further profit and further dividends into the future. The million-dollar question, then, has to do with the correct ratio between stock price and company earnings. Is a firm worth five times its profit? Ten times? Twenty times? Forty?

That's one critical question to answer, but there's another almost equally important one. Company profits, after all, are by their nature unstable. They'll be high during boom years, lower during lean ones. If you're seeking a measure of fundamental valuation, the instability of annual company profits gives you an uncertain foundation on which to build. The second question, then, is: how can you remove the instability from company profits without losing the crucial insight they give you into company value?

Shiller's work provides partial answers to both questions. His work involves two steps. The first is to generate a profit measure which averages a firm's earnings over ten years. That ten-year period will include good years and bad ones, exceptional losses and exceptional profits. The average figure, unlike any annual one, supplies an unvarnished estimate of its true trading position. Instead of looking at a regular price/earnings ratio, Shiller therefore prefers to use a 'cyclically adjusted price earnings' (CAPE) ratio – the same fundamental concept, but adjusted to remove temporary noise.

His second step was, quite simply, to do the math. He calculated his CAPE ratio for the entire S&P index for every month of every year from 1881 to the present. His results are shown in figure 13.2.

Those results are wonderfully illuminating. From 1880 to 1940, the ratio averaged 14.9. From 1940 to 1979, the ratio also averaged 14.9. Then, over the three decades of Planet Ponzi, from 1980 to 2010, the ratio has averaged 21.2, an average 42% overvaluation against historic norms. Since January 2000 it has averaged 25.9, an overvaluation of

Figure 13.2: Long-term value in the US equity market, 1881–2011

Source: Data available at irrationalexuberance.com.

74%. Just to be clear, there is no reason why this ratio should tend to increase over time. On the contrary: it should provide the most fundamental conceivable measure of value, and the ratio's stability over the century running from 1880 to 1980 should lay to rest any idea of long-term structural shift.

Such truths, of course, had little chance of taking hold on Planet Ponzi. In the last month of the twentieth century, the S&P 500 reached its highest ever CAPE ratio: a gravity-defying (and lunatic) ratio of 44.2. The extent of that bubble, its obvious absurdity, is clear from the graph above and is worth bearing in mind when you think about questions like 'When will the S&P return to 1500?' The question makes no more sense than trying to guess the number of African countries in the UN by watching the spin of a wheel. In fact, it makes considerably less sense. At least the spin of a wheel is random and unbiased. The level of 1500, on the other hand, was achieved when the equity market was in the grip of a once-in-a-century bubble. We might as well ask when the cheese mines on the moon will finally start to deliver. (The answer is probably around the time the government finally pays off its debt.)

In December 2010, the month in which Goldman was predicting a swift return to 1450, Shiller's CAPE ratio stood at 22.4, almost 40% above its historic average. The S&P has fallen back a little since then, but it still stands at just shy of twenty times cyclically adjusted profits, which is still more than 20% above the long-term average. These reflections suggest that the 'right' level for the S&P is around 900, a level which would be regarded by most well-known commentators as a ludicrously pessimistic prediction.

I'm not about to volunteer a prediction of my own. Equity markets have such a remarkable gift for self-deceit that, for all I know, stock prices will race back to 1500 before reality finally catches up. What I would say, however, is just what I said in relation to the housing markets. Why should we expect equity prices to normalize when we are living in extraordinarily abnormal times? The period in recent economic history which bears the greatest resemblance to our own is the troubled decade of the 1970s. The 1970s saw oil shocks, inflation, weak growth, high unemployment, and the breakdown of global currency systems. Between the oil shock of 1973 and the start of recovery a decade later, Shiller's CAPE ratio averaged just 10.2. If the S&P were to return to those bargain basement levels, it would need to fall by some 50% to around 600 or 700. If you think that a fall on that scale is impossible, you might want to take this book back to the place you bought it and ask for a refund. You can honestly say you've derived no benefit from it.

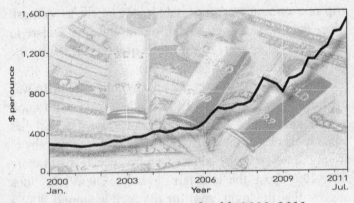

Figure 13.3: The price of gold, 2000–2011

Source: ThomsonReuters.

Meanwhile, if you'd be interested to know how you'd have done if you'd bought gold – the classic way to hedge against uncertainty and turmoil – you might want to study figure 13.3. You'll study it with relish if (like me) you bought gold way back in the early years of the millennium. You'll study it with mixed feelings if you didn't. And, of course, if you're the former British Chancellor of the Exchequer (and later Prime Minister) Gordon Brown, who sold around 400 tonnes of gold in 1999–2001, when the gold price was at a twenty-year low, you will probably review the chart with a little embarrassment. Equity returns over that period have been more or less flat. Gold is up over 500%.[5]

We're just about done on equity markets. The simple truth, once again, is that the assets promised by a Ponzi scheme are worth vastly less than they purport to be. Your house is worth less than the Ponzi-sellers suggested. Your equities and pension are worth less too. They were always worth less. It's just that for a long time there were enough Ponzi-ish buyers to keep the whole merry-go-round moving.

If you own any shares, either directly or via a pension fund, the thoughts contained in this chapter have probably done little to brighten your day. It wasn't you who led us into this mess, but you seem to be among those of us asked to pay for it all. Yet I wouldn't want these personal woes to conceal some of the policy implications that will follow from further falls in the equity market.

The most obvious issue is that people will feel poorer. People who feel poor tend to cut their spending. So firms will find it tougher to sell their goods. Profits will be under pressure, employees will be laid off. There's a vicious circle building there, emphasis on the word 'vicious.'

Secondly, of course, every decline in the equity market means a bigger hole in government and private pension funds. Those holes need to be filled. Corporations, which account honestly and openly for their pension funds, will need to dig into profits to find the necessary cash. Governments, which prefer to manipulate their figures, will simply find that their ever-swelling pool of commitments has just gotten deeper.

Thirdly, though, almost everything in Planet Ponzi traces back to the banks. If the banks were sound and strong, the economy could start to get going again. If the banks are little better than zombies, the economy is years from recovery. Japan's economy is still on intravenous support twenty years on from its crisis. And though banks operate through the markets for credit rather than equity, the equity markets are crucial to them nevertheless. We'll look closely at the financial sector in a future chapter, but for now you can just take it for granted that banks are hemmed in between their mountains of crappy assets and their oceans of excessive debt. Those mountains and those oceans aren't about to disappear.

In some crisis situations, governments have simply relieved banks of their bad debts. In others, banks have gone to the equity markets and raised capital. Either way, their balance sheets become freed up and capable of working once again.

Today, however, neither option looks at all easy. Governments simply aren't in a position to incur any more debts, to take on any more problems. Equally, however, declining equity markets make it fearsomely hard (and expensive) to seek capital. In September 2011, Bank of America announced a $5 billion investment by Warren Buffett. The market greeted the news with a surge of relief – which, however, faded rather quickly once the terms of the deal sank in. Buffett bought preferred stock, which paid an annual dividend of 6% (at a moment when the yield on ten-year Treasuries was just 2.02%). That stock will still be repayable even if the common equity sinks to zero. In addition, he was given no fewer than 700 million warrants, which gave him the right (but not the obligation) to acquire BoA stock at crisis levels. Those warrants are valid for an extraordinary ten years. At one point, following announcement of the transaction, Buffett's paper profits amounted to almost $4 billion. The scale of those profits indicates Buffett's genius – and BoA's desperation. In ordinary times, the bank would have rejected Buffett's offer as derisory or even exploitative. In the times we're in now, it seized the moment so greedily that the deal was agreed within twenty-four hours of its having been proposed.[6] As time goes by, and if equity markets stay under pressure, such deals will become ever harder to do. Banks will find it ever harder to prop up their balance sheets. The bad assets will remain frozen. The excessive debts will remain hard to clear. These aren't cheering thoughts, I know, but I'm in the truth business not the cheerleading one. As I said before, I did try to warn you.

Sorry. Again.

FOURTEEN

Planet Ponzi comes to London

I STARTED PART TWO of this book by pointing out the im-
probably large profits recorded by the financial sector in
the US. Those profits alone would provide compelling
evidence of a giant financial sector Ponzi scheme. The huge
destruction of value that has taken place since 2008 (and
which still has some way to run) comprises the inevitable
corollary of those bogus profits. When I moved to London
from New York in late 1999 I was motivated in large part by
a strong desire to get away from what I was coming to see as
a financial system out of control.

Unfortunately, Planet Ponzi followed me here. In the
UK, the growth in the financial sector has been equally wild
– and even more recent. A 2011 study for the Bank of
England looked at value added in the financial sector and
value added in the economy at large. The respective average
real growth rates since the start of World War One are as
shown in table 14.1.

For over half a century, the financial sector actually grew
less fast than the economy as a whole. For the quarter-
century after 1971, the financial sector grew a little faster

	Financial sector	Total economy
1914–70	1.5	1.9
1971–96	2.7	2.2
1997–2007	6.1	3.0

**Table 14.1: Growth in UK value added since 1914
(average annual %)**

Source: Stephen Burgess, 'Measuring financial sector output and its
contribution to UK GDP,' *Bank of England Quarterly Bulletin*, Q3 2011.

than the economy as a whole, but not all that much. Given
the growth in capital markets and the greater availability of
consumer finance, you can argue that the financial sector
was due a little catch-up time. But that's all. The rapid acceleration of the financial sector from 1997 essentially
represents the sudden turbo-boost of Planet Ponzi. In 1996,
the UK boasted a sophisticated, competitive and fully
functional financial system. It didn't need to catch up any
more. What happened in the period after 1996 was
historically unprecedented – and inherently implausible.

And remember that value added is a measure of output, not profit. If you examine profits, rather than value
added, Planet Ponzi's London division appears even more
distended. Between 1948 and 1978, financial intermedia-
tion (a subsection of the financial services sector) accounted
for around 1.5% of profits in the total economy. By 2008,
that ratio had risen *tenfold* to 15%. That's such an extreme
change as to be effectively impossible. Banks *weren't* making
those profits, they were simply pretending that they did:
manipulating their books to show profits that weren't, in
truth, ever there. The financial bust of 2008–9 showed what

happens when some of those wheels start to come off the wagon. The financial disasters we are starting to experience now show what happens when all the rest fall off too.[1]

If Britain copied America in the pell-mell Ponzification of its economy, London arguably exceeded New York in the grossness of its rewards for the new banking elite. A 2007 report in the *Washington Post* – that is, a report from that distant pre-crash era before bankers started to become PR-savvy about moderating their displays of wealth – made it clear just how gross those rewards could be.

> They call themselves 'the haves and the have yachts': rich London bankers and traders who drop tens of thousands of dollars for an evening of cocktails and hire 'personal concierges' to get their girlfriends dresses like those worn by movie stars.
>
> Long a hub for the world's ultra-rich, London has just welcomed an unprecedented number of newcomers into those ranks. Analysts here estimate that London's financial stars were paid a total of $17 billion in annual bonuses in recent weeks – including more than 4,200 people who received bonuses of at least $2 million each, on top of salaries already sagging under the weight of zeros.[2]

So gross were those rewards that Mayor Bloomberg of New York commissioned a report which argued that the light touch of regulation in London was making the city more attractive than New York as a hub for international talent.[3] Back in those happy pre-crash days, the waiting list for a custom-built Ferrari was three years. Auction houses were notching up records. Property prices were going crazy. Bankers were racking up cocktail bills of $36,000 in a single evening.[4] And it's all happening again today. There's a little more discretion, perhaps, but the money is the same, and in some cases property prices in central London are actually higher than in New York.

These things corrode a society. When talking about the financial industry in the US, I complained about weak regulation and the absence of consequences for bankers. When talking about regulators, I listed just some of the big-money lawsuits and settlements which have riddled the US financial industry in recent years. My own view is that neither the fines nor the lawsuits have been proportional or sufficient: people needed to go to jail. Yet at least the US is awash with such lawsuits. Where are their equivalents in Britain? Why are banks and bankers being allowed to ruin the country and then left to continue their Ponzi-ish activities with impunity? In an ideal world, any business leader who inflicts multi-billion losses on ordinary taxpayers should be deemed to have committed a crime, the only appropriate punishment for which would involve staring out of a barred window for a decade or two. If that's not possible, there should at least be a profound financial cost for the individuals involved. And if that's not possible, their firms should be fined huge sums of money.

There's nothing particularly vengeful in this logic. A kid who smashes a window once would expect to suffer. A kid who repeatedly smashes windows would ultimately expect to be locked up. Quite right too. Yet, in Britain, the firms and individuals which collectively caused damage amounting to tens and hundreds of billions of pounds have suffered almost not at all. That's crazy. If it's because the laws are too slack, the laws should be changed. If the laws are fine but are not being enforced, they should be enforced immediately. Indeed, lawsuits and criminal charges should be mounted even if the prosecution case is less than watertight. A judge can decide whether a charge is justified or not; the regulators should be seeking whatever penalties they can.

One of the striking differences between the financial cultures of London and New York is that, in America, at least regulators *attempt* to act with rigor. Those attempts often fail, because of weak laws or insufficient resources, but the will is there. In London, the opposite is true. Regulators are underpaid and often come from an academic background. Because economic theory tends (idiotically) to suggest that the financial world offers the most perfect possible example of markets in action, those theorist-regulators are woefully unsuited to tackle the grim realities of the financial sector. The situation will only change when regulators are better paid, have more real-world experience, and show real willingness to press for huge fines and, where possible, jail terms. At the moment, there's not the slightest hint of such a change.

Meantime, most of the issues we've looked at in the context of Wall Street hold equally true for London. The equity market in Britain is still too high. The housing market in Britain is way too high. The banks are overexposed to euro-zone sovereign debt and mortgages in particular. The various structural weaknesses of the financial markets – a lack of transparency, weak accounting rules, insufficient regulation, and much more – are every bit as true in the Square Mile as in Manhattan.

So much for Britain. Now for the world.

PART THREE

The Wider World

FIFTEEN

The rise and rise of Planet Ponzi

PLANET PONZI SOUNDS like a great title for a book. It's catchy, it's shocking, it makes a point. The cost of that catchiness is that it sounds phony. A marketing trick. It feels akin to those books called things like *How To Lose Twenty Pounds In Twenty Days And Never Even Feel Hungry*. You might choose to buy the book, but you're never dumb enough to believe the promise in the title. *Planet Ponzi* isn't like that. The title might sound shocking, but I challenge you to locate a more precise two-word descriptor of the financial history of the past three decades. You'll find it tough.

This chapter has a single mission. Its task: to demonstrate the growth of Planet Ponzi in country after country, decade after decade. Our principal data source is the McKinsey Global Institute, and all those data are available online. If you don't want to trust McKinsey, you can ferret out the original data yourself. I've made some of those checks. I didn't get exactly the same numbers as McKinsey – they may have used slightly different data sources or different exchange rates, or I may be looking at more recent

Type of debt	US 1990	US 2009	UK 1990	UK 2009	Japan 1990	Japan 2009
Financial debt	24	53	60	154	119	110
Household debt	59	97	65	103	66	69
Corporate debt	65	79	66	110	147	95
Government debt	57	67	32	59	59	197
Total debt	204	296	224	466	391	471

Table 15.1: The rise and rise of Planet Ponzi: debt as % of GDP

Source: 'Debt and deleveraging: the global credit bubble and its economic consequences,' McKinsey Global Institute, Jan. 2010.

data that have been slightly revised – but to an impressive degree my results converged with McKinsey's. In other words, the data we're about to look at are impeccable. If you've got a dash of the conspiracy theorist in you, you might wonder if the governments and central banks of the world are being altogether honest in their portrayals of debt, but if they're *not* being honest, they'll certainly be understating, not overstating, the real problem.

OK. Preamble over. Let's look at the data. And though the US boasts arguably the most bankrupt *government* in the world today, the United States as a *country* is by no means the most indebted. The precise winner is a little hard to call, but the United Kingdom and Japan are currently duking it out for the title of World's Most Indebted Country. Table 15.1 sets out the figures.

I'll talk a little about what precisely these figures denote in a moment, but for now let's just read the headlines. In the US, total indebtedness is around 300% of GDP. In Britain and Japan, the figure is closer to 500% of GDP. In all three countries, indebtedness has grown hugely in the space of just twenty years. In the US, indebtedness as a percentage of GDP has increased by around half. In Britain, it's more than doubled. Japan's figures have risen by almost a quarter from an already very high base. Looking only at government debt in relation to GDP, Japan has seen an increase of 235%, the UK of 85%, and the US of 18%. In the latter two cases, the post-2009 explosion of borrowing is driving those totals up higher still.

These figures are shocking. Or at least, they would be shocking if the remorseless growth of Ponzi-ish thinking hadn't driven us all senseless. In 1990, nobody in the world looked at America or Britain and thought, 'Gee, you know what, these economies would be a whole lot stronger if only there was more debt floating around.' On the contrary, any sane person in 1990 would have wondered why the heck government debt in America stood at 57% of GDP. We'd just won the Cold War, the economy was on a roll: debt should have been trending down to zero. Likewise, at the end of the 1980s, a decade when leveraged buyouts were all the rage on Wall Street, people were anxious that corporations had taken on so much debt that investment and growth would be inevitably impaired. People were worried about the incessant increases in credit card and mortgage debt, and the changes in culture that went along with that increase. These worries were neither flippant nor ill-founded. They were the right ones to have. Trouble is, our policymakers and regulators didn't respond when it would have been easy and relatively costless to do so. They were too toothless, too inert, too dumb, too cowardly. The result: a train which could have been braked gently to a halt can now only be halted by blowing up the track, with all the ugly consequences that will involve.

Or perhaps there is an alternative: the Japanese option. Japan's debt figures have hit a ceiling and are no longer rising. The country simply can't bear more debt. Banks can't lend, companies won't invest, the workforce is shrinking. Although interest rates are rock-bottom, the economy still isn't reviving. Indeed, the real tale in Japan is the way the government is simply running up larger and larger debts in the ludicrous hope that 'something will turn up.' We'll look at the hollowness of that hope in a while, but for now let's just acknowledge that there is an alternative to the track-blowing-up option. You can always try the zero-growth, rising-debt, ghost-economy option. Me, I'd blow up the tracks.

We'll look at some more scary numbers from around the world in a few moments – I know, I'm Mr Fun – but before we do so I should be a little more precise about what the figures mean. We also need to be very careful about what is and isn't scary about these numbers.

Table 15.1 shows gross debt in the economy broken down into the four main sectors: households, governments, corporations, and financial institutions. Crucially, the term 'gross' debt means that we're ignoring any assets. So although Japanese banks (for example) have debts equal to 110% of the country's GDP, they also have financial assets offsetting those debts. In fact, given that Japanese banks (to go by their published accounts) have got plenty of underlying capital, Japanese banks own assets that are greater than their overall liabilities.

Likewise, although households in America and Britain owe an amount equal to around 100% of their national GDP, those households will also hold a variety of offsetting assets: houses, bank deposits, stocks and bonds, pension assets. Those assets are, in both countries, considerably greater than the stock of debt. In the UK, for example, although the gross *debt* of households is roughly equal to 2009 GDP – an amount equal to approximately £1.4 trillion – the total stock of household *assets* was equal to around £6.3 trillion. The difference between the two figures – total household assets less total household debts – is close to £5 trillion, or well over three times the size of British GDP. A similar kind of equation holds true in the US, in Japan, and in the other countries we'll survey in this chapter.[1]

At this point, your reaction is likely to be one of confusion. After all, if households in all these countries are sitting on mountains of assets, who cares if they also happen to owe some money? OK, so banks may owe a lot of money, but if they hold assets that are worth more than their debts, then what's the problem? And corporations: some corporations may owe large amounts of money, others have got stacks of cash. Microsoft alone holds almost $40 billion of cash and short-term investments. It has nearly $90 billion in total assets. Although it does have some long-term liabilities, they're trivial in comparison.[2] In short, it can easily look as though these high levels of debt aren't a problem, given the amounts of assets floating around.

We'll come to that – perfectly reasonable – challenge in a moment. But first it's important to realize that, if you're looking at things on a global level, there will always be more assets than debt. Unless you happen to owe money to Martians or the Man in the Moon, your financial debt is bound to be somebody else's financial asset. The two things will always cancel out. At the same time, the world is full of lots of proper, tangible, valuable assets: houses, factories, offices, oil wells, power stations, and so on. It's also full of lots of highly valuable assets that have very little to do with tangible things. Apple, for example, has a market capitalization that is about $300 billion in excess of the net assets (mostly cash) on its balance sheet.[3] That doesn't mean that Apple is running some kind of huge Ponzi scheme; it simply means that Apple has some wonderful products, a terrific brand, and a dominant position in some of the hottest consumer segments of the moment. There's nothing phony about its market valuation.* In short, once you've canceled out the thicket of financial debts and financial assets, you'll be left with a whole heap of physical things (houses, offices, factories, and other stuff) and a whole heap of intangible things (patents, designs, brands, and so on), with loads of solid value in both piles. Taken as a whole, therefore, the world is not insolvent. That's not the issue.

Nor is the issue that America has been secretly taken over by China, or that Brazil has bought the United Kingdom, or anything like that. As of June 2011, mainland China held a little over $1 trillion in US Treasuries, only slightly more than Japan. That trillion dollars is certainly significant as an indicator of which way the economic wind has been blowing in recent years, but it still only amounts to a month or so of American GDP. If you broaden the issue and look at all overseas investments held by Americans and subtract all US investments held by foreigners, you'll find that the US has a net debt position of about $2.5 trillion. Clearly you'd prefer that the US wasn't in a net debt position at all but, given the size of the figures we've been hurling

* Not that I'd be a buyer at current levels. At Apple's October 2011 price of $400.00 per share, I would argue the market has priced in perfection for years to come. The real world doesn't work like that.

around in this book so far, $2.5 trillion here or there is hardly critical.[4]

The same goes for most of the other countries on Planet Ponzi. British government statisticians, for example, reckon that the country has a net 'international investment position' of minus £180 billion. That's equivalent to just over a month's GDP, little more than a rounding error in terms of the sums involved. And that's assuming you trust the figures. The government's statisticians don't possess the data to estimate a market valuation for all Britain's overseas investments and all foreign investments in Britain. For reasons we don't need to go into here, however, there are reasons to believe that if all investments, British and foreign, were estimated at their current market value, Britain would have a positive international investment position.[5]

All this leaves us with a puzzle. We've seen a frightening rise in the level of gross debt in the US, the UK, and Japan, but:

❑ financial assets have also increased;

❑ all three countries have a huge stock of valuable physical assets (houses, factories, offices, etc.) and of valuable intangible ones (brands, designs, patents, etc.);

❑ although individual countries may or may not owe money overseas, the quantity of any external debt is relatively modest.

In effect, what's happened in America is that a forest of financial debts has grown up, but those debts are largely owed to other American entities (individuals, banks, and corporations). To the extent money is owed overseas, American entities own offsetting claims so that the net position is more or less flat. The same is true of Britain. The same is true of Japan. The same is true of all the other countries we're about to survey.

The question is: does this matter? If we're owing money to ourselves, why the heck should we care? If it's all just circulating within the system, maybe gross debts could rise to 1,000% of GDP and we wouldn't have a problem.

You wouldn't expect me to agree with that proposition and I don't. It's catastrophically false, a financial insanity. An elementary-school kid would see through the deception – it's only our policymakers who are fooled. The issue is *not* the net levels of debt. The net levels of debt are always going to be OK, those things will always cancel out. The issue is the *structure*. The quantity of debt we have in our financial system creeps through it like some deadly ivy: poisoning, choking, constricting, and killing.

The collapse of Lehman Brothers proves better than anything why it's not the net levels of debt that count. As we've noted before, Lehman collapsed with net debt of 'just' $129 billion. In the context of the entire world's financial system, that $129 billion was a pinprick, nothing more. But it wasn't the net debt that counted. It was the gross debt. The gross debt of $768 billion. The derivative contracts with notional principal of a further $729 billion. When Lehman failed it caused a mass panic in the financial markets, because nobody knew where they stood.

Worse still, no one knew where other firms stood. So let's say you were in charge of the First National Bank of Alligator Gulch. You were owed money by Lehman, but you'd done your calculations and figured you were going to be OK. You'd take a hit, but you'd be fine. Unfortunately, though, your bank had also lent money to the Guaranty Savings Bank of Crocodile Canyon. You happen to know that the folks over at Croc Canyon had also been lending money to Lehman Brothers and, for all you knew, they'd lent too much. Maybe Croc Canyon was now in trouble. Which would mean that maybe your firm was now in trouble too. You couldn't take the chance. You'd have to play it safe. You'd have to wind down your loans to Croc Canyon and any other institutions which might have been weakened. Trouble is, you knew Croc Canyon – and every other bank which touched Lehman, or which touched banks which touched Lehman, which is to say pretty much every damn bank in the world – would be in the same position. So your ability to secure funds had just deteriorated, which meant . . .

Well, we know what it meant. It would end up meaning that the entire financial system ground to a halt. Even the really basic stuff that banks are meant to do – supplying cash to ATM machines, holding deposits, making mortgage loans – became uncertain. The problem arose because there was way too much debt, way too much complexity, way too little transparency, way too little oversight, no accountability.

There's another reason for strenuously opposing the rise in debt levels. Aggregate demand is made up of how much stuff we produce – that's the only real measure of how rich we are – plus any change in overall debt levels. So if we produce stuff worth $100, but take out a $10 loan, we can end up purchasing goods worth $110. That sounds attractive – the magic of credit – but at some point you have to pay back the $10 along with the interest. That means that aggregate demand will at some stage retreat from $110 to

$90 or less. Within a carefully planned family context, those things don't need to matter. At the level of an entire economy, such swings in demand make for a crunchingly painful recession . . . and it's no surprise, therefore, that the Western world has been hit with its worst recession since the 1930s and that many countries have *never* seen such a painful recession. The cause of the problem was way too much debt creation in the good years, a painful payback period now.[6]

So gross debt matters. In America, Britain, and Japan, debt rose to toxic levels over the course of two decades or more. And it's the same elsewhere. Using the same source – the McKinsey Global Institute – you get the picture across Planet Ponzi shown in table 15.2. (I've included the data for the US, the UK, and Japan from table 15.1 so the full horror can be seen all in one place.)

If I were being kind, I'd say that Canadian policymakers haven't made too horrible a mess. It's inexplicable to me how a resource-rich economy at peace with itself and its neighbors, with a colossal market lying just to its south, can possibly rack up government debt amounting to some 70% of GDP. Nor can I understand how policymakers thought it was sensible to allow the household sector to follow their American neighbors in rushing to take out mortgages, loans, and credit card debt. But let's not be too hard on the Canadians. They've done a bad job, but they've done the least bad job of anyone we've looked at. Their banks are safe. Their economy is growing. If they wake up one day and remember to start paying back their government debt, their country will be doing just fine.

Elsewhere, what can you say? The picture is so awful, it's almost impossible to exaggerate the problems. Japan is so

Country	1990	2010	Increase	Comment
US	204	296	+92	Debt increasing throughout the system. True government debt is way higher than these figures indicate.
Canada	210	259	+49	Excessive household debt, but well-managed banks and a resource-rich economy have kept things moving.
Germany	168	285	+117	Excessive growth in debt. The culprits are primarily the banks and the government.
France	208	323	+115	Excessive debt everywhere, except household sector. Banks fraudulently undercapitalized.
Italy	196	315	+119	Hideous levels of government debt and a seriously weak banking sector.
Spain	128	366	+238	Crazy banks, crazy property boom, overleveraged firms. Out of control country.
UK	224	466	+242	Prime Minister Brown's legacy to his grateful people. Insanity.
Japan	391	471	+80	A terrible record. The Japanese government makes Greece look prudent.
South Korea	157	333	+176	More insanity. Too much debt throughout the system, except at government level.

Table 15.2: Planet Ponzi goes global: total gross debt as % of GDP

Source: 'Debt and deleveraging: the global credit bubble and its economic consequences,' McKinsey Global Institute, Jan. 2010.

horrifically indebted, and has been for so many years, it looks like a shoo-in for the title of Supreme Ruler of Planet Ponzi. On the other hand, the British record is so alarmingly abysmal you'd have to say the champion of the East is about to be replaced by a new champion arising from the West.

But there'll be competition for the title. Britain boasts a huge and internationally significant financial sector, which tends to push up its figures. Spain doesn't have that excuse, yet has ramped up its debts to the same vastly excessive degree. South Korea has a penny-pinching government, but debt is running riot everywhere else in its financial system. In Germany, France, and Italy – in a period, please remember, when the Cold War ended, when there were no wars of existential consequence, when trade boomed, innovation flourished, and prosperity reigned – debt increased by trillions of dollars over and above the natural growth in GDP. That increase in debt amounted to more than an entire year's output for all three of those European countries.

By these abysmal standards, you could be forgiven for thinking that the United States is not in too bad a state. Except that, as we saw in the first part of the book, the published data on US government debt wildly understate its true position. If we added in all the extras we took a look at – state and federal pensions, social security, Medicare, Fannie Mae and Freddie Mac – the US debt numbers would increase by *hundreds* of percentage points.

Other countries, too, have liabilities of this sort. The trouble is measuring them. Only one country in the world provides an honest set of accounts. The UK government recently published its first ever 'Whole of Government Accounts,' which sought to account honestly for every part of government and for all liabilities: pension liabilities, provision against future liabilities, and so on. It's a stunning fact that Britain *first* did this in 2011 and that other countries don't do it at all. If a private sector company drew up a set of accounts which didn't consolidate all wholly owned subsidiaries and which didn't honestly report all its liabilities (including nonfinancial ones), that company would likely be committing criminal fraud. In the UK, where people are soft-hearted about these things, those found guilty of fraud can go to jail for seven years. In the US, where we take a more bracing approach, fraudsters can be sent to jail for life. Bernie Madoff's $18 billion racket saw him sent to jail for 150 years. The fraud currently being perpetrated by the US Treasury is at least a thousand times greater than that.

But I digress. Britain's Whole of Government Accounts report liabilities for public sector pensions at around 86% of GDP.[7] If you toss in various other liabilities – for nuclear decommissioning and the like – a round figure of about 100% is near enough correct. That figure is additional to the gross debt number in the table above. It represents court-enforceable debt obligations which are, from a financial point of view, little different from ordinary government bonds. I'd like to be able to give you similar data for every other country in that table. But I can't, because those other countries falsify and hide their accounts. That ought to be illegal. It's a practice which should lead to finance ministers and their civil servants being led away in handcuffs. But, on Planet Ponzi, what ought to be the case and what is the case are two very different things. Shame.

In any case, even if I had the data, they wouldn't give the whole story. The world is getting older. Baby boomers are aging. People are facing retirement in the expectation that they're going to collect a pension. But where are those pensions going to come from? To a frightening degree that question has been evaded by both private individuals and their governments. Remember, there is only one way to fund a pension and that is to put a little money aside each and every year of your working life, so there is a pot of money waiting for you on retirement. In principle, it shouldn't matter whether you do that for yourself, whether your employer does it on your behalf, or whether the government does it for you. What matters is that there's a pot of money with

Country	Private pension funds	Public pension funds	Total
US	72	18	90
Canada	65	9	74
Germany	5	–	5
France	0	2	2
Italy	5	–	5
Spain	8	6	14
UK	87	–	87
Japan	24	26	50

Table 15.3: The absent nest egg: pension provision as % of GDP, selected countries

Source: OECD, 'Pension markets in focus,' July 2011; GDP data from IMF, *World Economic Outlook*, April 2011.

your name attached to it, waiting for you when you retire.

And (most of) that money isn't there. Table 15.3 summarizes the total private and public provision for pensions in the West's principal economies. It's blindingly obvious from the table that France, Germany, Italy, and Spain have made effectively no provision at all for their aging populations. In effect, all four of these countries are running huge Ponzi schemes where current retirees are taking money from future retirees. When those future retirees come to draw their pensions, they're likely to find that there's no money left to look after them. That's the nature of Ponzi schemes: they always end up causing injury, and the bigger the scheme, the bigger the injury. That Italy and (to a lesser degree) Spain are mismanaging their pension obligations is hardly surprising. That Germany and France are doing so too is much more remarkable. It's true that this table notes only those savings which are formally held in pension plans. In continental Europe, there exist a variety of alternative pension funding methods, such as book reserves (a terrible idea: see below) and pension insurance contracts. These things, however, would add only a few per cent to the totals for France, Spain, and Italy, all of which effectively deal with pensions on a pay-as-you-go-basis. In Germany, the position is quite simply unclear, which is, if anything, even scarier.[8]

It's true, of course, that by comparison with the improvident British, Europeans are more likely to save their household income. It would be tempting to think that the true story of table 15.3 is simply that German savers, for example, are taking care of their own futures without going via some company pension plan. Unfortunately, that's simultaneously true and not true at all. True, savings rates are significantly higher in Germany than in Britain. But Brits are more likely to buy equities and property, while Germans are more likely to use low-yield savings accounts and euro bonds. The painful result: household wealth in Britain (as a multiple of disposable household income) is substantially higher than it is in Germany or France.[9]

The blunt truth, therefore, is that for all their apparent thrift, the *citoyens* and *citoyennes* of France, and the *Bürger* and *Bürgerinnen* of Germany are much less well provided for than they would appear to be. The aging populations of Europe are heading toward a future for which far too little money has been set aside. The principal problem has been one of Ponzi-ish thinking: neglecting future obligations because of the present pain it would cause to take them seriously. That failure alone should be enough to debar any current national leader from regaining office. It's a betrayal of an entire generation.

It's worth also noticing, while we're here, how untransparent the figures are. The OECD, arguably the best statistical outfit in the rich world, doesn't have data for German pension provision. The OECD doesn't have them, because no one has them. That's an amazing fact. We are entering a new era in world history – one with unprecedented numbers of elderly people, each of whom deserves a retirement of dignity and respect – and we don't even know how much money exists to look after them. That's appalling. What's more, the German notion that book reserves on a company balance sheet constitute a safe way to look after pensioners is simply untrue. I don't want to get too far into the technicalities, but if you happen to be ten or twenty years from drawing a pension, which would you prefer: professionally managed assets in a ring-fenced fund or an accounting reserve in a company's books, with no assurance whatever that that company would still exist in a decade or two's time?

In short, it's pretty clear that continental Europe is woefully and shockingly underprepared for its own near future. The famously thrifty savers of northern Europe are, in practice, in far worse shape than they think they are.

What's less obvious, however, from the data presented above is that America, Canada, Britain, and Japan are *also* running huge Ponzi schemes. (I don't have the data that would enable me to comment on South Korea.) For one thing, there's often a lot less in those public sector 'pension funds' than there appears to be. The US social security fund invests only in Treasury bonds, which are promises payable by future taxpayers – which is all a little like the German arrangement, only less transparent. But even if we take that public sector provision at face value, the sums involved are vastly less than they ought to be. In America and Britain, total pension assets are around 90% of GDP. If you think that's adequate, please imagine that you are ten or fifteen years from your retirement and that your pension pot – that's the capital you'll be able to invest, not the annuity it will pay out – is equal to just 90% of your annual salary. Does that sound like an attractive recipe for retirement to you? Or does it sound like the bitter joke at the end of a Ponzi scheme?[10]

Needless to say, because Western populations are rapidly aging, the probable future pension bills are mounting. Estimates of the sums involved range from 100% or so of GDP (in the case of the US and UK) to more than 200% for European countries. Those huge liabilities are excluded from the data on gross debt presented earlier in this chapter.[11]

In the end, the sad truth is that the true level of debt on Planet Ponzi is simply unquantifiable. I'd say that, if you wanted to take a highly conservative estimate for true indebtedness, you would need to add a minimum of 200 percentage points of GDP to every country's entry in table 15.2. That 200% might just about cover the liability gap facing the UK.* In the United States, it would be safer to add a minimum of 400%.† If you believe Laurence Kotlikoff,

* As discussed, the first 100% would just about cover the court-enforceable obligations relating to the retirement of public servants, nuclear decommissioning, and the like. The second 100% would just about cover the general state pension available to all retirees on retirement.

† To be clear about my arithmetic: I showed in chapter 4, 'A hole as big as the world,' that, on government data, there was a total public liability of around $75 trillion. About $15 trillion of that is financial debt, which is already accounted for in the data on gross debt. That leaves a liability of around $60 trillion or, very approximately, four times US GDP.

whom I quoted earlier, you'd be better off adding a sum closer to 1,000% of GDP. In Germany, France, Japan, and elsewhere – I just don't know. Until government accounts are consistently, transparently, and honestly prepared, we don't have a realistic set of figures which would enable us to determine these things.

Two further comments. First, most readers will have noticed some absentees in this chapter. There's been no mention of China. None of India. No mention of Brazil or Russia. All those countries have their challenges, of course. India has a problem with corruption, with red tape, and with its labor laws. China has a problem with murky accounting, fraud, and bad debt running rampant throughout its banking sector. Brazil has a problem with insufficient tax collection, bubbling inflation, and high social expectations. Russia's problems are more numerous still: corruption, violence, lawlessness, Vladimir Putin, murky accounting, murky everything. Putin has effectively been in power for twelve years already and is likely to be there a while longer. High oil prices have created a mirage of prosperity, but the underlying economy has stagnated or gone backwards.

Nevertheless, though all these countries have problems, they don't have a problem with excessive debt. China, the most indebted of the BRICs, has total gross debt of around 150% of GDP. As before, that figure aggregates the gross debt of government, households, corporations, and banks. Russia, the least indebted of the four, has a debt ratio of around 75%. (Its apparent debt-aversion has something to do with having gone bankrupt a decade or so back. These things leave their mark.)[12]

The debt-aversion of these four emerging market giants gives them huge strategic strength just as the developed world has chosen, quite needlessly, to incur a vast strategic weakness. I don't, as it happens, think that the United States and its allies have to watch passively as China and India take over the mantle of global leadership – but we do have some major housekeeping work to do. More about that in the final chapter.

Secondly, a warning. Because these debt numbers are so astronomical, there's a temptation to suppose that we can go on merrily kicking the can down the road in the hope that we at least will escape catastrophe. We can't. We're living in the catastrophe. I'm not aware of any developed country that has hit gross debt-to-GDP ratios of 300% or 400% and survived without turmoil. *Memento mori* is a Latin phrase meaning 'remember you will die.' There's an entire genre of art dedicated to representing that uplifting thought: a genre having to do with skulls, skeletons, ashes, clocks, and graves.

We don't need skulls or graves to remind us where we're headed. We have Japan. We have Iceland. We have Ireland. We have Greece. We have Lehman Brothers and AIG and General Motors and Bear Stearns and all the other casualties of the crisis. This can will be kicked no further. The road has ended at a big brick wall.

Up next: sovereign debt crisis in Europe and the next phase of collapse.

SIXTEEN

Giants unicycling on clifftops

WHEN, IN JUNE 2011, Standard & Poor's (correctly but belatedly) downgraded its credit rating for Greece to CCC, its press release chirpily reported that the country was now 'the lowest rated sovereign in the world – [having] fallen below Ecuador, Jamaica, Pakistan and Grenada.' Greece retorted with fury, contending that S&P's decision ignored 'the will of all Greeks to plan our future in the Eurozone.'[1]

S&P clearly wasn't all that fazed, nor did the will of all Greeks play a large part in its deliberations, because less than two months later the ratings agency announced another downgrade – this time to CC for long-term debt and to a paltry C for short-term debt. It also reaffirmed its previous estimate that the likely recovery rate for owners of Greek sovereign debt was around 30–50% of principal. (That is, bondholders could expect to recover something between €0.30 and €0.50 for each euro lent.) That recovery rate would place the Republic of Greece, birthplace of democracy, somewhat below Enron in the rankings of the bankrupt. Just to rub salt into the wounds, S&P further commented that the outlook for Greece was negative. No matter how low the country had sunk, in S&P's eyes the journey to the bottom still had a little further to run.[2]

It wasn't long before that dark prediction came true. On September 6, 2011, the country's deepening recession caused the bond market to worry that Greece wouldn't even be able to achieve the terms required by the latest European bailout package. Bloomberg quoted Michael Leister, a bond specialist at WestLB in London, as commenting: 'The consensus seems to be that the second bailout package for Greece might be obsolete before it has been put into law, which is obviously detrimental for sentiment.'[3] Either Michael Leister was misquoted or he was campaigning to win Understatement of the Year 2011. Detrimental for sentiment? Yields on two-year Greek bonds are hitting record highs of more than 100%. Greek bonds due for repayment in 2020 are being quoted at under 40% of face value with no real buyers in sight.[4] Personally, I wouldn't be a buyer of those bonds at any price higher than 5% of principal.

You can analyze the Greek disaster any way you like. Blame the falsified national accounts. Pinpoint the hopelessly lax attitude to tax collection. Call attention to the finances of the national railway, or the laws surrounding early retirement, or the feeble performance of an economy blessed with sunshine, shipping, tourism, and agriculture and wonderfully positioned to exploit the opening up of the Balkans. In the end, though, it comes down to these figures:[5]

Government debt, 2011	152% of GDP
Government deficit, average 2009–12	9.6% of GDP
Economic growth, annual average 2009–12	-2.2%

You don't need me to tell you that these are hideous numbers. A colossal debt, an impossible deficit, a shrinking economy. If you want a recipe for sovereign bankruptcy, you'll find it right here, in these three simple stats. A short lesson in how not to run a country. A poster-child for profligacy.

But Greece doesn't matter. It's small fry. It owes $472 billion.[6] If we optimistically assume that Greece's creditors will recover €0.40 on each euro, that represents a total impending loss of some $189 billion – representing, very approximately, a bankruptcy equal to about one and a half Lehman Brothers. If Greece's sister countries in Europe simply had to manage one and a half Lehmans, they would mutter a few (French and German) swearwords and get on with it, Greece could mutter a few Hellenic thank-yous, and everyone could move on.

Unfortunately, on the European corner of Planet Ponzi,

	Government debt 2011 (% GDP)	Government deficit 2009–12 (% GDP)	Economic growth 2009–12 (% change)	Borrowing costs 10-year bond (%)	Debt outstanding 2011 ($bn)
'Endangered list'					
Portugal	91	6.9	-0.2	14.1	214
Ireland	114	16.6	0.5	8.2	243
Italy	120	4.4	1.2	6.8	2,623
Spain	64	8.1	0.8	5.7	949
France	88	6.6	1.6	3.3	2,410
'Safe havens'					
Germany	80	2.5	2.7	2.1	2,819
UK	83	9.1	1.7	2.3	2,052
US	100	10.8	2.8	2.0	15,154

Table 16.1: The ugly facts

Source: IMF, *World Economic Outlook*, April 2011 (data include estimates for 2011/12); data on bond yields from *Financial Times*, extracted 6–7 Sept. 2011.

the problem is worse than one small country getting into a mess. There are a few other countries who are watching Greece's descent into financial Hades with some trepidation. You can see this if we boil the entire debt problem down to the same few simple statistics, adding just a couple more figures to do with the cost of the borrowing and the absolute dollar size of the debts. The ugly facts are set out in table 16.1.

The table is arranged with the grisliest cases (as measured by the degree of panic on the bond market) at the top. I've added in Germany, Britain, and the US by way of comparison. I should also add that I've drawn my economic growth estimates from the IMF *World Economic Outlook* database published in April 2011. Without exception, growth estimates have declined since then, and equity markets have plunged, Germany's by around 30%. The market is currently afraid of a double-dip recession unfolding in both North America and Europe, and I personally suspect that recession has already started.

So, bad as these figures look, the reality is worse. Sorry.

Portugal and Ireland

Table 16.1 makes grim but interesting reading, roughly the way a murder victim must look to a forensic pathologist. Portugal is pretty much gone. It's not as thoroughly bankrupt as Greece, but that's hardly a comfort: nobody is as bankrupt as Greece. Even Pakistan looks a better bet. From the bond market's point of view, the way to think about Portugal is as follows. It owes roughly 90% of GDP. The interest rate on that debt is 14%. So simply in order to pay interest on its existing debts, the country has to hand over 14% of 90% of GDP – or about 12.5% of its annual income. To put that another way, every single person in the country has to work from January 1 to February 14 and hand over every single penny of their earnings to (primarily foreign) bondholders.[7] They can't use any of that money for eating, heating, or anything else. The government can't use any of that money for health, education, or anything else. Shareholders can't use any of that money for dividends or reinvestment in their businesses. From January 1 through February 14, the entire national product has to be handed over to bondholders.

That kind of sacrifice is something a country could probably make if it were necessary to get it out of a hole . . . but the lethal twist here is that Portugal could do all that and still be at the bottom of its hole. All it would have done would be to have kept current on its interest payments. It wouldn't have repaid a single penny of its debt; and, worse still, since the economy is shrinking, the sacrifice needed the following year merely to achieve the same stasis would be even greater.

If the Portuguese want to get out of their hole, they'll need to start repaying principal. Trouble is, in order to do that, the government will need to act more aggressively: raising taxes or cutting spending. Which is where a second vicious little twist arises: each time the government takes these (drastically unpopular) austerity measures, it hammers the economy. Total production in the economy shrinks, while the absolute burden of debt service remains unchanged. You can hardly blame the citizens of Portugal if at a certain point bankruptcy were to appear more attractive than soldiering on.

For Ireland, something like the same logic applies. Ireland is a little better off in that its economy (aside from its banks and its property sector) is flexible, efficient, open, and productive. My own hunch is that the scale of Irish indebtedness, combined with the current cost of borrowing, is simply too much for any country to bear. Nevertheless, at least the Irish can comfort themselves with the thought that their problems are primarily financial as opposed to financial *and* structural. They'll be OK in the end. It's just that the road there will be painful.

Italy

Next up, Italy. There are two things you need to know about Italy. The first is the scale of its debts. It owes $2.6 trillion, or well over three times what Lehman owed at the time of its collapse. (And where Lehman owned over half a trillion dollars' worth of saleable financial assets, the assets belonging to the state of Italy are primarily things like wonderful beaches, Roman ruins, and Renaissance art. Nice things to have, but not so easy to sell.) On some measures, indeed, Italian government bonds form the world's third largest bond market, after the US and Japan. The market is so huge and so liquid (for the time being) that few bond investors of any scale can afford to be out of it. That's helpful, assuming that there are no concerns about creditworthiness. If there are such concerns – and there are – financial contagion on a massive scale is pretty much guaranteed.[8]

The second thing you need to know about Italy is the state of its politics. Indeed, this book went off to be typeset containing a couple of paragraphs about Silvio Berlusconi.

About his clowning, his trials, his media empire, his some-times bizarre political views. I took the view – and I still take the view – that no country could be viewed as creditworthy with such a clown at the helm.

Unsurprisingly, however, events caught up with me. In November 2011, Berlusconi was tipped unceremoniously out of office. He was displaced not by his voters but by the bond markets, working, on this occasion, in collaboration with the horrified duo of Angela Merkel and Nicolas Sarkozy. His government has been replaced by a techno-cratic government containing not a single elected official. I'll talk more in a later chapter about the democratic failures of the current crisis, not only in Italy but across the globe. For now, though, consider this. The people of Italy have not voted in favour of austerity or economic reform. No leading politician has cogently delineated the problem or set out a game plan for reform. No election campaign has pitted rival ideas against each other. The electorate has not been forced to look at the current reality and endorse a particular solution.

The result is that the current Italian government lacks a popular mandate. The people of Italy can hardly be unaware that the bond market is raging at the door and that their position within the eurozone has never looked more perilous – but an awareness of disaster is far from being the same thing as a plan, broadly shared by the electorate, of what to do about it. Indeed, one of Berlusconi's most toxic legacies has been the way he chose to infantilize politics, the way he made it seem less important than the next bungabunga party.

All this matters because countries need leadership in times of danger, and the danger facing Italy is now acute. By mid-November 2011, interest rates on Italian ten-year bonds were pushing towards 8%, nudged upwards by worries of an economic slowdown and insufficient government zeal in tackling the country's excessive debt, and exacerbated by the uncertainties of the eurozone's stumbling response to crisis.[9] These are times of almost breathless risk for the world economy. To understand those risks, you need, once again, to see things through the eyes of the bond market.

Italy has a decaying economy. Some of its best industries are located in segments, notably shoes and clothing, where production is shifting remorselessly to lower-wage economies. Italian *firms* will do fine. They'll simply offshore their production to the degree required – indeed, typically alert and nimble, they are already doing so. The outlook for the Italian *economy* is far less rosy, however. The south of the country is backward, corrupt, and still prey to organized crime. The north of the country has some fantastic enterprises, but is still hampered by a creaky state sector, a lack of innovation, and too many uncompetitive industries. Between 2000 and 2010 the Italian economy managed growth of a puny 0.25% a year, or a little more than 2.5% in a decade. The German economy is perfectly capable of generating that much growth in the space of a few strong months.[10]

Dazzling economic growth is not, therefore, remotely probable either now or in the near future. (The one gift Berlusconi did unquestionably bring his country was a period of real political stability. It is unforgivable how little use the country made of that.) So the only plausible way out of Italy's growing budgetary hole is for the government to slash its spending. In the months before Berlusconi's departure, Giulio Tremonti, the Italian finance minister and a highly capable individual, understood the imperative and prepared a budget packed with deficit-slashing measures amounting to some €40 billion ($55 billion). Those measures included many which would hurt the pockets of the least well off: increased health charges, reduced cost-of-living increases in some state pensions, a probable increase in sales taxes, reductions in local authority budgets, and so on. These things hurt. They hurt ordinary people in real ways and the hurt is lasting, not temporary.

So imagine the shock when detailed analysis of the budget revealed that Berlusconi had smuggled into it provisions that stood to save his media company, Fininvest, some €750 million by postponing damages it was due to pay. It was alleged – I don't know with what truth – that neither Mr Tremonti nor Berlusconi's political allies had been told of this clause, but in any case Berlusconi withdrew it amid the inevitable uproar. The episode is instructive. Even under extreme economic pressure, the Italian government is so dysfunctional it is capable of behavior that would shame many an African kleptocrat. What's more, the bulk of the budget's cost-cutting measures were reserved for 2012, hinting that there might well be an intervening election – in which case, there is no guarantee that a new government would feel obliged to honor the pledges of its predecessor.[11] It's true that this unseemly episode took place when Italy was still being led by Berlusconi, but *he* isn't the point. The point is the political system which allowed him to get to the top in the first place. That system remains entirely unchanged – and, indeed, for that reason the arguments of this section (and this chapter) remain valid no matter what further changes of leadership there may be.

It is against this background of limp growth and budgetary uncertainty that Italian bondholders are obliged to form their judgments – judgments which leave the country teetering on the edge of a precipice. If bond yields stay at their current levels of close to 7%, the mathematics of indebtedness (the same kind of logic we looked at in relation to Portugal) would seem to imply that the government's debt has become insupportable. That the country has become insolvent. If bond yields fall back below 5% and stay there, the government's position is arduous but probably tenable.

If Italy were to find its Margaret Thatcher, and if that leader were to have a strong and united parliament at his or her back, and if the country at large were broadly supportive of strong medicine and harsh measures, the country would be fine. It would be not merely one of the pleasantest countries in the world to visit or live in, it would also become a financial and economic success, a safe haven. But it has no Thatcher. It has no unity. It lacks any sense of common purpose.

The country could still go either way. It could survive and thrive or it could go the way of Greece. I hope it flourishes but I'm not hopeful. When Italy needed a lion, its people elected a clown. The new government may or may not have lionhearts in its number – but the Italian people still have yet to speak.

Spain and France

All this is getting very gloomy, so I'll be as brief as I can. In Spain and France, the outlook is not as dire as in Italy. Yes, growth is far too weak. Yes, debt is too high. Yes, budget deficits are yawning. But still, it's better to have debt at 65% or 90% of GDP than to have it at Italy's crazy 120%. In both Spain and France, politicians may have been too slow to get a grip on their problems, but their leaders are no Berlusconis.

Because Spanish growth is lackluster and (aside from a crazy property boom) has been for some time, the outlook for Spanish bonds is worse than for French. Though the problems in Spain are less severe than they are in Portugal, the difficulties are clearly analogous.

France, by contrast, has far more strong international companies than does Spain. It has a hugely impressive ten in the global Fortune 100, including Total, AXA, Carrefour, and Peugeot. Spain has only three.*[12] France is also more politically influential. It has long been seen as one of the twin engines of Europe, alongside Germany.

In part because of its size and importance, bond markets have largely chosen to see France as a safe haven, Spain as imperiled. In the summer of 2008, French bond yields came close to 5%, but have fallen a long way back since. In the summer of 2011, Spanish bond yields spiked at well over 6%, a level close to which one has to start doubting the long-term solvency of the Spanish government. In brief, therefore, the two countries share problems similar to those of their neighbors, but to a lesser degree. Bond markets judge that Spain is in greater danger than France – a fair assessment – but as of now (early November 2011) the markets are

---

* America has twenty-nine. Britain has eight. Germany and Japan eleven each. Italy just the four. Adjusted for the sizes of their relative populations, France is significantly better than the US at creating world-beating companies, which challenges a few hoary old stereotypes, *non*?

betting on a generally positive outcome, not a disaster.

And perhaps that's correct. Perhaps that is, indeed, where the balance of probabilities lies. The trouble is that, as we know, markets aren't ultimately guided by a balance of probabilities. They're guided by reality, and both France and Spain are sailing through seas that are heavily mined. The mines in question are partly political, partly financial.

In France, the political danger is simply that a government comes into power which lacks either the will or the ability to do what needs to be done. French socialist contenders for office seem to have difficulty in recognizing elementary realities. Arnaud Montebourg thinks banks should be forbidden from speculating with clients' deposits. (So they couldn't make any loans, presumably.) He wants to abolish ratings agencies. (Because they tell the truth, I guess.) And he berates financial markets for wanting to turn France 'into their poodle.' (Actually, Arnaud, the bond markets don't want a dog, they want to know they're going to get their money back. You know: the almost $2.5 trillion that France borrowed.) Meantime Martine Aubry wants to fix the looming pensions crisis by bringing the pensionable age down from sixty-two to sixty. François Hollande wants to create 300,000 public sector jobs. And French voters appear to be partial to this nonsense. Almost three-fifths of the population want higher trade barriers to be erected unilaterally. The same number think trade with India and China has been bad for the country.[13] Nicolas Sarkozy, supposedly a politician of the center-right, came to power promising sweeping structural reform and has delivered almost nothing. His popularity at home is bumping along the seafloor, yet from a bond market perspective he still looks like the least bad of the possible leaders.[14]

In Spain, the political dangers come from the street. In May 2011, tens of thousands of Spaniards, mostly young ones, took over central squares in sixty cities across the country. *Time* magazine's story about the protests went under the headline 'Has the revolution come to Spain?' If it has, I've a lot of sympathy for the protesters. Appalling, discriminatory, and stupid labor laws have allowed unemployment to rise to 21.3% and youth unemployment to an outrageous 46.2%. Those kids who do have jobs tend to have poorly paid and insecure ones. The politicians seem to care more about taking kickbacks (over 100 candidates in recent local elections were under judicial investigation) than about solving these problems.[15] Holders of government bonds, meanwhile, care only about one boring thing – getting their money back – and political turbulence on the current scale is hardly reassuring.

So much for the political mines. The financial mines are, if anything, more dangerous. The French government has debt of around 90% of GDP. The country also boasts a number of very large banks. BNP Paribas, Crédit Agricole, Société Générale, and Banque Populaire/Caisse d'Epargne are all members of the global Fortune 100. Yet no one truly knows if these banks are solvent. French bank shares are down by 33% since the start of 2011. Spreads on credit default swaps – a measure indicating the probability of default – have increased to levels last seen in the fall of 2008.[16] And we know what happened then.

❖

In a hard-hitting recent speech, Christine Lagarde, the head of the IMF, estimated that unrecognized losses on European bank balance sheets amounted to more than €200 billion and called for urgent, compulsory recapitalization of the banks.[17] From an international policymaker, this was bruisingly direct talk – but pessimists in the private sector make her look like the sunniest of optimists. A note released by Goldman Sachs in mid-August 2011 argued that European banks might need as much as €1 trillion in new capital.[18] And forgive me for stating the obvious, but a trillion euros is a lot of money. Cast your eye back to table 16.1 on p. 266 and its summary of the financial position of Europe's principal economies. Neither Italy nor Spain can risk taking on a penny's worth of new debt. France and Germany might be able to find a hundred billion or two between them, but neither country can afford to be profligate. Quite simply, there is not a trillion euros' worth of available public capital in Europe. If Europe's banks need a bailout on that scale, it's not coming from the taxpayers.

It's not clear, however, that private investors are likely to open their wallets up either – nor that they should do so in order to finance irresponsible lending practices and weak managements. Through the summer of 2011, equity prices in Europe lost one-third of their value. Bank stocks sharply underperformed the overall index. Those drab facts hardly suggest that investors are falling over themselves to plug any funding deficits. Indeed, the real truth is worse, because, as share prices plunge, any capital-raising has to be done at increasingly depressed prices. Since capital-raising under these circumstances would heavily dilute the ownership position of existing shareholders, those shareholders – the people who ultimately call the shots – will be heavily resistant to taking the only course of action liable to avert Armageddon. In short, the banks may need a huge amount of money, and no one has any idea where it might come from. Bank chiefs and financial regulators are currently working with a strategy that can be summarized as eyes shut and fingers crossed.

These things haven't exactly escaped the attention of the financial markets. All through 2011 there's been a growing sense of jitteriness – mirroring to an uncanny degree the anxiety felt in the months between the collapse of Bear Stearns and the Lehman bankruptcy. That nervousness has manifested itself in an acute risk-aversion. American money market funds are pulling their cash out of Europe. Interbank loans have become ever shorter in duration, meaning that ever larger volumes of money have to roll over every week. French banks, indeed, have effectively lost their access to this market. And these things matter. As so often in this book, I find myself making statements that sound boringly technical. *European bank funding is becoming more short-term*: I mean, do you really care? Has a statement like that ever bothered you in the past? I'm guessing not. But these things are likely to affect you personally, and massively. Your job, your pension, your savings, your government may come to depend on these things.

The disaster scenario is this. A big bank – let's say a mythical French one, the Banque des Grandes Baguettes (BGB) – announces unexpectedly large losses on its sovereign loan portfolio. It has become highly reliant on short-term funding, but money market funds and the interbank market now cut it off completely. BGB is now totally reliant on funding from the European Central Bank, and the ECB in turn comes under acute pressure to force a restructuring or bankruptcy filing. Maybe the ECB caves into that pressure, maybe it doesn't, but either way the market is in a panic. In Italy, the Banco Bunga Bunga announces that it too has lost the ability to fund itself. In Spain, the Caja Sangria is in trouble. In Germany, it's the Weisswurstundpilsner Landesbank.

As these events unfold, the government bond markets will slide into a state of panic. The huge Italian bond market, for example, is likely to freeze almost completely. The market for Italian credit default swaps may well begin to resemble the current market for Greek CDSs. No lender would trust that any other lender was solvent, so the inter-bank market would be more or less extinguished.

This is the point of catastrophe. The financial system is, very largely, constructed like those circles of people each of whom is sitting on the lap of the person behind them. If everyone is stably seated, there's no problem in maintaining the circle. But as soon as you start pulling out individuals, the circle collapses. When Bear Stearns and Lehman disappeared, Wall Street lost its two weakest players, but the consequence was that even the strongest ones were on life support. Goldman Sachs, remember, for all its boasting that it required no government bailout, nevertheless found itself accepting $69 billion worth of funds from the Federal Reserve.[19] That's not quite the same thing as avoiding a bailout, if you ask me.

And the situation today is precarious in the extreme. Don't take my word for it. Ask Josef Ackermann, the CEO of Deutsche Bank, the world's second biggest bank by assets (and, by the way, a well-managed one, though with much more leverage than I personally would like[20]). At a meeting of bankers on September 5, 2011, he said: 'It's stating the obvious that many European banks would not survive having to revalue sovereign debt held on the banking book at market levels.'[21] Notice what he's saying. Remember that the market price for a government bond is the fair price for it. If the market priced a bond too high, people would sell it and take their profits; if the market priced a bond too low, people would buy it, on the expectation of gains. So the market price for bonds – just like the market price for anything else – is the fair price. It's the only realistic one you can use. But European banks aren't using that price, because they can't. Instead, they value these loans at a fantasy price when they draw up their accounts, because if they didn't they'd be bankrupt.

Actually, that's the wrong way of putting it. If a company is bankrupt, it's bankrupt. It's not a question of what the accounts do or don't say, it's a question of whether the company's assets are worth more than its liabilities. In effect, the head of the world's second largest bank is confirming that 'many European banks' are bankrupt and are presenting fantasy accounts in an attempt to keep reality at bay for that little bit longer. That's scary in two ways. It's scary because the world can't afford another colossal financial crisis. And it's even more scary because of the Ponzi-ish assumptions underlying Ackermann's comments. On Planet Sane, if a bank were bankrupt, you'd either seek to wind it up, or merge it with a stronger competitor, or seek to attract additional capital. One way or another, you'd aim to fix the problem. On Planet Ponzi, however, none of these options are among the ones that come to mind first. You'd much rather present accounts which you know to be misleading. And you'd seek ways to defer the sovereign defaults which you know are coming (Greece for sure; Ireland, Spain, and Portugal quite likely), even though deferring the problem will make it bigger and worse. And you persuade the European Central Bank to lend yet more cheap money to weak banks against rotten collateral. And you put pressure on the ratings agencies to avoid telling the truth. And you deny that the crisis is anything like as bad as it quite obviously is. And so on.

Ackermann (whose bank is probably not at risk) is prey to this kind of thinking himself. He is hostile to an IMF proposal for a mandatory recapitalization of the banks, a proposal which might actually fix the problem. He also dismisses the threat to the global economy. One report of Ackermann's speech stated: 'The Deutsche Bank chief said he doesn't expect the global economy to slip into a recession. Germany and most other European countries will have "stable growth and I believe we also won't slip back into recession in the U.S.," he said. "So this spreading of panic and fear-mongering is simply mistaken."'[22] Really, Josef? *Simply mistaken?* So the dreadful employment figures in the US are simply irrelevant? The collapses in British services output make no difference? The Europe-wide fall in business confidence and the one-third decline in European equity prices, all that is 'simply mistaken'?

The trouble with avoiding reality is that sometimes reality comes to seek you out whether you like it or not. In 2008, total disaster was arrested because of the willingness of governments around the world to halt the crisis in its tracks by borrowing vast amounts and by printing trillions of dollars out of thin air. This time around, the potential problem may be on a far larger scale, and the ability of governments to take firm action is acutely limited. Indeed, that phrasing doesn't quite capture what happened. It sounds so positive – 'firm action,' 'halt the crisis' – but what actually happened was the opposite. Firm action would have involved facing up to the crisis. Forcing creditors to take losses. Making shareholders lose everything. Telling Wall Street and the City of London and the financial sector generally: 'We're sorry to hear about your problems, guys, but we didn't cause them: you did. We don't think ordinary taxpayers should help retrieve your mistakes and we certainly don't think that ordinary taxpayers should end up funding your bonuses or your unsafe lending practices.' There would unquestionably have been huge economic fall-out if governments had adopted this courageous position, but instead they did what everyone born on Planet Ponzi does: they kicked the can down the road. And because Ponzi schemes only survive by expanding, every time you kick the can down the road, you create a bigger problem than you had before.

In short, Europe's problems today are scary. In Spain, there is a huge problem with bad debt arising from bad real estate deals and it's still unclear to what degree the second-tier Spanish banks will be able to survive those losses. My view is that many of these banks are grossly understating their exposures, but that the government will not be in a position to nationalize or recapitalize them – or, if it does, it will be using massive leverage and risking taxpayers' funds only to prolong the inevitable and necessary defaults and subsequent painful process of deleveraging. In France, if politicians keep their cool and if their banks prove stronger than they appear, those banks may survive. I'd expect both countries to have a tough few years – slow growth, fiscal austerity – but nevertheless to come through OK. But that happy outcome is by no means assured. It's not even possible to ascertain the likelihood of disaster. Only the banks know how strong their balance sheets truly are – or do even they really know? As we saw earlier, Citigroup's senior management did not understand how weak it was. Nor did the managements of Lehman or Bear Stearns. Nor did the management of Britain's Lloyds Banking Group understand what a dog they'd bought when they took over HBOS. (It managed to lose £10 billion in a single year.[23]) There may well, in other words, be a large European bank, or several large European banks, that are even now sliding toward the waterfall, utterly oblivious of what's about to happen. And if one large bank goes over the edge, there are countless more in danger of following. When and if the banks start to collapse, the fiscal consequences for governments will be horrendous, no matter how prudent they seek to be. A European banking crisis will therefore also be a European sovereign debt crisis – which in turn will make the banking crisis even worse.

This survey won't have cheered up too many readers. It's also raised countless questions. What about Germany? What about the current European bailout fund, the EFSF? What about the euro – can the European currency even survive?

Those are big questions. Too big and too important for this chapter.

SEVENTEEN

The *aureus* and the *as*

FOR FIVE HUNDRED years around the birth of Christ, Europe had a single currency. The Roman republic and, later, the western Roman empire issued coins that ran from the golden *aureus* through the silver *denarius* and the brass *sestertius* and *dupondius* down to the copper *as*. The Roman coinage was universal across the empire, but it also had extensive sway beyond its formal boundaries. Because the Roman empire was potent, its currency too was potent. Although the coins were made of precious metals, their value was greater than the metal they contained.

The system was beautifully simple. A Roman emperor didn't need to worry too much about fiscally incontinent barbarians in Germany. There were no fiscal problems which a few thousand Roman legionaries couldn't sort out. That's the first kind of currency union you can have. One in which fiscal discipline is created and enforced from the center — with spears and siege machines as required.

But that's not the only way to build a currency system. The United States has a federal system, albeit one with a strong center. Although the Federal Reserve has responsibility for controlling monetary policy and is theoretically independent of government, its independence is purely notional. The US president appoints the Fed's chairman and the US Senate approves the nomination. Nevertheless, despite the power of the center, the system remains genuinely federal.

At the moment, there is no provision in US law for American states to go bankrupt. Although various US states defaulted on their debts in 1841–2 and 1873–4, those defaults did not trigger full-scale bankruptcy. (Though they did cause plenty of mayhem and led to the spread of balanced budget clauses in many state constitutions.[1]) At the moment, it feels like 1841 all over again. California has a $25 billion spending deficit and a hole in its unemployment insurance fund that's expected to reach $13 billion this year.[2] Though California is in the worst position among US states, there are plenty of others that are also in a bad way. But the way things stand at present, they can't go bankrupt.

Although bankruptcy is wrenching, it's also cleansing. The whole point of the process is that, under the supervision of a court, you get to wipe out unpayable debts and leave yourself with a sustainable financial structure. Possessing a bankruptcy option could even help the negotiating position of individual states. At the moment, public sector unions can bargain hard against a state that has no credible way out. If states could threaten bankruptcy there would be two credible parties at the negotiating table.[3] Though it sounds weird to say it, a bankruptcy option would probably improve the fiscal position of the states in the long term, and serious legislative thought has gone into creating the option, Newt Gingrich being the most vocal proponent of the idea.[4] The notion is hardly outlandish. After all, municipalities can already file for bankruptcy. Orange County famously did it recently.[5] New York

City came within a whisker of having to do it in 1975.[6]

So let's just assume this change had gone through. Let's say there was a bankruptcy law that states could use. If California did file for bankruptcy, no one anywhere would think that had any implications for the dollar. When New York City almost went bankrupt, the papers weren't printing panicky articles demanding 'Where now for the dollar?' The dollar would be totally unaffected. The bankruptcy would happen under court supervision. California would emerge with sustainable finances. Some creditors would lose money because they had lent money to an outfit that had mismanaged its finances. Which, you'd hope, would remind lenders that they need to think before handing over their cash.

So that's the second model for a common currency. Everyone takes responsibility for their own finances. No one bails out anyone. No need for legionaries and siege machines. If California (in the US version of this scenario) or Greece (in the European one) files for bankruptcy, the bankruptcy process is handled in the ordinary way, with no implications for the currency whatsoever. The currency just continues.

Bear in mind that bankruptcy does not mean the extinction of a nation. It does not mean that a fleet of trucks drives overland from Germany and Switzerland to Greece to start carting off ancient monuments and ripping up the national railroads for scrap. In fact, almost nothing visible would change. Countless US passengers have flown on the planes of bankrupt airlines, most recently American Airlines. Those planes were fueled, serviced, piloted, and cleaned. You couldn't tell from the flight whether the airline was in the bankruptcy court or not. Same thing with GM when it went bust. Its cars didn't stop working. Dealers still had cars to sell. Production lines stayed moving. The bankruptcy court has no interest in arresting ordinary productive labor or trashing ordinary productive assets, because its ultimate aim is the preservation of value. That requires those planes to fly, those cars to move. It's the same thing with countries. Assets remain bolted to the floor, businesses continue to operate, private depositors remain entitled to their cash.

The point is that bankruptcy is a financial problem which needs a financial solution. That solution is painfully simple. Creditors need to recognize that they are not going to get their money back in full. They need to acknowledge their losses. The debtor needs to commit to a new payment plan which will ensure that the new, lower level of debt will be properly serviced. And that's it. Everyone moves on. Because sovereign default has been perfectly common over the years, there are well-established mechanisms for handling these things. The so-called 'Paris Club' handles debts owed by a sovereign borrower to sovereign lenders. (For example, if Greece owed money to the German Federal Republic, that debt would be renegotiated via the Paris Club.) The London Club does the same thing for sovereign debt owed to the private sector. The IMF supervises everything, supplying stopgap funding where necessary.

If Greece had been left to go bankrupt, anyone holding Greek government debt would have taken a hit: they'd have been legally obliged to recognize their losses on their balance sheet. Outside Greece itself, relatively few banks would have been tipped over into insolvency as a result. Some might have taken a hit large enough to force them to seek new capital or merge with a stronger partner. The really mismanaged ones could have been left to fail. Which would have been good. Greece would still be in the euro. Germany and the other strong countries of Europe would not have had to bail out a small, reckless, improvident country. Some stupid lenders would have been taught an important lesson.

On Planet Ponzi, however, the golden rule is: never, ever, acknowledge a financial loss. Because bankruptcy forces the recognition of losses, it's the least favored solution on Planet Ponzi. So instead we have a chain of bailouts, which are extraordinarily costly to taxpayers in the provident countries and which cannot possibly fix the problem. They can't fix the problem, because Greece isn't like some fundamentally sound business with a temporary cashflow crisis. If that were the issue, loans from European taxpayers might make perfect sense. But it's clearly not the issue. The country owes more than 152% of its annual income. Ratings agencies estimate that just 30–50% of that debt is collectable. That's not a momentary embarrassment over cashflow; that's bankrupt, bust, broke, insolvent, ruined. It's kaput. Πτωχευση.

Worse still, this reality denial makes everything worse for longer. Greece is forced into firesale privatizations in a scramble to raise funds. As a result those privatizations are poorly planned and raise far less than they should. The Greek government is compelled to cut spending so savagely that the country's economic fabric is permanently impaired. Banks, which ought to be raising capital and fixing their businesses, are left pretending that things are OK.

There's another problem with the European bailout program, which is a tad technical, but bear with me as I explain it. The main European bailout tool is the European Financial Stability Facility, or EFSF. The EFSF has, in theory, the ability to issue bonds worth up to €440 billion. Because its bonds are guaranteed by eurozone member states, those bonds will carry an AAA rating.[7] That's the good news. The bad news is that the potential demands on its services vastly exceed its capacity. Take a look at figure 17.1. (And note, by the way, I haven't even placed France on that chart, or Belgium, or any other countries that might get into trouble if the turmoil became too much.)

In one way, I'll admit that this graphic exaggerates the problem. Greece is bankrupt, but that doesn't mean it can't pay a proportion of its debts. Likewise, though Italy's finances are ropey, any writedown on Italian sovereign bonds won't need to be anything like the 50–70% write-downs anticipated in Greece. Yet it's still the case that the EFSF is insufficient. It's built to withstand a gale, when the radar is showing a hurricane. And it's at its limits. The EFSF enjoys its AAA rating thanks to the financial capacity of its AAA-rated members, such as France, Germany, and the Netherlands. But the Netherlands is not a large country. If it incurs any more debt via the EFSF, it will be at risk of losing its AAA rating, which in turn would mean that the burden

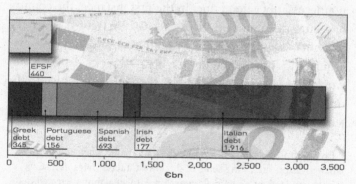

Figure 17.1: The European Financial Stability Facility
Source: IMF, *World Economic Outlook*, April 2011.

of maintaining that rating would fall on France and Germany. France would probably not be able to sustain that additional burden, so it too would lose its rating. Germany alone couldn't swallow over €440 billion of additional debt (and, as a political matter, would almost certainly not want to), so the EFSF would lose its own rating and its ability to raise funds would be vastly diminished.*

In short, not only is the bailout program utterly misconceived – because it's about deferring a problem, not fixing it – it is woefully underpowered. Because financial markets recognize these facts, the entire European banking sector is aswirl with fear and uncertainty. That fear causes banks to restrict their lending and hoard their cash. It causes consumers to defer purchases. It prompts companies to avoid investment and refrain from hiring. The uncertainty itself is like a tax charged on the entire economy, destroying jobs and preventing growth.

There is one last option, not yet discussed. Greece could ditch the euro, reintroduce the drachma, leave behind the experiment with a common currency. It's a real option, but not necessarily a good one. In the first instance, the country has euro-denominated debts. If Greece returned to the drachma, that new currency would trade at a very low level against the euro. Taxing in drachmas to repay debt in euros would not be remotely credible, so in effect to return to the drachma would be to admit insolvency. Since Greece's problems don't in fact arise from the common currency at all –

* Even as it is, that fundraising ability is utterly untested, at a time when investors are facing some of the lowest interest rates in history. Would you lend, at a minimal interest rate, to an acronym created in panic by the Brussels Eurocracy? I doubt you would, and most investors are likely to feel the same.

they arise from mismanaged public finances – a return to the drachma would accomplish almost nothing that simply declaring bankruptcy could achieve. What's more, since Greece has a bizarrely small export sector, a return to the drachma wouldn't do much to boost the overall economy – indeed, it would simply inflict on the country all the costs of possessing a small, pointless currency on the edge of a huge common-currency area.

Naturally, the same kind of question arises in the opposite direction. At a certain point, will the north European economies not get fed up being bound to their untidy and reckless southern neighbors? Will there not come a point where exit from the euro, for all its cost and grief, will not be preferable to the status quo? Some economists at the Swiss bank UBS attempted to quantify the pain of leaving. They reckoned that if Greece were to go, it would suffer costs equal to around 40–50% of GDP the first year and around 15% in each subsequent year. If Germany were to leave, they reckoned that first-year costs would be 20–25% of GDP, and subsequent-year costs about 10%.[8] Even to my mind, those costs seem pessimistic in the extreme, but the exercise serves to make a point. The euro as it stands today has a central bank but no central treasury; the countries who use it have politicians who won't lead and governments with no room for maneuver, and include bankrupt nations that deny their bankruptcy; the system suffers from countless banks that are insolvent but in denial, and an almost complete lack of transparency or accountability. Such a currency must surely implode. It cannot last. At the same time, because the alternatives are awful, the present system will endure – and propagate its own version of awfulness – for some time to come. It's not a pretty picture, however you care to look at it.

But it's time to leave these thoughts. Enough of the euro and the EFSF – and enough of Greece, Ireland, and Portugal too. Readers in Germany and the Netherlands will be wondering about the implications of all this for them. It's all very well being prudent, diligent, and competitive yourselves, but what happens when all those around you are wildly mismanaging their affairs?

It's a fair question. As it happens, there's room for optimism. Canada's banks survived the 2008–9 financial crisis just fine. They had no subprime mess, no tidal wave of foreclosures, no gigantic bank failures. The economy couldn't be unaffected by American travails, but the effects were limited.[9] It does, of course, help to have 178 billion barrels of oil under your feet.[10] Except for that oil, German, Dutch, and Scandinavian policymakers today are in broadly the same position as their Canadian counterparts of 2008. Their governments have responsible fiscal policies. The economies enjoy some strong, well-managed businesses. Their citizens know that rewards come from hard work intelligently directed – and haven't forgotten there was once a time when you needed a wheelbarrow full of cash to buy a loaf of bread. As a result, no postwar German or Dutch government has yet applied for citizenship of Planet Ponzi. Quite likely, no German or Dutch government ever will. It's not in the genes.

Yet these sane and stable countries are trading nations located right at the heart of Europe. Canadian banks were somewhat shielded from American contagion not simply by better regulation and an old-fashioned sense of discipline but also by a different currency. Canadian banks accepting Canadian dollars from Canadian savers weren't particularly tempted to start investing those deposits in mortgage assets denominated in US dollars, because of the resultant currency mismatch. Many banks in Germany, however, were tempted – too tempted – to acquire 'high-yielding' euro assets as a way of boosting profits. The largest German banks are probably fine, but the *Landesbanken* (regional wholesale banks) and local savings banks may well be overextended in a number of cases.[11] It's impossible to say which banks are in trouble, because the various bank 'stress tests' which have been applied were all devised on Planet Ponzi – so that, for example, the European stress tests of July 2011 excluded any consideration of losses on sovereign debt portfolios. Since all banks holding sovereign debts in the troubled eurozone countries would have lost money, those stress tests were effectively meaningless.[12]

Nevertheless, strong economies and well-managed governments can get through these messes. If some banks need to be recapitalized, the German and Dutch (and Scandinavian) governments will have ample resources to do so. Growth will be injured by the turmoil. Joblessness will be higher than it ought to be, growth and household incomes lower. But still. There may be rain and bad weather in Berlin and The Hague. That's still preferable to the gales and thunderstorms that are coming to Paris, or the typhoons and worse which will visit Madrid, Lisbon, and Athens. And in Germany and the Netherlands, the government can still afford a raincoat.

Up next: the United Kingdom – and this time, and for the first time in this book, we have some real good news to explore.

EIGHTEEN

Choosing second

THERE'S AN OLD JOKE which runs like this. Q: Why did New York get Wall Street and New Jersey get the toxic waste dumps? A: Because New Jersey had first choice.

Something similar applies in Europe. Both Britain and Germany are impressive in their ways. Germany is the second largest exporter of goods in the world (after China), an extraordinary achievement for a country with a population smaller than that of either Japan or the United States.[1] Britain, on the other hand, has a somewhat average manufacturing sector but a quite remarkable service sector. Britain is the world's second largest exporter of services, behind the US but well ahead of Japan, Germany, and all the emerging market giants.[2] Although Britain is strong in nearly all service sectors, the global heft of its financial services sector is simply extraordinary.

Now, there's no question which of these two positions you'd rather be in. Having a large manufacturing sector, particularly one whose eminence is based on quality rather than price, is a gift for any economy. Having one of the world's two leading financial centers in your country, on the other hand, is like sharing your home with a hormonal gorilla.

The animal is impressive as heck, but you know you're going to lose some china. The financial sector in Britain wasn't as utterly out of control as its counterpart in the US – no subprime horrors, no CDOs of CDOs – but being 'better managed than Wall Street' is hardly a badge of managerial excellence. On pretty much every metric you care to look at, Britain has too much debt. Too much government debt. Too much household debt. Too many large and leveraged banks. Way too much mortgage debt. Even its corporations are too ready to borrow.

Having said all that, however, Britain is still in better shape than the troubled economies of southern Europe. It doesn't have the hideous government debt of Greece or Italy. It doesn't have the structural rigidities of Spain. It's still Europe's chief magnet for inward investment. It remains a good place to do business, ranking tenth in the World Economic Forum's annual competitiveness survey (neck and neck with the US, Germany, and Japan).[3] What's more, the country isn't in the eurozone. Germany's current challenges very largely revolve around how it can manage its relationships with its fiscally incontinent, low-growth eurozone partners. Naturally, Britain has extensive trading relationships with the eurozone, but its banks are at least somewhat insulated.

The bond market, at the time of writing, is allowing the British government to borrow at just 2.3% p.a. for a ten-year bond. France borrows at 3.3%, Spain and Italy at 5.7% and 6.8% respectively.[4] Those borrowing costs reflect the market's current estimate of risk, and are confirmed by the ratings agencies. Britain's international debt rating is affirmed at AAA by all the major agencies (thereby placing it above the United States), and there are no rumors of looming downgrades dogging the country, which cannot be said of France, for example.

These things are, on the face of it, mystifying. Britain's government debt is about the same as France's. Britain's government deficit is worse. In the short term, its growth prospects seem equally feeble. Its banks don't have huge exposure to either Greece or Portugal, but they do have massive exposure to the almost equally troubled Ireland. And of course, it shares house with a hormonal gorilla and there's a lot of broken crockery littering the carpet.

The bond markets are right, however. The ratings agencies too. Personally, I wouldn't give Britain an AAA rating, simply because I don't think any nation on Planet Ponzi deserves such a rating. The risks are simply too great, not just in the UK but across the board. Nevertheless, despite those debt figures, despite that horrendous deficit, and despite that gorilla, Britain is showing signs of wanting to exit Planet Ponzi. To take the pledge. To push away the bottle. In plain language, Britain is the first leading country on Planet Ponzi to show convincing evidence that it wants to return to a path of fiscal rectitude and sober banking. (Germany and Canada are largely fine on both counts, but they always were.)

The story of Britain's conversion to fiscal teetotalism is worth telling in some detail, because it shows what can be done. In 2009 the government deficit stood at £144 billion, an extraordinary 10.3% of GDP. The following year, that deficit rose a notch to 10.4%. Government debt, inevitably, was starting to spiral upwards. The economy shrank abruptly, by 4.9%, in 2009. In 2010, growth returned, but feebly, at a rate of just 1.3%.[5]

In these ugly circumstances, an election was held in May

2010. The Labour government was, deservedly, beaten. It lost because it was seen as having contributed to the banking crisis by regulating too little and borrowing too much. Prime Minister Gordon Brown was seen as bullying and detached from reality. According to his Chancellor of the Exchequer Alastair Darling, when the global financial crisis blew up Brown predicted that it would all blow over in the space of six months – a prediction which even then seemed extraordinarily out of touch.[6]

On the other hand, the incoming government struck many observers (including this one) as underwhelming. The new Prime Minister, David Cameron, had no real experience of the private sector. He was a PR man turned professional politician. His background was privileged. He was surrounded by colleagues with similarly patrician origins. Worse still, his Conservative Party didn't even have overall control of Parliament. It was forced to enter coalition with the Liberal Democrats, a left-leaning party of protest with no previous track record in government. Its leader, too, was a man of privilege with virtually no experience outside government. Given the vast scale of the problems facing the country, this new government seemed underweight and underexperienced. Catastrophe loomed.

Loomed – but has not, as yet, arrived. The new government didn't just talk tough, it actually delivered. It told voters bluntly that savage cuts were needed and that taxes would need to be raised. It set up an Office for Budget Responsibility, an independent agency to vet the government's budgetary figures. It unveiled a spending review which promised to slash £81 billion from government spending over four years, an amount equal to 6% of British GDP. Government departments (excluding health and education) would lose an average of 19% of their budgets. American, Italian, Spanish, and French readers will want to reread that sentence – no doubt with incredulity. The British government is calmly proposing to cut (in inflation-adjusted terms) some 11% from the education budget; 25% from the Home Office budget; 20% from the policing budget; 25% from the Justice Department budget; 7% from the defense budget; 15% from the transport budget; almost 30% from the business budget; *over* 30% from the communities and local government budget. Alone among the major departments, health was spared any cuts in spending.[7]

These figures exclude various mandatory expenditures ('annually managed expenditures' in the jargon), which departments have to administer. Thus, for example, the relatively small Department for Work and Pensions (with an annual departmental budget of around £7 billion) manages a huge welfare budget of between £150 and £160 billion. Nevertheless, those mandatory expenditures are also being cut. Pension ages are rising. Welfare rules are tightening. Investment budgets are also being reduced.

The upshot of all this is a dramatic drop in government borrowing. The independent Office for Budget Responsibility estimates that the yawning government deficit is going to dwindle almost to nothing within four years (see figure 18.1).[8] Over the period covered by these forecasts, government debt is forecast to peak at 85.5% of GDP, before starting to drop back.

There are two different ways you can look at these figures. You can look at them with Ponzi-ish eyes. You can forecast the dissolution of the state, the collapse of public order, the decay of education, the destruction of a generation. These are the kinds of forecasts which have fueled the

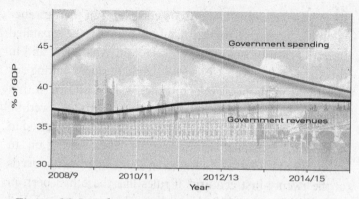

Figure 18.1: What responsible government looks like: UK government revenues and spending, 2008/9–2015/16

Source: Office for Budget Responsibility.

insane levels of government spending right across the developed world. They are the kinds of forecasts which are causing politicians problems right across southern Europe; the kind which in the US prevent Democrats and Republicans from coming to any shared view of the direction forward.

Alternatively, you can look at them with the eyes of sanity. Government revenues are holding broadly steady. Government expenditures are simply falling back to where they were in 2003–7. In 2003–7, nobody thought that the state was dissolving, public order collapsing, or a generation being destroyed. If anything, it felt as though the government could economize quite happily if it needed to.

Nor have the politicians stopped at getting a grip on their own finances. The banks, too, are to be overhauled. In September 2011, the Independent Commission on Banking published a report into the future of the banking industry.

Its precise recommendations are complex, but their essence is simple. Ordinary, routine retail banking is to be separated from the casino banking so prevalent on Wall Street and in the City of London. Consumer banking and banking for small and medium-sized companies will be housed within the ring-fence around retail banking. Those 'fenced-in' banking operations will be closely regulated and required to hold plenty of capital against possible losses. And so on. In effect, it's like a British Glass–Steagall Act fitted to the needs of the twenty-first century.[9] If rules like these had been in place in the US in 2008, the crisis would have wrecked Wall Street but left Main Street largely untouched.

There are other good things in the pipeline too. The set of zoning rules which governs new construction developments has been cut down from over 1,000 pages of regulations to just 52.[10] Red tape, more generally, is to be cut. The British economy labors under the burden of some 21,000 different regulations. The government has announced a commitment to reduce that burden over its time in office. A government website invites people and companies to identify which regulations they want to be junked, saying bluntly: 'Once you've had your say, Ministers will have three months to work out which regulations they want to keep and why. But here's the most important bit – the default presumption will be that burdensome regulations will go.'[11] If they really mean that, it'll be a reversal that no government in my lifetime has managed to achieve.

Thus far I've been positive, so I ought to admit to a couple of doubts – serious doubts. First, I don't think that the British government will achieve either its revenue or its spending target. Its projections are based on far too rosy a picture of economic growth. The simple fact is that if you drink a bottle of whiskey each day from Monday through Saturday, you're going to have one hell of a hangover come Sunday. The British economy is in that position now. Past growth has been pumped up by excessive reliance on government spending and household debt. Firms need to figure out how to engineer growth in a climate that's prudent, not Ponzi-ish. That's not an impossible brief – Germany manages it – but it's an art that needs to be relearned. The learning will be slow.

Secondly, although the banking reforms are fundamentally sound, they are being introduced painfully slowly. The reforms won't be complete and in place until 2019: that's eight years from the date of the report and more than a decade from the banking crash. I can understand that measures need to be introduced properly and without imposing unnecessary costs of transition – but *eight years*?

Thirdly, despite the astonishing progress on certain fronts, there are still huge issues left unaddressed. The government has brought in no measures to constrain house prices. Since Britain is as fond of housing bubbles as it is of royal weddings, it seems crazy not to get a grip on the housing market, which lies at the heart of so many of the country's economic and financial troubles. Additionally, household debt has become too free, too easy. The government needs to find ways of limiting further growth. The credit card economy is no way to build stability or prosperity in the long term.

Fourthly, in October 2011 the Bank of England's monetary policy committee agreed to approve the printing of £75 billion in a vain effort to wake up the economy.* Such

* The leading advocate of such quantitative easing in the UK has been the MPC's sole American member, Adam Posen. He's acting like Ben Bernanke's Mini-Me in the United Kingdom.

policies might in theory have a positive impact if they serve to unblock the flow of credit to firms, but they're utterly senseless to any other end. And in Britain today, firms are not seeking to take on debt (because they're terrified of a worsening recession) and banks don't want to lend (because they know they have capital and liquidity issues which corporate lending would only exacerbate). Indeed, there exists no credible evidence that monetary loosening has had any positive effect in either Britain or the US since the credit crisis began, while the risk of fanning inflation is already high and rising. Once again, we see academics and politicians with minimal real-world experience combining to conduct theoretical experiments with real economies. Such experiments can only end badly.

But in the context of where Britain's been for the past thirty years – at the heart of Planet Ponzi – it's one hell of a good start. The US government needs to copy David Cameron's lead. Italy, Spain, and France should take careful notes. Even Germany, whose banking system is not as robust as it ought to be, should be watching with interest.

And the best thing about all this? The single most positive aspect is that, with the exception of some public sector unions, everybody's on board with the project. The Labour Party, now in opposition, has converted from fiscal recklessness to something closer to fiscal prudence. True, it wants the fiscal tightening to run more slowly than the Conservative plan. It has a tendency to oppose individual cuts without proposing other specific measures in their place. Yet right across the political spectrum, it is under-stood that taxes have got to be increased (but modestly) and expenditures cut.

Indeed, compared with what I've seen elsewhere, British

politicians have suddenly discovered a remarkable capacity for honesty. During the 2010 election campaign, there was a televised debate which saw the Chancellor of the Exchequer, Alastair Darling, go up against his rivals from the Conservative and Liberal Democrat parties. One of the exchanges during that debate ran as follows:[12]

'Do you agree that cuts we are going to be facing will be deeper than the cuts that Mrs Thatcher had to put through Britain?' TV presenter Krishnan Guru-Murthy.

'Well, I said last week they're going to have to be pretty deep.' Alastair Darling MP, Chancellor of the Exchequer.

'The answer is yes.' Vince Cable MP, Lib Dem Treasury spokesperson.

'The answer is yes.' George Osborne MP, Shadow Chancellor.

Given that the Thatcher era is etched into British political folklore as a time of dramatic budgetary cuts, this frankness is astonishing – and accurate. Independent analysts have indeed confirmed that the plans of all three parties imply a fiscal tightening much more severe than Mrs Thatcher ever achieved.

And the British public has responded to this honesty with intelligence and stoicism. The Conservative Party is a little behind Labour in the polls, but less than you'd expect for a government in mid-term austerity mode. There is no popular movement against the cuts in general (though specific issues, of course, get people heated). The riots that disfigured London in the summer of 2011 had nothing to do with cuts or the austerity program; they had nothing to do with politics of any sort, in fact. What we saw then was an outbreak of criminality reconceived for the age of social media. Almost three-quarters of those charged with offences following the riots had a criminal record.[13] The riots were so bad only because police struggled to adapt their tactics to the fleeting, mobile, Twitter- and BlackBerry-driven criminals of the modern age.*

What this proves, of course, is that if politicians only dare to be honest, voters will respond with intelligence themselves. Perhaps the greatest lie on Planet Ponzi is that voters and taxpayers have only themselves to blame for the messes their governments make. That's simply not true. Democracy is great – but if all it offers is a choice of idiot, the poor old voters aren't in a position to get things fixed.

For thirty years, and through administrations of both political colors, politicians allowed Ponzi-ish thinking to creep into every aspect of British economic life. Government debt stayed stubbornly high, when it should have all but disappeared. Household debt became excessive. Property became (and still is) bubblicious. The City of London came to rival Wall Street as a manufacturing center for financial WMDs. The regulators actively boasted of their 'light touch'

---

* Sentencing also has a little way to go. Two men were jailed for four years for inciting riots via Facebook, though the riots in question never materialized. Sir Fred Goodwin, the 'world's worst banker,' whose bank, RBS, reported pretax losses of almost £41 billion for 2008, enjoys a tasty pension and has quietly returned to business. (See 'Facebook cases trigger criticism of "disproportionate" riot sentences,' *Guardian*, Aug. 17, 2011; 'Who's the world's worst banker,' *Slate*, Dec. 2008; RBS losses from restated annual accounts ending Dec. 2008; 'Sir Fred Goodwin given job by Scottish parliament architects RMJM,' *Guardian*, Jan. 16, 2010.)

regulation. That thirty-year road has now come to an end. Politics and the economy are in clear-up mode, much like London after the riots. There's broken glass everywhere – broken glass and shattered businesses.

But the clear-up is, in a strange way, inspirational. Tough political decisions can be made. Politicians can be honest. Voters can be trusted to understand what has to be done. The lobbying power of the banking industry can be kept at bay.

If I'm honest, I'd like this UK government to do more, to do it faster – and ideally to throw a few bankers in jail. But I'll settle for what's on offer. The American (and European) public needs politicians with similar courage. It needs political parties with a similar sense of national purpose. It needs voters to reward them. These things are present in Britain right now. They could yet come to America.

The alternative isn't pretty. The alternative is Japanese.

NINETEEN

A van for Fukushima

I USED TO WORK in Japan. I loved it. I liked the politeness, the tidiness, the sense of safety. I liked the food. I liked the sense that kids respected their elders, that society had a place for the aged as well as teenagers. I even liked the kimono-clad girls who used to stand by the elevator doors and bow, covering their mouths with their hands as they giggled at me. (I never figured out why they did that, either the bowing or the giggling. Or what I was meant to do when they did.) So I like Japan and its people. I'd love to see the country succeed. Yet almost everything that's happened since I left the country in 1988 has been detrimental to its chances of success. I would say that it's a tragedy, except that tragedies are meant to be whizz-bang affairs: a few swift acts, then a stage slippery with blood. Japan's agony is so much slower than that. It's been a full generation now since the country skidded into catastrophe and there's still no real sign of change.

Let's start, as ever, with some facts. In the twenty years to 2011, Japanese GDP per head has grown by just 0.7% per annum. Inflation has averaged less than 0.1%. Households and firms are not grossly indebted by any means, but their banks have distended balance sheets – in relation to national income, banking debts are twice as high as they are in the US. Worse still, gross government debt is a crazy 229% of GDP in 2011 and is forecast to rise to more than 250% of GDP by 2016. Now, it's quite true that *net* debt is much less than this. Much of Japanese government debt is held by different, interlocking units of government, so that the government's level of net debt (that is, total debt minus total financial assets) was 128% of GDP in 2011, and is projected to rise to 164% in 2016. You can find champions of the Japanese government arguing that even these lower figures overstate the true level of indebtedness because, if you look only at debt held by the public (i.e. excluding debt held by Japan Post, the Central Bank, the National Pension Fund, and so on), the figure falls even further, to around 60% of GDP.[1]

But we're not going to be so easily soothed. For one thing, we've already learned that the structure and gross amount of debts matter very much. Mountainous piles of borrowing combined with a weirdly convoluted system of public finance combine to form a huge problem in the making. And in any case, net debt stands well in excess of Italian levels. Worse still, that figure is projected to rise and rise. It's extraordinary that the Japanese yen is seen as a safe haven for investors when simple mathematics show the country to be in worse shape than Italy.

That basic problem is compounded by three further issues. The first is that Japan has simply stopped growing. Its economy is a mere ghost of the roaring tiger of the 1980s. Very high levels of debt could be quickly demolished if the economy were growing strongly; but not only has growth been largely absent for two decades, there is not, even now, a plan for restoring it. I know that the country has a culture of consensual decisionmaking and careful planning, but *twenty years*?

The second issue is that Japan hovers between very low inflation and actual deflation – that is, a situation in which prices fall year on year. You might think that since inflation is a bad thing, *de*flation must be a good thing, but that's not true at all. For one thing, if consumers believe that they can buy stuff (TVs, trainers, washing machines, cars) more cheaply next year than they can this year, they've got every incentive to defer purchases, which holds back demand, which holds back growth. Deflation also makes it less attractive for firms to invest. So if, for example, you were a car company wondering whether to expand capacity, you'd be in the position of having to pay for your plant and equipment upfront, while knowing that the products you are intending to make will likely sell for less and less each year. That's not a tempting prospect; so it's no surprise that investment has fallen steadily in Japan over the past two decades.[2]

The third issue is Japan's feeble political class. Including the current prime minister, Yokishiho Noda, Japan has had six prime ministers in the past five years. There has been a change of governing party in that period, and multiple shifts of factions and power-brokers. But nothing changes. Indeed, because political factions seem somewhat more important than parties in Japan, it's not even clear that voters have any real input into who governs them or how policy is conducted. The feebleness of the resulting governments is hard to exaggerate. Here, for example, is an account of one tiny incident arising from the Fukushima disaster:

Immediately after the earthquake and tsunami on March 11th that crippled reactors at the Fukushima Dai-ichi nuclear power plant, all but one of the devices to measure radioactive matter in the area were knocked out. So the authorities in Tokyo sent up a vehicle stuffed with gauges to assess how dangerous the leakage was.

Bewilderingly, says Goshi Hosono, a politician recently appointed to oversee Tokyo Electric Power (TEPCO, the utility that runs the plant), the vehicle got stuck in traffic. It then ran out of petrol at a time when the tsunami had led to a nationwide shortage of fuel. Because of this, the government abandoned the mission. Later, the government declared the Fukushima incident to be on the same level of seriousness as the accident at Chernobyl 25 years ago.[3]

This is just extraordinary. You have in your country a nuclear disaster that's as bad as or worse than Chernobyl and you can't get some measuring equipment to the site in a timely way? If circumstances had been genuinely impossible, one would have to have sympathy, but journalists had no difficulty in getting to the scene. If they ran out of petrol, they simply bought some more. Or borrowed a car. Or found a helicopter. Or did something else. The point is, they fixed the problem. It's what they were paid to do. Yet the government of the country – which boasts an army, a navy, and an air force; plus a full range of civilian emergency services; plus some of the most technically advanced companies in the world; plus a large nuclear industry; plus an astonishingly stoic and hardworking population – was unable to get a van to the site. This inertness, this feebleness of action isn't just pathetic. It's appalling.

And in a way, Japan's debt problem is eerily analogous to its nuclear problem. It is now clear that TEPCO, the nuclear utility in question, has been slothfully, shamefully managed. The basic problem was not simply one of reactor generation and design. Poor management allowed problems to fester and persist. For a long time, that didn't seem to matter. Then something went terribly, tragically wrong – and it became clear how very much it mattered.

The country's debt is the same kind of issue. At the moment, approximately 95% of Japanese government bonds are bought domestically.[4] That sounds like a strength, but it isn't really. From the point of view of domestic savers, very low interest rates plus negative inflation have seemed to make a perfectly sane investment proposition. Yes, you get a low return on your money; but then the money itself is becoming more valuable, year on year, as prices fall. And that's fine – until it reaches the tipping point where it's not actually fine at all. Japanese bond yields today have effectively no premium at all for risk. Bond investors simply assume they have a 100% chance of getting their money back. That's why interest rates in the ten-year bond are as low as 1%.[5]

But remember that net debt is projected to carry on increasing – to Greek levels and beyond. Remember too that the Japanese population is aging, and as it does so it will be more inclined to draw down on its savings, thereby starting to close off a critical source of funding. As those domestic sources of funds become harder to tap, the country will need to start looking to overseas investors; yet those investors have no reason to buy Japanese bonds at their current levels. (Of the 5% of government bonds held by foreign investors, the large bulk is held by central banks. True private sector overseas investment in Japan is essentially nil.)

And that's the nightmare scenario. Domestic savers lose the capacity or will to fund the government. In order to lure in investors from abroad, interest rates have to rise. But as soon as they do, the sustainability of a 150% net debt ratio starts to be called into question. Which means that the days of a zero per cent risk premium are gone for ever. Which pushes interest rates up again. Which makes that debt ratio seem ever less sustainable.

Plus, of course, these vicious circles contain spirals within spirals. If the Japanese government finds itself in a position of having to reassure foreign investors of its creditworthiness, it will have to start cutting expenditure or raising taxes. Doing so will produce a temporary improvement in government finances, but at the cost of imposing cuts on an economy that is already growth-free and prone to deflation. If consumers are unwilling to spend and investors to invest in today's economy, they will be even less willing to do so in an economy marked by weak government finances, budgetary austerity, and sharp deflation. The country risks combining the debt levels of Greece and the growth levels of Portugal.

If you want an even scarier spiral-within-a-spiral, try this. Japanese banks made losses solidly for ten years from 1993. They then dipped into loss again in 2008. In a low-growth, deflationary economy, their opportunities for genuinely profitable loans are restricted, with the result that (with frightening lack of imagination) they invest much of their customers' deposits in government bonds, to such an extent that banks comprise some 45% of the total market for these bonds. Which is fine – someone needs to buy those bonds – but if your major customers are perennially loss-making firms, it won't be too long before those customers disappear. Even in Japan, you can't make losses for ever and expect to survive.[6] And if banks fail or are forced to shrink their balance sheets, their purchases of government bonds will inevitably tumble.

Finally, domestic investors aren't idiots. They're looking to safeguard their money, to create a store of wealth for old age and perhaps to turn a profit. Historically, the Japanese authorities have treated their savers as somehow 'locked in' – but this is a lock without a key and a prison without walls. As soon as Japanese savers consider that their money might be safer elsewhere, that's where they'll put it. Given that the yen has risen steadily against other currencies, those savers have made prudent investments so far, but a turn in the currency could precipitate a rapid change in mood. We haven't reached that tipping point yet, but remember: all Ponzi schemes feel OK while you're in them. But they implode fast, and catastrophically. The ratings agencies are already starting to warn of the problem – and not only are they absolutely right, on this occasion their message is timely.[7] It's timely because there is actually scope to act before it's too late.

The main lines of action are utterly obvious. The government needs to throw every lever likely to restore economic growth. Japan's manufacturers are excellent, but its service industries are feeble. There's too much regulation, too much monopoly, and a lack of innovation quite remark-able in a country whose innovative abilities in other fields are so striking. Government bureaucrats, who have a strange habit of stifling any change that doesn't suit them, have got to get back to doing their jobs: executing the policies decided upon by the country's elected leaders. And those jobs need to be tackled with vigor. If a van needs to be sent to Fukushima, that van has to get to Fukushima.

It's truly hard to exaggerate how anti-growth and anti-openness the Japanese civil service can be. Following the Fukushima disaster, one bureaucrat chose to speak out rather than continue to collude with the cover-ups, the hostility to competition, the outright corruption. In the words of a blogger for *The Economist*:

> Among those who deserve honour is also a humble bureaucrat at the trade ministry. In a system that prizes remaining nameless, faceless and not rocking the boat, Shigeaki Koga chose to step forward and reveal some of Japan's ugliest secrets.
>
> After [the Fukushima disaster of] 3/11, Mr Koga decided to speak out about the awful practices he had experienced while working on Japan's energy policy. The disaster at the Fukushima nuclear plant, run by TEPCO, is symptomatic of a wider malaise. The utility companies buy the academy by sponsoring research, buy the media through mountains of public-service advertisements and junkets, buy big business by paying top-dollar for everything, buy the bureaucrats and regulators by handing them cushy post-retirement jobs.
>
> Talking to him one gets a chill down the spine. Often, bureaucrats are regarded as lemming-like

self-interested do-nothings or devious micro-managers. But Mr Koga's brave words and deep understanding of how energy companies pad their costs, block competition, keep energy prices high and ultimately strangle Japan is an antidote to that image.[8]

It's important to understand that what Mr Koga (who has been transferred to a meaningless job, whose views have been ignored, and whose policy recommendations have been disregarded) described is not an exception. The problems he exposes are ubiquitous across vast swathes of Japanese industry and government.

The solutions to these problems aren't a secret. All Western governments need to manage their energy suppliers, procure competition, ensure stable energy supply, and so on. They've developed policy tools to do these things, some better than others, but almost all better than Japan's. The sad truth is that the Japanese no-growth economy is an easily fixable problem and yet no one in Japan has the guts to fix it. It's a terrible shame.

All of which suggests that most of all, more even than a gale of deregulation, the country needs a change of culture. It needs a change away from the culture of inertia and timidity that has developed in recent decades and back to something closer to the culture of zing, energy, and inventiveness that propelled the country into the top rank of industrial nations. Sony is the world's second biggest maker of LCD televisions, but for years it has lost money on every set it's sold. The company's music-player business has been crushed by Apple. Its mobile phone division, Sony-Ericsson, has likewise lost its way. In America, those problems would drive investors crazy. They'd demand swift, radical, decisive action. In the case of Sony, you have a boss, the Welsh-born Sir Howard Stringer, who wanted to take that action. Who had a plan for doing it. Yet the company's hierarchy impeded that plan at every step. Radical change wasn't the 'Japanese way.' Obstruction (and death by asphyxiation) was better than bold, decisive change.

Most bosses viewed the recession of 2008–9 as a disaster, yet Stringer welcomed it, commenting: 'When this crisis came along, for me it was a godsend, because I could reorganise the company without having to battle the forces of the status quo.' He's fired staff, closed factories, and re-organized product development to eliminate the old internal company 'silos.'[9] None of that stuff is fun, of course, but it's how capitalism works. You can't have dynamic companies without change. You can't get creation without destruction.

And of course you don't need foreign-born business-people to take the lead on these issues. Hiroshi Mikitani, one of Japan's richest men and brashest, boldest entrepreneurs, recently decided to quit Keidanren, the country's leading business association. In a symbolic gesture, he announced his departure via Twitter, before following up with a letter. He said, 'I am doing business to drive Japan to new Japan, and they [Keidanren] want to protect old Japan. So I felt that for fundamental issues, I don't share the values of the cur-rent Keidanren ... It is a fundamental philosophical difference, I don't think it's right to stay there.'[10] As I said ear-lier, I've lived and worked in Japan and systemic cultural issues of this sort are familiar to me. The Japan I knew was a society of whispers – and too little has changed in the quarter-century since.

And that, truly, is the nub of the issue. If the old

Keidanren philosophy is permitted to linger – if companies resist change, if banks are content to make losses, if bureaucrats block vigorous action, if government debt continues to sidle upwards, if secretive obstruction continues to be preferred to openness and change – the country will hit a tipping point, and an Italian-style credit crisis will ensue. Japan's leaders are not as laughable as those in Italy, not as openly rancorous as those in the United States. But in some ways laughable is good, openly quarrelsome is good: at least it makes the problem visible. Japan's core problem is a kind of ghostliness, an invisible decay. In Spain, crowds of young people – *los indignados*, the indignant ones – have taken to protesting in public squares.[11] Japan's voters need to find some of that spirit for themselves – the willingness to challenge authority. The old 'more of the same' philosophy is killing the country. More of the same is strangling its firms. More of the same means a leaderless nation, aimless elections, and ever-increasing debt.

More of the same means a van getting stuck on the way to Fukushima and nobody doing anything about it.

TWENTY

The man who ate a supermarket

THUS FAR, OUR discussions have, in a strange way, rendered people themselves invisible. It's all very well to calculate debt ratios, examine growth statistics, and suggest policy prescriptions, but all these things can feel far removed from voters themselves, like a parent talking to a doctor while the little six-year-old patient is left to swing her feet and wonder why she feels bad.

Yet in the end, governments can't accomplish anything at all if they lose popular consent. In 2010 the then deputy prime minister of Greece, Theodoros Pangalos, said: 'My friends, we all ate together.' I think he was trying to say that everyone helped create the problem and everyone will have to help resolve it. But that's not how Greeks themselves see it. In the protests in 2011, protesters were reported shouting: 'You lying bastard! You're so fat you ate the entire supermarket.'[1] It's all very well for European politicians to meditate solutions, all very well for the IMF to require austerity and budgetary reform, all very well for think-tanks to suggest ways to revitalize the Greek economy. The simple fact is that if voters lose their patience, none of these things will happen, or at any rate not the way the IMF would like them to.

And the voters are right; the voters are always right. It's all very well for outsiders (like myself) to comment that the Greeks spent ten years living high on the fruits of a eurozone Ponzi scheme. It's true; they did. But that's not quite the point. No Greek voter ever had the choice fairly put to them. 'Hi, Agamemnon (or Bellanca or Christoforo or Demetria), would you like to live beyond your means for ten years, knowing that at the end of the decade your country will be plunged into an appalling recession and probable bankruptcy, your kids will lose their futures, and you will lose your pension?' No voter in the world, let alone in Greece, has answered 'yes' to that question. Right at the heart of Planet Ponzi there lies – well, lies. Untruth. A refusal to be honest. Government accounts that aren't truthful. Accounts of major financial institutions which routinely conceal losses and even insolvency. Credit ratings that are overblown. Central banks extending cheap loans against collateral which they know to be rotten.

Also, there's a lack of accountability and transparency. An unwillingness to face up to big issues and deal with them directly. You see that everywhere. Politicians choosing to dodge the financial consequences of their actions. Regulators unable or unwilling to do their jobs. Bank bosses who trash their institutions but still, somehow, seem to come away with hundreds of millions of dollars in 'compensation.' Bailout money that surges out of the government's coffers and somehow seems to end up sticking to the same people who caused the problems in the first place.

Lies, lack of accountability – and a torrent of fake

money. Securities mis-sold at wrong valuations to stupid investors. Government debt that trades as high-quality investment grade when in reality it's junk. Government debt shooting up. Pension liabilities and other off-balance-sheet debts shooting up. Central banks printing money. Banks taking on ludicrous degrees of leverage.

Forgive me if I'm wrong, but I don't think any voter ever voted for any of this. (Well, OK, a few Wall Street bosses probably did, but I'm talking about the kind of voters whose liquid assets don't run into eight digits.) That's why I've got sympathy for the man in the street, the Greek protesters, the Spanish *indignados*, the American Tea Partiers. These popular movements are howls of rational protest against the irrationality of their rulers. If I were a Greek protester, I'd probably figure it wasn't me that ate the supermarket. If I were one of the 46% of Spanish young people without jobs, I'd be occupying the public squares too.[2]

The more voters distrust their governments, the more belligerent those protests are likely to be. Why would Italians be willing to accept the necessity of austerity, when their prime minister loads his budget with cuts for them, money for him? What would you feel as a French voter asked to take some pain, when you read that former president Jacques Chirac and former prime minister Dominique de Villepin have been accused of accepting huge bundles of cash from African leaders?[3] (Both men deny the charges, which are unproven, though they do come from a well-placed source. Both men have also faced – or are still facing – a variety of other corruption charges.) Why would you, as an American, listen to men like Treasury secretaries Robert Rubin and Henry Paulson, who have earned count-less millions on Wall Street and whose policies have systematically tended to boost Wall Street's Ponzi-ish profits?[4] Why, for that matter, would you listen to academic economists like Larry Summers (another former Secretary of the Treasury and more recently director of President Obama's National Economic Council), when Summers was paid over $5 million from a hedge fund in the space of little more than a year?[5] Or take advice from Obama's chief campaign strategist, who has received income of $1.5 million and a buyout pot worth over $3 million, through offering services to such patriotic organizations as the Association of Trial Lawyers of America?[6] Heck, you can't even have much faith in the regulators when one of them – the SEC's Eileen Rominger – reported $57.5 million in income from Goldman Sachs in 2010/11 (prior to her shift to the SEC) – and that's not counting her multi-million-dollar investment earnings.[7]

The bottomless gulf between the lives of ordinary people and those of the individuals in charge of decision-making is even more extreme when we turn from government to Wall Street. The CEO of Citigroup, Vikram Pandit, seemed all set for Wall Street sainthood when, acknowledging that his firm had received the most government support of any bank, he offered to accept a salary of just $1 for his labors. That sounded great – the guy was only going to be overpaid by $1 – except that a dollar doesn't mean the same thing on Wall Street as it does to you or me. In July 2011, Bloomberg commented:

> Pandit's $80 million is the last of the $165 million New York-based Citigroup agreed to pay for his share of Old Lane [a hedge fund] four years ago. The bank has since awarded him compensation, including stock and options,

worth about $63 million when he received them. This includes a $1.75 million salary he got in January, replacing the $1 he told Congress he would take in February 2009 until the bank turned a profit. In May, he entered into a company profit-sharing plan which will give him an additional $25 million if the company meets analysts' estimates.[8]

If you think that Pandit's grateful shareholders wanted to reward him for creating huge value for them, you probably want to refresh your memory of the Citigroup stock price. Take a look at figure 20.1 overleaf. If you performed that badly, you'd be fired.

These things aren't restricted to American firms. Bob Diamond, then the CEO of Barclays, snapped at a British parliamentary inquiry:

I really resent the fact that you refer to this as blackjack or casino banking or rogue trading. It's wrong, it's unfair, it's a poor choice of words. We have some fantastically strong financial institutions in this country and frankly they deserve better.[9]

Would those, I wonder, be the same fantastically strong financial institutions who cost the country at least £850 billion?[10] Would Mr Diamond's own bank be the same one that has seen its share price slump by four-fifths since early 2007?[11] And yet, somehow along the way, Mr Diamond has collected more than £50 million in salary and other payments.[12]

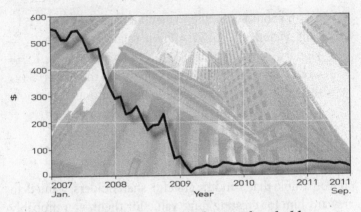

**Figure 20.1: How to reward your shareholders:
Citigroup stock price, 2007–2011**

Source: ThomsonReuters (data widely available online).

Such sums are so utterly remote from most normal people's lives that it's impossible to read stories like this without a by now familiar mixture of feelings: shock, disbelief, outrage, anger – and a kind of weary fatalism. Voters have come to realize that they'll take the pain for someone else's gain, while the gainers will be left remarkably untouched. Those gainers will, frequently, have done the exact opposite of what they were paid to do (destroyed their firm instead of preserving it, wrecked profits instead of boosting them, accumulated rotten assets instead of good ones) – yet somehow those things deserve a 'performance-related' bonus.

But at some point, voters will react. If governments are to step from Planet Ponzi into reality, they're going to have to make tough, unpopular decisions. They're going to have to copy the Brits in cutting back some government departments' budgets by 20% or 30%. They're going to have to watch taxes rise, banks lose headcount, businesses struggle, unemployment rise. These things are the consequences of any Ponzi scheme played out on the scale and duration of this one, but they're inevitably unpopular. And at some point, in some countries, given the scale of insult they've had to endure, voters will dig their heels in. They'll throw the brakes on government reform plans. Things that need to be done won't be done.

It's impossible to predict precisely where that protest will take place or what form it will take. In Britain in September 2000, a bunch of people got angry at the huge taxes their government was imposing on top of a surging gasoline price. Some lorry drivers started to blockade the ports and refineries that brought oil into the country. Pretty soon, garages in London and across the country were running out of fuel. The country came to a standstill. The government backed down.[13] That protest had little to do with Planet Ponzi, but it shows the essentially random nature of these things – and that protest unfolded in a country noted for its normally phlegmatic and uncomplaining people. What happened in Britain during a time of plenty will certainly be repeated in numerous countries during this time of arduous sacrifice and absent growth. We're already seeing something similar in the United States in the guise of the Occupy Wall Street protests, which are currently spreading from New York to a reported 146 other cities across the US.[14]

Those protests are utterly understandable – and may also be utterly disastrous. If a given government's debts are supportable, but only just, a mass protest movement could tip the country over into insolvency. At the same time, popular protests levy a kind of uncertainty tax across a nation – and the world. The absurd, staged, artificial confrontations between congressional Democrats and Republicans over the 2011 debt ceiling vote frightened investors and made the US economy a less certain place to do business. If you were a CEO contemplating whether to approve a major investment in the US, that political charade would have tilted you away from doing so. If you saw fuel protesters blocking refineries or city squares crowded with angry youngsters, you'd feel that bit less inclined to hire staff, invest money, bet on growth.

And, of course, this atmosphere of protest is not confined to the Western world. The Libyans toppled a dictator by force of arms. The Egyptians did so by force of will. Through 2011 we have also witnessed dissident action in Syria, civil war in the Yemen, Saudi troops in Bahrain, angry protests in Iran, a continuing battle against Islamic militancy in Saudi Arabia itself. Iraq continues to be deadly and unsettled. Israel has seen Turkey, once an ally, turn against it. Violent protests forced it to evacuate its embassy in Cairo.[15]

Many of these developments betoken good things. I'm hopeful that Libyans and Egyptians are to enjoy freely and openly elected governments. I'm hopeful that Syrians will soon win the same freedoms for themselves. Yet financial markets are unsentimental. They don't care about freedom; they do care about oil. And the oil market is very delicately balanced at present. Saudi Arabia claims to maintain a cushion of 3–4 million barrels a day of idle capacity, yet the stark truth is that demand for oil is exceeding the current supply and oil prices are acutely vulnerable to supply shocks.[16] All it would take for oil prices to explode would be a terrorist strike on a Saudi pipeline or an Iraqi port – or an Israeli attack on Iran – or unrest in the northern Arab

Emirates[17] – or, indeed, any one of a hundred other night-mare scenarios, each of which is highly possible. US foreign policy in the Middle East has been persistently naïve, and the well of hatreds and suspicions has only gotten deeper.

Nor is it as though the oil-producing world beyond the Middle East is safe and stable. Russia, let's remember, is still facing low-level war in the Caucasus.[18] Nigeria is facing a serious and rising threat from Islamic militants, to add to an age-old problem in the oil-producing delta region.[19] Violence in Mexico has become worse, just as oil production has declined and investment collapsed – so much so that the country may cease to function altogether as an oil exporter.[20] Venezuela, the world's eighth largest oil producer, has so badly managed its natural riches that there are widespread fears the country will go bankrupt, while its chief oil firm has witnessed an abrupt fall in production.[21] Of course, none of this means that there *will* be some kind of disaster which forces oil prices through the roof, but you'd be crazy to bet against it.

Thus far in this chapter, I've dealt only with dangers arising directly from human action, yet there are indirect dangers too. I've spent a portion of my professional life working in environment-related fields, creating the Voluntary Carbon Standard and helping to develop the markets that have resulted. You can't be in that field and not be highly aware of the looming environmental costs facing the planet. For example, as the planet warms, hurricanes – which gain their power from warming seas – are expected to become more frequent and more intense. Hurricane Katrina cost the US federal government some $105 billion in repairs and reconstruction.[22] Timber damage alone cost perhaps as much as $2.4 billion.[23] The oil price also spiked, following an unprecedented degree of destruction inflicted on rigs, pipelines, underwater installations, and refineries.[24]

So when you think about the future, you need to make allowance for the potential costs of more storms and other climate instabilities. Then too there are the wars and civil unrest so often associated with those instabilities.[25] Nor should you ignore the consequences of rising food prices, water shortages, and the proliferation of extremist ideologies and cheaply available weapons. If you add to all these things those natural disasters (like the recent Japanese tsunami) which don't have any link to climate warming but are still violent, tragic, and destructive, you are looking at financial contingency costs running into the hundreds of billions of dollars.[26] Indeed, if a natural disaster were to be implicated in interfering with oil production or some other highly valuable commodity, the costs of disaster could easily run to many hundreds of billions.

The failure of the nuclear reactor at Fukushima shows how close a major industrial country can come, not merely to human tragedy, but to profound economic turmoil. When the nuclear catastrophe first hit, the Japanese prime minister was looking at worst case options which would have involved the evacuation of 30 million people from the Tokyo area. Prime Minister Kan commented in an interview: 'It was a crucial moment when I wasn't sure whether Japan could continue to function as a state.'[27] Kan's understated concern contrasts with the continuing feebleness of TEPCO's efforts to control its damaged reactor. According to a recent report in *The Economist*,

> in the crucial hours after the tsunami, TEPCO
> failed to add water to cool the reactor cores. It

was unable to restore steady back-up power until days later and inexplicably delayed venting a build-up of pressure that eventually led to hydrogen explosions. As if that were not bad enough, TEPCO withheld information from everyone, including the then prime minister, Naoto Kan, who stormed into its headquarters yelling: 'What the hell is going on?' A meltdown began several hours after the tsunami struck, but wasn't officially disclosed until nine weeks later.[28]

I've talked enough about the problems of obstructive secretiveness in Japan already, but the economic costs of natural disaster require further comment. It remains probable that there is, in the words of one expert, a 'massive problem' with contaminated water at the stricken site. Current estimates put the cost of dealing with that water at over $500 billion, but since every estimate has been underweight to this point, it would arguably be safer to double that number.[29] And that's not to count the cost of the evacuations, the damaged farmland, the uncertainty over power generation, the disruption to supply chains, or – most worrying of all – the sense that TEPCO and the various government bureaucracies are more slothful, more feeble, more timid than the courage and endurance of the Japanese people deserve.

I don't want to overplay these things, because they're possibilities, not certainties. Nevertheless, they serve to emphasize a point I made earlier about the necessity of low government debt. If a nation is not facing an existential threat, it should be seeking, little by little, to reduce its national debt to zero, or even (like Sweden and Norway) to accumulate national assets. When unforeseeable disasters happen – when Katrina hits, when the tsunami strikes, when the oil price soars – governments in a strong financial position have the ability to respond decisively, in whatever way makes most sense. The financially constrained governments of today have lost that flexibility. If the world stays cool, that loss may not directly matter. But ours is not a cool world.

TWENTY-ONE

Doing a Caporetto

OUTSIDE ITALY, the name of Luigi Capello is not well-known, which is a pity. Anyone who really stands out in their particular line of work deserves all the fame – or notoriety – their actions have earned. And Luigi Capello, an Italian general of World War One, stands out equally for his smug overconfidence, his calamitous decisionmaking, and the vast losses he inflicted on his own side.

His story is this. Up until late autumn 1917, Capello was regarded as one of the finest leaders of the Italian army, personally brave and tactically astute. The Austrian invaders had been held at bay. The Italian army had ceded very little territory. The enemy was, in many ways, on the verge of collapse. The German commanders, seeing the gravity of the situation, chose to send fresh troops to reinforce their Austrian allies and mount an attack on Italy.

Capello's duty at Caporetto was clear and simple: to resist the attack. He didn't need to do or achieve anything else. Simply to maintain the status quo would count as a wonderful victory. Furthermore, Capello was blessed with reliable intelligence reports. He knew that an attack was coming, and where, and when. His superior officer ordered

Capello to take up a defensive position to resist the assault, but Capello – smugly overconfident – decided he'd set up an offensive one instead. If the German assault had been a feeble one, that would have been a clever move. As it was, however, it proved disastrous.

German forces ripped through Capello's line. More than thirty thousand Italian troops were killed or wounded. More than a quarter of a million were taken prisoner. Over three thousand artillery pieces – more than half the Italian stock – were lost. To this day, Italians use the term 'a Caporetto' to signify a disastrous reverse. We're going to start counting our own lost artillery pieces in the next chapter, where we'll survey the extent of the coming damage to the world's financial system. But before we do that, we should spare a thought for our generals. After all, they were the ones who led us here: to towering governmental debt, a broken financial system, a colossal, job- and savings-destroying recession.

You can, if you like, regard these things as the outcome of mere ignorance. Not many politicians have had a background in finance. President Obama was a law professor. His predecessor was theoretically speaking an oilman (though practically speaking an idiot). Angela Merkel was a chemist, Gordon Brown a history lecturer, Nicolas Sarkozy a family lawyer. On the other hand, politicians need to grasp many more subjects than economics. Like the current German chancellor, Margaret Thatcher was a chemist by profession. Unlike the current German chancellor, however, Thatcher was never frightened of making a tough decision.

Perhaps, instead, we should focus on our leaders' most senior advisors. In the US particularly, there's come to be a tradition whereby each new leader recycles a gallery of failed, or evidently biased, advisors. Larry Summers, for example, has advised Ronald Reagan, Michael Dukakis, Bill Clinton, and Barack Obama. Summers was one of the key players who torpedoed the better regulation of financial derivatives, a decision so bad that it should have prevented him from ever having an influence over policy again. Timothy Geithner reportedly refused his president's order to develop a plan for the winding-up of Citigroup – a failing which, if the accusation is true, should be regarded as no less treasonous or destructive than a battlefield general refusing a direct order from his commander-in-chief. Since Geithner regarded the banks as 'his longtime constituents,' however, maybe he figured his loyalties lay elsewhere.[1]

Or perhaps we would do better to focus on the conflicts of interest: the torrent of Wall Street lobbying cash and the revolving doors between Wall Street and Washington, Wall Street and the regulators. These conflicts are at their worst in the US, but they're present in the UK, where the Conservative Party is essentially the City of London's lapdog.

In the end, however, it comes down to the simple matters of transparency, accountability, and enforcement of the rules.

Transparency first. It remains extraordinary that governments are prepared to issue accounts that barefacedly deny the existence of countless real liabilities. Politicians should not accept that. The media should not accept that. Voters should not accept that.

It's also astonishing that the accounting rules applied to banks allow them to record assets at values billions of dollars distant from their real worth. If a financial system is allowed to hide its losses in this way, it's tough for any regulator to gain the political support needed to address its flaws. These things are true at the corporate level, but they're no less true at the level of every individual subunit. If the mortgage desks that pumped out their toxic crap had been forced to hold their leftover assets at realistic values, those desks would have crumbled long before the crisis grew to the extent that it did.

Transparency should apply at the level of entire markets as well. Michael Lewis calls the bond market a 'pit full of pythons' because it is so opaque. Yet the equity market functions fine with a very high level of transparency. Nothing bad happens. Companies aren't suddenly unable to raise money, investors aren't deterred, market-makers don't go out of business. So the simple discipline of price discovery should be brought into as many markets as possible. The worthwhile markets will succeed. So too will traders and investors who bring some added value to those markets. Everyone else will be driven out of business, financial markets will be less volatile – and the world will be the better for it.

While we're still talking about things that ought to astonish us, we have to take note of the amazing fact that the US monetary authorities have long been prepared to live with the system as it stands today. The Fed is happy to lend hundreds of billions of dollars to crisis-struck banks without any real economic return. It's incredible that the European Central Bank should fight for its right to accept bankrupt Greek debt as collateral for its loans. Any real banker would fight for the exact opposite. It is (to use a fine Britishism) gobsmacking that the Bank of England is willing to further debauch the pound by quantitative easing, at a time when long-term bond yields, the target for such nontraditional measures, are already at record lows.

'Moral hazard' is a term much used in economics. It means that if you reward people for ineptitude or remove penalties from failure, you will encourage precisely the behaviors that you least want to see. Central bankers and regulators should be the fierce guardians of moral hazard: the angels with the flaming swords. They've become the exact reverse. One congressional inquiry, for example, saw the following interchange between Representative Alan Grayson and Elizabeth Coleman, the Fed's Inspector General. (You can see the whole thing on YouTube, if you care to.)

Q: You are the Inspector General. My question is specifically do you know who received that $1 trillion plus that the Fed extended and put on its balance sheet since last September? Do you know the identity of the recipients?

A: I do not. No. We have not looked at that specific area . . .

Q: What have you done to investigate the off-balance-sheet transactions conducted by the Federal Reserve which according to Bloomberg now total $9 trillion in the last eight months?

A: I'll have to look specifically at that Bloomberg article. I don't know if I have seen that particular one.[2]

Q: That's not the point. The question is have you done any investigation or auditing of off-balance-sheet transactions conducted by the Federal Reserve?

A: At this point we are conducting our lending facility

project at a fairly high level and have not gotten to a specific level of detail to really be in a position to respond to your question.[3]

Wow! These guys overseeing the Fed are so high-level they can't even screw their eyes up enough to find the odd few trillion that they've been throwing around.

This extraordinary laxity is the inevitable result of a system designed to be as opaque, as untruthful, as possible. Accountability is the flipside of transparency. If politicians were obliged to present honest government accounts, they couldn't escape the voters' judgment on any mismanagement. If banks were forced to present honest accounts, their bosses could hardly justify their lavish remuneration or even, often, remain in their jobs. If traders' profits were linked to proper accounts, they'd be a lot more careful about prudent risk management. If markets were transparent, not opaque, investors too would be exposed to the cold blast of truth.

Since these things are both obvious and largely costless to achieve, it's bewildering that it hasn't yet happened. And in the end, we have to come back to the generals, to the Luigi Capellos who have led so many different governments in so many different parts of the world to their own Caporettos. It's hard to avoid believing that politicians would rather snuggle up close to special interests, give way to the lobbyists, and avoid challenging their legislators, activists, or voters. Perhaps politicians think they're more likely to be re-elected that way. Perhaps they're right to think so. I wouldn't know.

But presumably people enter politics originally to bring about change. To lead the country to something better, not something merely comfortable. Margaret Thatcher was a crucial leader for Britain because she didn't give a damn about what was comfortable or what lobbyists wanted from her. She knew what was right, did it, and was prepared to reap the consequences, good and bad.

By contrast, the political leaders of today seem to lack almost any desire to *lead*. That's been comically obvious in Italy and saddeningly so in Japan. But Chancellor Merkel, who is neither a buffoon nor an incompetent, presents another version of the same basic deficiency. Her timidly evasive approach to the eurozone crisis has done nothing but exacerbate the problems. She hasn't even had the courage to *kick* the can down the road; she's insisted on nudging it, a centimeter or two at a time – and you can imagine for yourself how much the financial markets love *that* approach. A bolder leader would, two years ago, have propelled Greece into formal default, ring-fenced Italy and Spain, and placed Portugal and Ireland on probation. That action, taken swiftly, properly explained, and fully committed to, would have snuffed out the crisis. Some creditors would have lost money, which would have reminded them of the importance of trying harder next time. Some banks would have gone bust, which would have reminded bank boards and shareholders that their job is to ensure their charge is properly managed. Those outcomes would have been painful but good – a phrase in the lexicon of every true leader, but one that has slipped from use today.

In the United States, it's hard even to single out individuals for blame. Do I cite Bill Clinton for abolishing the Glass–Steagall Act and systematically opposing any real constraint on Wall Street's power to destroy trillions of dollars' worth of value? Or George W. Bush for his countless fiscal follies? Or Barack Obama for his changeless change, his stimulus plans that have stimulated little but the flow of red ink? Or Nancy Pelosi for her refusal to contemplate entitlement cuts of any kind? Or Messrs Greenspan and Bernanke for their love of the bailout and the printing press? For their inability to keep track of their trillions? Or the entire Tea Party movement for its obdurate attitude to tax reform? Truth is, all these people stand guilty as charged; but the real issue is a political atmosphere so corroded, so poisoned with partisan posturing, that the poor old truth is left wheezing and battered in a corner. If a political leader had the guts to speak the truth, it's doubtful that anyone would even hear it. Politicians react to the environment by throwing up smokescreens. The intense wars of class, culture, ideology, and party function as a way to distract everyone – voters, media, Congress – from the fundamental reform issues which we have discussed in these pages.

The only country on Planet Ponzi that actually seems to have some leadership is Britain. I'm not by any means a fan of the country's leadership over the last couple of decades. Britain is, as I've argued previously, in many ways a contender for the dubious accolade of World's Most Indebted Nation, which tells you all you need to know about its management in the recent past. But if its leaders (of both political persuasions) led the country into its current mess, its leaders of both political persuasions seem ready to lead it out. To slash spending, to take a pragmatic approach to taxation, to restrain the banks, to do what needs to be done.

And the truly weird thing about this? *These things are not unpopular*. The exact same politicians who are doing all these terrible things *are not unpopular*. It's way too soon to call the next election, but the low political calculation which seems to sway politicians from Yosemite to Yokohama could simply be based on a false assumption. Maybe lying, dissembling, and evasion are not the most effective ways to win an election. Maybe transparency, accountability, and leadership are. You won't know until you've tried it – and in Tokyo, Berlin, Paris, Rome, Madrid, and Washington it might by now be time for a new approach. It'd have my vote.

TWENTY-TWO

Crunching the numbers

IT'S TIME TO add up. This book has thrown around so many huge numbers that you may be feeling a bit dizzy. So let's summarize.

Twenty or thirty years ago, the world went crazy. Wall Street started to turn itself into a giant Ponzi scheme. Washington started to rack up uncountably large – and wholly unpayable – obligations that now total somewhere between $80 and $200 trillion.* The other nations of the world chose, more or less, to follow suit. As the Ponzi scheme started to collapse, it inaugurated what is certainly the greatest and most dangerous recession since the 1930s.

In normal recessions, output usually returns to its 'core' level fairly swiftly. That is, though the recession causes injury for a few years, output tends to spring back to its original trajectory, thanks to an extra spurt of growth in the first year or two of recovery. Recessions caused by banking crises tend not to be like that. Output is permanently

---

* And by the way, isn't it amazing that we don't know this figure even to the nearest *hundred* trillion dollars? Even those high-level guys at the Fed might start to get twitchy at this degree of unknowing.

stunted. Although growth will one day resume, there's no extra spurt, no return to that original trajectory. It's hard to measure the present value of that lost output, but what is absolutely certain is that it is staggeringly huge. One estimate prepared by the Bank of England puts the figure at somewhere between $60 trillion and $200 trillion. As the author of that paper dryly comments, 'to call these numbers "astronomical" would be to do astronomy a disservice: there are only hundreds of billions of stars in the galaxy.' Quite so. Only bankers can destroy that much value. Black holes are wimpish by comparison.[1]

That measure of loss affects us all – or rather, it affects almost everyone who isn't collecting a Wall Street bonus. But, important as it is, it's not the measure we'll focus on in this chapter. Our concern now is to understand just how bankrupt the world's financial system is. If it seems strong enough to get through the current crisis, we can have some expectation of having seen off the worst, of limping through to better days ahead. If, on the other hand, the system has been more gravely weakened by what has happened so far, then, the worst is yet to come; the destruction is not yet over. So let's examine some facts.

The world's banking system holds approximately $100 trillion in assets. Those assets are supported by $5.4 trillion in capital. The banking system as a whole earned pretax profits of around $700 billion in 2010, which means that if banks were able to stop paying dividends to their shareholders, you'd expect bank capital to grow by approximately that amount each year. That's the global picture. This book, however, has not been interested in tracing developments in China, Brazil, or other key markets of the future. Our interest has been with Planet Ponzi, and

	Bank assets ($bn)	Bank capital ($bn)	Banking profit ($bn)
US	13,145	1,034	114
Eurozone	31,848	1,297	86
UK	9,705	449	36
Japan	11,928	561	43
Planet Ponzi total	66,626	3,341	279

Table 22.1: The vital statistics

Source: 'Top 1000 World Banks,' The Banker, July 1, 2011.

the key data for Planet Ponzi are as shown in table 22.1.[2]

In summary, then, the banking system on Planet Ponzi has approximately $3.3 trillion of capital as a buffer against possible losses. It has $66.6 trillion of assets, from which those losses are liable to come. Readers of a superstitious bent will note that 666 is the number of the beast, but I'm not superstitious.

We're about to start examining the scale of possible losses still to come in the current credit crisis; but before we do so, I need to make a couple of important points. They cut two ways. First, it is not only the banking system which holds poor-quality assets. Many of those assets will have ended up with insurance companies, pension funds, and central banks, for example. In the 2008–9 phase of the credit crunch, about two-thirds of the total losses ended up being absorbed by the banking system, and about a third by insurance companies and other investors.[3] In the absence of a better guess, I'd say that the same division of probable losses to come still holds true.

That first point is helpful. Systemic risks stem largely from the banking sector, so if losses are shared more widely, the banking sector is that little bit more robust. The second point, however, pushes us in the opposite direction. Looking at *total* bank capital is helpful in the sense that it quantifies the total size of the buffer available, but that can also be misleading. Because institutions are not all equally weak, some strong ones will be impaired but broadly un-affected by a wave of losses. Others will go under. When those weak ones go under, their creditors in turn will start to endure losses. Some of those creditors (already hit by sovereign debt losses and the other problems we've spoken about in this book) won't be able to take the additional hit and will go under themselves, triggering a further wave of insolvencies. Again, you only need to think back to 2008, when financial meltdown was triggered by Lehman Brothers with its net losses of just $129 billion. In a more ordinary climate, those losses wouldn't have triggered disaster, but in a system weakened by heaps of other losses, they proved catastrophic.

So what scale of losses would trigger the apocalypse this time round? I don't know. Worse than that, nor does anyone else. It would be nice to think that there's an office some-place – in the IMF, in the Federal Reserve, in the Bank of International Settlements, maybe somewhere in Brussels – where some wise officials have all the necessary data to hand. But there is no such office. Remember that Citigroup was astonished by its own insolvency. Senior officials at the bank were amazed to find themselves chopped off at the knees. Dick Fuld never thought Lehman would go under.* James Cayne of Bear Stearns thought the same of his firm (and said so, in language that would make a lumberjack

---

* Fuld's compensation for the decade in which he wrecked his firm and destroyed the financial system: $484 million.

blush*).[4] What we can say with confidence is that if there is a wave of losses that looks large in relation to bank capital – let's say a trillion or so – and if one large and visible lender goes under, we will be even worse off than we were in September 2008: facing a nuclear chain reaction, where each new detonation threatens to cause a still larger explosion down the chain. And this time, there are no bunkers.

So let's take a look at the losses that are potentially coming our way. We start with the grim probabilities of sovereign default.

Sovereign defaults

By this point in the book, you may be starting to suspect that I have a slightly negative view of the world. Personally, I'd disagree with that contention. I think I'm realistic. In addition, as we'll see in due course, I think there are solid reasons for optimism in the medium to longer term. Nevertheless, I want to keep my personal view strictly to one side, so we'll focus here instead on what the financial markets themselves expect, using the most recent data available.

The data we'll use rely on credit default swaps, which as we've already seen are essentially a way to buy insurance against the risk of default. Because these swap prices are publicly displayed, it's possible to see what insurance

*Cayne's compensation: $155 million in the five years to 2007. Forbes estimated the value of his stock in Bear Stearns at $966 million in 2007. What Cayne said about Geithner is too obscene to reprint but the end-notes point you to a source where you can find it.

premiums are being demanded and paid. Clearly, the higher the premiums charged, the higher is the implicit risk of default. Indeed, it's possible to use credit default swap pricing to estimate the 'cumulative probability of default' for all sovereign debt markets. The cumulative probability of default (CPD) is exactly what it sounds like. It's the chance that a default happens at some point within a given period – in our case, we're looking at the next five years.

Table 22.2 overleaf presents these data. The cumulative probability of default data has been crunched by an outfit called CMAVision, and is available online. Government debt data are sourced from the IMF and are also publicly available. The third column simply multiplies the risk of default by the amount of government debt outstanding.

A few comments about these figures. First, I've tried to be kind. I've ignored all non-European borrowers whose public finances are questionable. I've also ignored all European sovereigns (notably France) where the risk of default is currently considered to be under 15%. Those are big concessions to unreality. France's debt is already the subject of market gossip, and table 22.2 simply assumes that the country's debt is unchallengeably strong. That's not the case, but I'm assuming that it is. Additionally, there are numerous non-European sovereign borrowers that would be at risk in the context of a global credit meltdown – Venezuela, Argentina, Pakistan, Ukraine, Dubai, Iraq, Lebanon, El Salvador, the Dominican Republic, Vietnam, Egypt, and the State Bank of India, to mention only those countries with a risk of default at 15% or greater.

Secondly, the way I've presented the data tends to suggest, wrongly, that the risks are uncorrelated. In practice, the risks will be very closely correlated. If Portugal goes under,

Country	Cumulative probability of default (%)	Government debt ($bn)	Possible scale of default ($bn)
Greece	91	473	430
Portugal	61	214	131
Ireland	46	243	112
Italy	33	2,623	866
Hungary	31	102	32
Croatia	30	29	9
Spain	28	949	266
Romania	26	66	17
Iceland	25	14	4
Bulgaria	24	10	2
Latvia	20	11	2
Lithuania	20	18	4
Belgium	20	486	97
Russia	19	162	31
Poland	18	282	51
Turkey	18	314	57
Total Europe		5,996	2,111

Table 22.2: The cost of sovereign default

Source: Debt statistics from IMF, *World Economic Outlook*, April 2011;
default data from CMA, *Global Sovereign Credit Risk Report*, 3rd
quarter 2011 (full details available from www.cmavision.com).

the pressure on Spain will become almost irresistibly strong.
If Spain goes under, the likelihood of default by France and
Spain will rocket to levels where the markets will freeze,
funding ceases, and insurance becomes all but unbuyable.
This point is both hopeful and scary. It's hopeful in the sense
that if the creaking institutions of the eurozone do manage
to get to grips with the countries currently on their most
endangered list, the prospects for everybody else immediately improve. (Though since intense financial pressure is
the only thing forcing reform in Italy, for example, any relief
on that front is of questionable long-term value.) But it's also
scary. Thus far, European institutions have proved hopelessly inadequate to deal with the mounting crisis. Unless

they show a lot more leadership very soon, the chances of Europe-wide contagion will rapidly increase.

Finally, I don't want to pretend that these figures are more precise than they are. For one thing, the scale of losses, *as finally realized*, will be significantly lower than the total scale of default. So, for example, a Greek sovereign default would likely affect all $473 billion of outstanding debt, but the affected creditors would nevertheless expect to get some portion of their money back. (At the moment, the ratings agencies are predicting between 30 and 50 cents on the dollar.) You could therefore argue that the overall figure of more than $2 trillion is unrealistically gloomy. To some extent I can agree with that, except that if a bank holds the debt of a government in default, that asset becomes almost worthless until some clarity is reached on final payouts. The debt can no longer be used as collateral. It won't be tradable, or at least certainly not in any sizeable volume. For a significant period, the asset will be effectively worthless, no matter what the finally realized value may one day prove to be.

Besides, although the data in this table are the best available, that doesn't make them good. Because there are huge vested interests seeking to minimize the scale of the crisis (I would number among them every European government, the British and American governments, and every European, American, and Japanese bank), the markets themselves are highly subject to manipulation. After all, some readers will have wondered why I've made things so complicated. Why look at the cumulative default probability as predicted by spreads in the CDS market? That sounds like technobabble. Why not take the *face value* of European government bonds, then subtract the current *market value* in order to derive the total destruction of value? That would be a beautifully direct and unanswerable calculation.

Indeed it would. Unfortunately, however, there are no dependable prices for these government bonds available anywhere. If I call a broker today and request a bid/offer price for, let's say, a ten-year Portuguese bond, I will be quoted two prices: a price at which that broker is prepared to buy bonds and a price at which they're prepared to sell. But if I actually seek to take them up on that bid, I'll often find that they're prepared to trade a maximum of one single bond. In the context of the government bond markets, that's a little like a grocery store only being prepared to sell rice by the grain. And let's suppose, for the sake of argument, that I'm happy to trade bonds in that way. If I actually seek to close a deal, I'll often find that brokers suddenly declare themselves unable to complete a trade. They'll make up some kind of story why their bid prices have disappeared, but it's not the story that matters – it's the disappearance. Indeed, if there's one thing more scary than a grocer willing to sell rice only by the grain, it's a grocer who doesn't even have the guts to do that.

It's issues of that kind that have pushed me into the slightly convoluted calculation mechanism used above – but although the CDS markets are less prone to manipulation, that doesn't mean they're not suffering from it. If there were a transparent market in these things, I'd expect the figures emerging to be very significantly worse than those I've just given you.

But you've already got me tagged as a pessimist and I don't want to add any further to your suspicions. So we'll take the market data as being objective fact and simply note that, according to current prices for credit default swaps, the financial markets are braced for possible defaults of around

$2,111 billion. If dominoes start to fall, that number will increase very rapidly indeed, so we might want to add an extra trillion or so into our worst case scenario. (Though in fact, a real 'worst case' would be substantially worse than that.)

As we saw in table 22.1, the total capital in the European bank markets is just $1,297 billion. If sovereign defaults affect some $2–3 trillion worth of bonds, the destruction of value could well be in the region of $1–2 trillion. Or, to put these facts in plain English, the loss of value in the European sovereign debt market could more or less destroy all the capital available in the European banking sector.

The US housing market

The size of the US mortgage market is $13.7 trillion. Of that total, some relates to non-residential mortgages (including farms). Now, we've already discussed the fact that the commercial property sector is in serious difficulties, but we're simply going to set that aside for the time being – all $2.4 trillion of it – and simply examine the $11.3 trillion residential mortgage sector.[5]

We saw in an earlier chapter that the US housing market is in serious trouble. Almost a third of all home sales are triggered by financial distress. Almost a quarter of all homeowners are suffering negative equity. The noted economist Robert Shiller suggests that further house price falls of 10–25% are perfectly feasible.[6]

The truth is that house price falls of 25% simply don't bear thinking about. If prices sank that low, countless homeowners would seek to walk away from their mortgages, or sell their houses, sooner than service their debts. It would be appropriate and orderly to do so. Mortgage companies could hardly even offer a threat of repossession, because to repossess something is pointless unless you figure you can sell it, and under the scenario we're discussing the market would be all but bombed out.

But still, at least the math is simple. A loss of 25% applied to a mortgage market of $11.3 trillion implies total losses of an additional $2.8 trillion. Since the total quantum of capital in the US banking sector is just $1 trillion, on this scenario the US banking sector has also disappeared.

I think it's fair to argue, however, that $2.8 trillion seems harsh. Not all the loss in housing value will end up impairing mortgage values. Equally, a 25% fall in house prices is at the bottom end of Shiller's range of estimates. Perhaps it would be fairer, then, to assume that the loss of value arising from the US housing market would be more contained at, let's say, $1–2 trillion. The US banking sector has still disappeared, but at least there'd still be a handful of genuinely well-managed banks poking out above the waters, like Ararat after the Flood.

European housing markets

As we saw in the chapter on housing, however, US house prices are sensible compared with those now prevalent across parts of Europe and much of the rest of the world. Some European countries with large mortgage markets (Germany, the Netherlands, Italy) have fairly sober house prices. They're either minimally overvalued or, in Germany's

	Residential mortgages outstanding ($bn)	Overvaluation (%)	Scale of possible losses ($bn)
Britain	1,882	27.8	523
France	1,012	48.5	491
Spain	931	39.2	365
Total	3,825		1,379

Table 22.3: The coming European housing crash

Source: Mortgage data from European Mortgage Federation.

case, actually undervalued. (I'm using *The Economist*'s figures, which use the long-term ratio of house prices to rents to derive a 'fair' valuation.[7]) We can therefore ignore those happy markets and restrict ourselves to focusing on the three markets – Britain, France, and Spain – where the volume of outstanding mortgages is large and where the extent of house price overvaluation is extreme.

The potential for losses in these markets can be summarized as shown in table 22.3.[8] These data, in line with my practice throughout this chapter, are deliberately optimistic. I'm ignoring all the smaller mortgage markets where prices are crazy (Sweden's 36% overvaluation, Ireland's 23%). I'm assuming that markets simply revert to their long-term mean levels, without overshooting on the way down as they overshot on the way up. If house prices fell to just 20% below their long-term value – which is well within the range expected by Robert Shiller for the US market – the losses wouldn't be $1.4 trillion, but more like $2.25 trillion. But still. I'm an optimist. You can be gloomy if you like; me, I'm prepared to settle for losses of $1.4 trillion . . . which would almost precisely wipe out the European and British banking sectors . . . except that, as we've seen, those have already been blown out of the water by sovereign debt problems, so there's nothing much left to be wiped out. Which is good news, I guess.

Nonperforming loans

So far, we've restricted ourselves to two sectors: lending to governments and lending against houses. Naturally, however, banks are involved in a far wider range of activities than just that. They lend to individuals via personal loans and credit cards. They lend to companies, large and small. They offer firms mortgages collateralized by commercial property. In times of economic distress, naturally both firms and individuals may struggle to service their debts. The more extreme the economic turmoil, the greater the likely rate of default.

Unfortunately, we lack any easy way of putting numbers to those likely defaults. Remember that banks need to fund their operations through extensive interbank borrowing and use of the various securities markets. If lenders and investors start to scent that a bank is in trouble, they'll immediately begin to withdraw funds or demand higher rates of interest. Either of those outcomes will severely hinder the chances of a weak bank making it through a difficult time unscathed. The result is that banks, particularly the weak ones, have a strong incentive to hide any troubled debt. The good news is that auditors and regulators do require disclosure of any 'nonperforming loans,' which means that any problems should, in theory, be out in the open.

Only they're not. The bad news is that it's easy to disguise a bad loan as a good one. Let's say you've lent $10 million to a borrower who's struggling. That borrower needs to pay back $3 million this year to stay within the terms of your original agreement, but he calls to say that the $3 million simply isn't there. What do you do? Well, roughly speaking, you have three options. The first is the nuclear one. You call in your loan. The borrower can't pay. You put the company into liquidation and an administrator tries to salvage what he can, right down to selling the company's office furniture, if need be. You won't get your money back, but you'll get something.

Option two is honesty. If the borrower reckons he can find about $6 million in total over the next few years, you could choose to accept that $6 million and tell your auditor to book a loss of $4 million for the money that you will never see again. You don't put the company into administration (an action which in itself is quite likely to impair the company's value). Instead, you let the company go on managing its business, get what money you can, fess up to the losses, and everyone moves on. No one likes option two, but it's still by far the best and most honest alternative.

The final option, however, is commonplace. There's probably a technical term for it somewhere but I call it 'deceit' or, if you prefer something a little catchier, 'extend and pretend.' Here's how it works. When your borrower tells you that he simply doesn't have the $3 million available to service his loan this year, you tell him not to worry. You say he can pay you next year. Or the year after. You rewrite the loan agreement, in fact, to defer all those payments he can't make and will never be able to make to sometime in the future. In cold, hard, economic terms, nothing has improved. You've still lost money on the loan. You know it, your borrower knows it. But crucially, the loan is no longer in default. Because you've rewritten the loan agreement, the borrower now looks like a model client who's made every single payment on time.

Perhaps you think such a thing would never happen, or certainly not on any real scale and not with any banks of substance and reputation. But you'd be wrong. A study, conducted by Barclays Capital and reported by the *Financial Times*, took a group of twenty-seven banks and examined those loans which seemed to be nonperforming (e.g. where interest wasn't being paid or where maturities had been extended). For the first quarter of 2011 – and bear in mind that only twenty-seven banks were involved in this study – the total of nonperforming loans was some $200 billion as compared with the *reported* total of $129 billion.[9] That's potentially as much as $70 billion smuggled away in games of extend and pretend.

Misrepresentation on that scale is somewhat alarming, to put it mildly. On the other hand, in the context of the figures we've been looking at so far, $70 billion sounds manageable. But don't be fooled. The IMF estimated the total losses arising from the first phase (2007–10) of the credit crunch (more on this at the end of the chapter). Excluding sovereign losses (which didn't play a part in that phase) and residential mortgages (which we've already covered), the IMF estimated that losses in the corporate and other consumer sectors amounted to approximately $2.2 trillion, of which about $1.4 trillion ended up pounding bank balance sheets. If there is a new global recession unfolding now, or soon, I'd expect it to be more severe than last time, simply because the effects of the previous collapse were cushioned so heavily by governments borrowing and printing money. Since governments are now out of cash, there's no more cushioning left. A cautious estimate of possible losses would therefore be for the same again – another $2.2 trillion. A worst case scenario would add at least a trillion to that, or let's say $3.5 trillion for the sake of a round number. As before, not all of these losses would afflict the banks themselves. Some would be borne by other parts of the financial system, but all the same, the losses could be of a system-crushing scale.

Japan

So far in this chapter we haven't mentioned Japan. The bond markets still regard its government debt as super-safe. I don't regard it in that way at all – I think an Italian-sized mountain of debt piled on to a stagnant economy and managed by temporary prime ministers and secretive, obstructive bureaucrats is a recipe for disaster.

The same goes for Japanese banking. A recent note by Fitch commented:

> Unless major Japanese banks are successful in bolstering their core capital, their ratings will likely remain constrained by their weak capitalisation . . . The agency remains concerned over the weakening asset quality at major Japanese banks and the impact it may have on the banks' modest profitability and weak core capitalisation . . . Furthermore, the Japanese government's strong encouragement for banks to increase lending and/or to restructure loans to SMEs [small and medium-sized enterprises] could also put

> pressure on their loan quality . . . Fitch notes that
> their large stock investments remain a significant
> risk on the banks' balance sheets and that the risk
> is currently understated in terms of the capital
> charge these investments attract.[10]

This short note refers to many of the themes we've already discussed. The dead hand of the Japanese government interfering in a negative (and behind-the-scenes) way with ordinary commercial operations. Poor asset quality, arising in part from past government interference and in part from a stagnating economy. Shoddy and even deceitful accounting techniques, which mean that large risks (banks holding equity stakes) are poorly handled in terms of disclosure and risk management. Everywhere you look in Japan, you sense that whiff of historical and traditional relationships overriding commercial good sense – which means, of course, that bad commercial decisions are made, leading to poor credit quality, weak and unambitious banks, and finally to an economy stifled by lack of credit where credit is most needed.

Nevertheless, creditors can be reassured by one thing: namely that everything Japanese happens in slow motion. I think a credit crisis is brewing in Japan, and one on a potentially horrendous scale. (Recall that Japan has gross debts outstanding of $13.3 trillion, and net debts of $7.4 trillion.) But the crisis isn't imminent. When debt yields start to nudge upwards, and when domestic savers start slimming down their holdings of government bonds, that's the time to run for the hills. I personally wouldn't hold Japanese bonds because I don't like playing a timing game – holding something I know to be toxic in the expectation that I'll be able to get out in time. But that's me. I'm cautious that way. This chapter's mission, however, is to examine the scale of losses likely to hit the world's banking system over the next few years and, for once, I'm optimistic. A credit crisis in the West combined with serious recession in the world economy will cause some injury in Japan, of course. But the damage will be limited. A hundred billion dollars. Maybe two. But that won't be the real issue. The real issue is a few years away, but is at least an order of magnitude larger.

US federal and state debt

Similarly, I haven't made any allowance for any US default. Again, that's not because I think everything's fine. As a matter of fact, I consider the US 100% certain to default on its obligations, but it's important to be careful about precisely what we mean by that.

As we saw earlier in the book, the US government has obligations equal to somewhere between $80 trillion and $200 trillion. Of those, some obligations – such as its Treasury bonds or pension commitments to its employees – are set in stone: court-enforceable obligations which must be paid, no matter what. Other obligations, however, are less binding. At the moment, the government makes certain moral commitments on social security, Medicare, and Medicaid, but those things are subject to reversal. Pension entitlements can be slashed, the provision of health care withdrawn. Such actions would constitute an ethical default. They would mean that the government is betraying all those countless Americans who have trusted its promises, but you can't take the government to court for such breaches of trust.

Inevitably, therefore, that's how the government will choose to default. It will, at some stage, be forced into a massacre of entitlements, simply because those entitlements were unaffordable when they were promised and are ever less affordable now. Even if tax rises are forced through or exemptions slashed, the massacre will happen because the funding gap is so enormous. As a matter of fact, what we'll see is the precise reverse of the past thirty years. For three decades, our politicians have cut taxes and expanded entitlements. The tax cuts weren't real (because they were made at a time of national debt). The entitlements weren't real either (because they were never achievable). Nevertheless, for three decades, voters have lapped up the sweet delusion that these impossible things could all happen together, like the Oscars and the Superbowl and Christmas Day all arriving on the one same miraculous morning. In the default phase of Planet Ponzi, we'll experience the opposite. Years will go by with no Oscars, no Superbowl, no Christmas. Tax increases *and* entitlement cuts. Our poor and elderly citizens will feel cheated and lied to, and they'll feel that way because they have been. That's the first type of default that's going to happen, and it'll start happening very soon.

The second type of default has to do with the dollar. If the government can't pay its debts in good old-fashioned dollars, it can always seek to trash the currency instead. It's a sweet little trick, when you think about it. You borrow money that has some value, repay it with money that doesn't. You've cheated your lender, obviously enough, but nobody can touch you for it, because you're paying the money back, dollar for dollar.

If you wanted to achieve such a default, you wouldn't

want to just go ahead and blurt it out. You'd be a little subtle about it. The first thing you'd want to do is tweak those inflation figures, so that inflation *looked* stable whereas in fact it was galloping away at 10% or more a year. You'd want to cover your manipulation in plenty of complicated talk about statistics, but the talk wouldn't signify a string bean.

The second thing you'd want to do is to start churning out new dollar bills. You'd print like crazy. You wouldn't talk about trashing the currency, of course; you'd talk about price stability, about quantitative easing, about Operation Twist and bringing down the long end of the yield curve. Ideally, too, you'd have someone in charge who really believed in the value of what he was doing, someone who didn't really live in the real world. Maybe a professor of something. A guy who had studied a period of history from eighty years ago and who's been yearning all his life to save the world using techniques which might or might not have worked back then, but which certainly don't make sense in the present day.

Needless to say, these things are going on right now. Ben Bernanke, chairman of the Fed and student of the monetary history of the Great Depression, is in charge of our money supply. He truly believes that rolling the printing presses will make a difference – and he's right, of course, it will: just not in the way he thinks. For each new dollar that the Fed creates, the dollar in your pocket will lose a little value. Creditors will lose out. Worse still, ordinary Americans will lose out. If median household incomes are now back where they were in 1996, a good part of that awful record lies with the destruction of the dollar.

That's the second type of default the government can pull, and it's already happening.

The third type of default involves a failure to make scheduled payments on court-enforceable obligations. As we've just noted, that term includes financial debts, such as Treasury bonds, but it also includes pension liabilities. Because these things can be enforced in a court of law, any failure to pay would be unambiguously serious. That point of ultimate seriousness was almost reached in early August 2011, when a bunch of congressional lunatics decided to play a game of chicken with national prosperity. Since the debt ceiling increase was passed and since no default did take place, most commentators assumed that no damage had been done. In practice, of course, it had: huge damage. Starting up new businesses, hiring new staff, and investing in new projects requires a degree of confidence in the future: 'animal spirits,' in Keynes's evocative phrase. The sight of elected American lawmakers happily tossing around high explosive right by the beating heart of American prosperity would not make me, as a business owner, more likely to invest in the US. I suspect most business owners feel likewise. So damage – real, job-killing damage – has already been done.

Nevertheless, actual default on financial obligations did not happen and I continue to think it is probably unlikely to happen, at any rate in the near term. I don't, however, think that this third and most serious type of default can be ruled out in the longer term. Our politics has become so dysfunctional, our leadership so obsessed with re-election and party dominance, our legislators so bitterly divided, that all bets are off. Financial default is unlikely to happen soon. It probably won't happen later. But that's the most you can say. (And these remarks apply only to the federal government. At a state level, I'd say that default is almost certain to happen.)

Since our objective in this chapter is to count up the scale of financial losses likely to hit banks and other investors in the next few years, and since we're trying to be as cautious as we can in our predictions, I'm going to assume that state and federal governments will pay their bills for the next few years. Default on health and pension commitments will certainly happen. The destruction of the currency has already started. The mountain of financial debt will be a horrendous problem for the future. But for the purposes of the present chapter, I'm going to estimate financial losses on US government debt at $0. Optimistic to the last.

Summary

In April 2009, the IMF started to sweep up following the first phase of the credit crisis. It published a note summarizing the estimated scale of financial sector writedowns over the period 2007–10. Its figures were as shown in table 22.4.

Bluntly summarized, the first phase of the credit crisis caused losses of $4.4 trillion. A large chunk of that devastation was borne by insurance companies, pension funds, and the like, but banks alone suffered losses of $2.8 trillion. Given that the banking sector as a whole has capital of just $3.3 trillion (and had less in 2008), you could pretty much say that the first credit crisis destroyed the solvency of nearly all American, European, and Japanese banks.

Total catastrophe was averted by government action on an extraordinary scale, but since few of the fundamental problems were addressed, the problems are still there. Only this time governments have no room for further action. I've

	Writedowns ($bn)		
	Total	Banks	Other
United States			
Residential mortgages	1,421	810	611
Other consumer	368	228	140
Corporate	433	265	168
Commercial mortgages etc.	490	302	188
Total	2,712	1,605	1,107
Europe			
Residential mortgages	387	238	149
Other consumer	193	120	73
Corporate	477	295	182
Commercial mortgages	136	84	52
Total	1,193	737	456
Japan			
Consumer	65	58	7
Corporate	84	71	13
Total	149	129	20
Emerging market assets held by US, European, Japanese banks	340	340	–
World total	4,394	2,810	1,583

Table 22.4: The end of civilization, Part I

Note: The figure of $490 billion for 'commercial mortgages etc.' in the US includes losses of $80 billion for municipal debt.

Source: IMF, *Global Financial Stability Report*, April 2009.

summarized the problems we might be facing today in table 22.5.

In our cautious best-guess scenario, the banks are kaput. In our (not very severe) 'worst case' scenario, the banks are so kaput that they couldn't be much kaputter. These figures make no allowance for potential problems in Japan or in the US. They make no allowance for any emerging market losses triggered by problems in the West. Some people will feel I'm being overoptimistic here – but, what the heck, let's enjoy a little sunshine.

The problems in the banking sector are so serious that

	Total losses ($bn)
Sovereign debt problems	1,000 - 2,000
US mortgages	1,000 - 2,000
European mortgages	1,000 - 2,000
Everything else (mostly commercial mortgages, corporate debt, and other consumer debt)	2,000 - 3,500
Japanese government debt	–
US federal and state debt	–
Total cost of catastrophe	5,000 - 9,500
Share absorbed by banks	3,300 - 6,300

Table 22.5: The end of civilization, Part II
Source: See discussion in text.

the only plausible rescue could come from government action; but, as we've seen throughout this book, Western governments no longer have the resources to find a few trillion dollars from anywhere.

And that's that: the end of Planet Ponzi. We turn now to what comes after.

PART FOUR

Solutions

TWENTY-THREE

The end of days

I AM FREQUENTLY ASKED when I talk about the themes of this book: What happens now? How does it end?

Those are fair questions and I wish I knew the answers, but I don't. So much depends on chance and circumstance, all one can really address is the probabilities. The coming crisis is almost certain to play out first in two areas: American mortgages and European debt.

Take the mortgages first. Because the economic news is so relentlessly bad, because there is no room for fiscal or monetary stimulus, and because of the plague of uncertainty that weak leadership and political bickering have spread across our usually confident nation, the US housing market is going to weaken further. Like unstable mountain ice slowly thawing in the sunshine, that creeping weakness will at some point cause an avalanche. Bear in mind that the wreckage from the last slump hasn't yet cleared from the system. There are still almost 2 million foreclosed or delinquent homes not yet released to the market. Some commentators reckon that although Bank of America has already taken losses of some $30 billion on its US mortgage book, the total damage could run into the *hundreds* of billions.[1] Damage on that scale could yet capsize a major lender even without further housing weakness; any further house price dips will make that outcome more probable and more rapid. As the roughest of rough guides, each 10% dip in house prices is inflicting $1 trillion in losses. Not all of those losses will be borne by the banking sector. Homeowners will take their share. Investors dumb enough to have bought bubble-era mortgage debt at bubble-era prices will take their share. But such comforting thoughts run only so far. You can share the pain of a $1 trillion loss all you like: the losses that remain may still be enough to blow some weak banks sky high. And when they go, others will go too. That's how the avalanche will start.

Same thing in Europe. We've already heard the head of Deutsche Bank expressing his opinion that numerous euro-zone banks are already insolvent. That terrifying comment means that the system is already dead; all that remains is for the corpse to recognize the fact. That act of recognition could be prompted in any number of ways. A sovereign default could trigger the formal bankruptcy of some local banks, which in turn would propel losses through the financial system, swelling as they go. Or some crooked trader working in a bank with hopelessly inadequate risk management systems could cause a collapse in confidence, a run on deposits – and bankruptcy. Or it could emerge that a big French lender has become entirely reliant on funding from the European Central Bank, causing another huge loss of confidence and the kind of panic we saw in fall 2008.

Or something else. You can't predict which melting snowflake causes the whole snowfield to disintegrate. All you can do is watch the snowfield and try to avoid the collapse.

It's also worth repeating that nothing will be left untouched by anything else. The financial system is *global*. Americans can't watch catastrophe in Europe and feel unharmed. Quite the opposite. Small things matter today as they've never mattered before. Take Greece, for example. Even in European terms, the economy of Greece is small enough to figure as little more than a rounding error, yet the fate of that small country is currently terrorizing the continent – and Europe's terror is America's fear. The same is true the other way round. The collapse of Lehman brought devastation to Europe. If a big American lender goes, the consequences for Europe will be immediate and violent. The truth is that the financial system is barely surviving as it is. It only needs one significant lender to declare bankruptcy for there to be a repeat of 2008–9 on a worldwide scale. The only difference this time is: there isn't any safety net.

People tend to listen to me politely as I say all these things, then interrupt before I'm quite done, saying, Yes, but *what will actually happen*?

Well, bankruptcies. To some extent, policymakers will try to magic up capital from nowhere by getting their central banks to roll the printing presses and conjure up money from the void. Some of that money will be used to nationalize banks and set them back on their feet – a task which, as we saw in 2008, often enough means that you start with a corpse and end with a zombie.

But it seems unlikely that, in the current climate, voters will have patience for more such nonsense. Without fiscal or monetary resources, policymakers will probably just have to let companies fail. Those failures will cause other failures – and those failures will just have to be tolerated too. The economic downturn will get worse. More companies will fail, house prices will sink. For a few years, we'll live in genuinely uncomfortable times. But bankruptcies are cleansing. GM's bankruptcy saw it bounce back with a clean balance sheet and renewed management vigor. It could start investing, start hiring, start growing.

Indeed, the reason why people press that question at me – *What will actually happen?* – is because they are still prey to a little Ponzi-ish thinking. That thinking says that bad things never really have to happen, because the government will always step in to fix things. It's the kind of thinking which says that house prices have to go up, that banks can't fail, that government promises can be relied upon, that there will always be enough money to put things right. That thinking is nuts. It comes straight from Planet Ponzi.

The simple truth is that I don't know precisely what's going to happen, or when, or how. No one knows that. All we can say is that bad things can happen, and they will, and that events in Europe and the housing market in America are equally likely to provide the initial trigger. What matters much more, of course, is what we – politically and personally – should do about all this. The question is not: When will the end days come and how will they unfold? Rather, it's the question the millenarians want to put to us: Are you Rapture-ready?

That's the issue we turn to next: first at a policy level, next at a personal one.

TWENTY-FOUR

What is to be done?

In 1902, a young Russian revolutionary – Vladimir Ilyich Ulyanov, better known to history as Vladimir Lenin – wrote a pamphlet entitled *What Is To Be Done?* In that work, Lenin argued that it was no longer enough for workers to struggle against the owners of capital. The struggle had to become politicized, made conscious. From that pamphlet, the Bolshevik movement – and later the Communist Party proper – was born.[1]

Now, I'm an American hedge fund manager, so you wouldn't expect me to share Lenin's politics and I don't. On the other hand, there are some telling parallels between his day and ours. Lenin was frustrated because the various micro-battles of Russian workers against Russian capitalists seemed to neglect the broader political story. In the same way, we've watched the world go bankrupt once (in 2008–9), and I've argued that we're about to see the same thing unfold all over again, only this time more nastily.

Naturally, recent events haven't gone unnoticed. Politicians debate deficits. Banking regulations are rejigged. Bonus payments provoke annoyance and stern op-eds in the major newspapers. But there's a weird disproportion between the scale of the wreckage on the one hand (vast, gargantuan, the biggest in world history) and the scale of response on the other (timid, piecemeal, ineffectual).

This book has been two things. It's been an exercise in financial mathematics and contingency and scenario planning: looking round the world, country by country and sector by sector, and totting up the likely scale of damage coming our way. That's a dry exercise, a little technical at times, but nevertheless worth doing – particularly when, at the end of your labors, you notice that the world is about to end. But this book is also a call to arms, a summons to political action. It's my own (American, hedge fund) version of Lenin's pamphlet. And the central message is the same. It's time to end the tinkering. It's time to look up from those various important micro-battles and attend to the big picture, to challenge the culture, to hurl out one whole generation of politicians and the assumptions which they and we have come to accept. Time also to challenge Wall Street's way of doing business, to reject it as unethical – to name it as morally and financially bankrupt. Naturally, there are a host of individual changes to make: reforms to banking rules, changes to government accounts, and the like. But none of that matters as much as the headlines. And the headlines are simple. We need honesty in government, honesty on Wall Street, and honesty in the media. And transparency. And regulations that bite. And accountability that's visible.

Voters and taxpayers have to understand the issues so they can insist on the necessary changes. If politicians try to sneak on to Planet Ponzi again by the back door, they need to be thrown so far out of office they splash down somewhere in the south Pacific. If bankers try to boost returns by selling worthless assets for phony profits, they need to be fired, and probably prosecuted, and ideally have past bonus payments clawed back. And although this sounds revolutionary, we should remember that Planet Ponzi is only three decades old. For most of American history – for most of British, or German, or Japanese history, if it comes to that – Planet Ponzi had no traction. Governments turned to debt in time of war; and not itty-bitty wars but real life-or-death, existential struggles. Everything else was financed out of current income, while debt was steadily and relentlessly paid down. Countries, such as Sweden, that have pursued that logic with calm resolution find themselves with no net government debt at all. They are countries who have paid off their mortgages, who have savings in the bank, who could face any future disaster with brimming resources and calm confidence.

Likewise, there is nothing inherently evil in the financial sector. For most of recorded history, bankers did what they were meant to do. Banks accepted deposits and lent money. Investment banks sold securities and made markets for bonds and equities. Those things had their place in a complex, mixed economy. Those involved earned a little money for themselves. They added a little to national welfare. Everybody was better off.

Then, sometime around 1980, things changed. The culture changed. Wall Street became a place where Salomon Brothers, the leading firm of its day, could cheat the US government on a colossal scale. It became a place where awful subprime securities were sold by salesmen who knew these things were awful – and nobody went to jail. It became a place, indeed, that could bankrupt the entire world's banking system – yet still, mesmerizingly, astonishingly, inexplicably, nobody has gone to jail. Indeed, the very same people who did these things are gazillionaires. They made their money by bankrupting the planet and we've let them keep it, all umpteen gazillions of it.

It wasn't always like this. Wall Streeters always had fancy jobs that paid more money than people earned elsewhere and which were imperfectly understood by those outside the financial world, but those disparities weren't utterly out of line with other inequalities. Lawyers also had abstruse jobs with big pay packets. So did ad execs and heart surgeons. It's only recently that the lawyers and the admen and the surgeons came to look like poor country cousins compared with the plutocrats of Wall Street.

So change is necessary; and change is possible. The question we're left with is: what change? We start with government.

Change in government

The first thing government needs – the main thing, the central issue – is honesty.

The US government likes to draw attention to its 'debt held by the public' figure, which stands at around $10 trillion. And the figure is fine, as far as it goes – except that's not very far. There's all the other stuff we looked at. Debt held by the government. State pension liabilities. Fannie Mae and Freddie Mac. The FDIC. Medicare liabilities. Social security liabilities. Financial guarantees and other contingencies. A whole plateful of extras which cumulates to something like $80 trillion, if you believe the government, or $200 trillion, if you believe Laurence Kotlikoff.

These confusions are wholly unnecessary. The government should publish audited accounts, every single year, that show *all* the government's assets on the left-hand side of the balance sheet and *all* the government's liabilities on the right. That's how it works everywhere in the private sector. That's what the British government has started to do. That's what any organization with complex finances needs to do in order to understand its own financial position. Every government in the world should do the same. There are no excuses for doing anything else, no excuses for not doing it *now*.

Second, the whole analysis of government budgets and deficits needs to be torn from the hands of politicians. Although the Congressional Budget Office is notionally independent, that independence is tightly constrained. If a law says that certain tax cuts are due to expire, the CBO is obliged to draw up projections on that basis, even though everyone on the Hill and elsewhere knows that the cuts are likely to endure indefinitely. So those rules need to go. The CBO, or some successor entity, needs to have real independence and a substantially enhanced budget. It needs to create projections that reflect the private sector consensus – and 'worst case' projections that reflect what happens if things go wrong. It needs to have enough resources to commission its own original investigations. It needs the authority to determine what it'll investigate, and how, and when. And it needs to issue regular bulletins that announce a 'fiscal gap computation' of the sort pioneered by Laurence Kotlikoff. That type of computation is the only way of crunching the numbers that can't be manipulated, because it considers all liabilities, not just debt obligations. That one innovation would force a huge and positive change in our political climate. It would provide a non-negotiable baseline metric for fiscal conservatism. Under a sound government, the fiscal gap would close. No ifs, no buts, no opportunity for manipulating the system. Under a George W. Bush or a Barack Obama, that computation would show an unmistakably widening gap – in public, for all to see.

Third, this policy of honesty needs to be driven into every corner of government. States need to produce honest assessments of their liabilities. Accounts need to be drawn up, audited, and published. Where there are enormous holes, state governors and legislators need to be held to account. The same goes for campaign finance. The current US legislation on 'campaign limits' imposes no real limits whatsoever. Campaign spending needs to be properly transparent, subject to rules that have bite – and rules that are enforced.

If honesty is the first requirement, action is the second. Costs and revenues need to be brought into alignment. On the tax side, there needs to be a massacre of exemptions. All existing loopholes need to be closed and a fair, simple, and balanced system introduced. Tax rates can stay where they are, or even fall, but taxation should be there to make money for the country, not for tax lawyers. At the moment, too many companies and individuals are escaping their fair contributions to the nation's coffers. At a time of budget deficits, there's nothing conservative about maintaining exemptions.

Likewise, everyone knows there is a fundamental problem with the cost of US health care, yet nobody makes any serious attempt to fix it. That inertia simply has to end. American businesses can't sustain the cost of looking after their employees. The uncertainty surrounding future healthcare costs is a huge disincentive to invest and hire, particularly for the smaller and medium-sized companies we depend on for growth. Nor can the government any longer sustain the cost of Medicare. Individuals are being ripped off by a bureaucratic system that charges huge prices to deliver unacceptably poor care. I'm not an expert on the health industry. I don't pretend to offer a specific solution. But no country in the world matches American health spending and nearly all first world countries have significantly better health outcomes, so it's pretty obvious that things can be improved. It really comes down to a problem in business management: how to re-engineer the system to deliver more and cost less. That means looking at the plumbing and fixing it. It also means facing down the health-insurance cartel and their highly paid lobbyists, who will do all they can to resist change.

Needless to say, any such re-engineering won't *feel* good. It will be attacked not only by the vested interests of the insurance and health bureaucracy, but also by politicians seeking lobbyists' dollars and votes. Those politicians will want to pose as protectors of the ordinary American, yet they'll be no such thing. Ordinary Americans have not been protected by the politics of Planet Ponzi. They've been destroyed. Their living standards have stagnated, their homes and savings have lost value, their jobs have been lost or become precarious, their kids' prospects have deteriorated, their banks have become unsound, their government is bumping up against the limits of its creditworthiness, their currency is being debased, and foreign competitors are gaining ground, unable to believe their luck. Recall that comment of Arthur Levitt, former chairman of the SEC. He said that individuals 'never knew what hit them.' Individuals aren't even aware of the battles that they're losing, aren't aware of what's at stake, aren't aware of the cumulative damage already done and still being done.

If honesty and transparency are to become the first watchwords of government, they need to become the watchwords of voters too. A bankrupt system isn't capable of being saved. You can't cut entitlements that will never be delivered. Tough action needs tough politicians. It also needs tough voters.

The same lecture applies to social security. The long-term liabilities being generated by the system as it currently stands need to be eliminated. That means we need either to pay more or to accept a cut in entitlements – or, better still, a bit of both. Other countries have taken tough and credible action on this front; there's no reason why it can't be done in America.

As with health care, the only plausible way ahead involves some cooperation between Democrats and Republicans. We need a bipartisan commission, with real authority and proper funding, to explore reforms and make recommendations – and an administration and a Congress with the guts to enact those recommendations. No partisan sparring, just doing what needs to be done. Tough politicians backed by tough voters. That's how you create solutions.

Change in regulation

Simultaneously, Wall Street needs to be restrained. That means a new Glass–Steagall Act, redesigned for the twenty-first century. One type of bank will be the old-fashioned,

Main Street sort: the type that takes deposits, makes loans, and generally handles the business of individuals and firms. These banks should be prohibited from entering into most risky transactions. Financial weapons of mass destruction need to be strictly monitored or prohibited. Capital needs to be kept at safely high levels. Deposits would continue to be insured by a recapitalized FDIC. Supervision of these banks would need to be close, intrusive, and relentless.

Outside that firewall, however, Wall Street should be allowed to be Wall Street. Capital requirements should be increased, but for the most part the Masters of the Universe should be left to play with their toys. With one proviso, however. The new banking regulations should explicitly prohibit government assistance for the industry. Bailouts should be made slightly more illegal than dealing crack cocaine. If a firm gets into trouble – it dies. Its shareholders should be wiped out. Its junior creditors would take their hit. If necessary, the pain would reach all the way up to senior creditors.

As a matter of fact, I'd like to see a rule whereby anyone who has earned more than, say, five million bucks from a firm would have their personal assets placed at risk if the firm failed due to their incompetence, or following losses incurred when they were at the helm. That way, you wouldn't have to face the sight of multimillionaire bosses walking away intact from the wreckage of their failed firms. You wouldn't want to make them destitute – but if you left them with half a million bucks or so in personal assets, they'd still be vastly richer than most Americans. They could buy a nice-looking bungalow someplace not too expensive – I'm thinking Detroit, Baltimore, Oakland, Flint – then take a nice productive job that contributed something to society:

pizza-deliverer, mailman, roofer, nurse. We'd all be winners.

There's a further implication of these changes. Bankruptcies for financial firms in the US and elsewhere haven't worked because the current court process is way too slow. In most industries, that hasn't been a problem. Airlines have sailed the skies, GM's factories continued to bash out SUVs, Enron's pipelines continued to pump gas, all while the parent companies were dragging their weary way through bankruptcy proceedings. Banks aren't like that, however. Their businesses depend on trust, and if trust dies – as it can in the space of a weekend – the business has died too. In aerodynamics, you say that a plane stalls if its airspeed falls below the minimum necessary to generate lift. At that point, you no longer have a plane; you have a chunk of metal falling out of the sky. It's the same deal with banks. The second they hit stall-speed, they're no longer banks at all; just a pile of financial obligations and some fancy real estate.

There's only one way to solve this problem and that's via the 'living will': effectively, a prepack bankruptcy plan which can be triggered on Friday and completed by Sunday. Naturally, if you move at that speed, there are legal niceties which are going to be trampled underfoot. That's too bad. Those legal niceties benefit lawyers and accountants and absolutely nobody else. Fast, decisive bankruptcies are essential to a well-functioning financial system. That also means that no firm will ever again be 'too big to fail.' If a firm fails, it fails. Too big to fail is too big to exist. Creditors who lent their money to a failing firm will get the most appropriate possible reminder about why credit analysis matters. And in the meantime, taxpayers will be able to watch the whole drama unfolding on the weekend news, knowing that they themselves won't contribute a single dime.

These rules will accomplish much of what is needed, but financial markets are complex enough – and fast-changing enough – that more detailed regulation will always be needed. The basic architecture of the regulators themselves is probably fine as it stands. What doesn't work, however, is the basic structural weakness of the system, which pits underpaid, under-resourced regulators against hugely wealthy firms replete with thousands of smart people and expensive lawyers, constantly seeking ways to play the system. And there's another twist to this imbalance. Ideally, you'd think that regulators and legislators would be natural allies: working together for the common good. In practice, however, regulators are so easily bought by the money, glamour, and influence of Wall Street, the watchdogs continually find themselves neutered by their masters.

There's no good solution to that problem, but there is perhaps an acceptable one. Regulators need to have their budgets trebled or quintupled. (Wall Street should pay those costs, one way or another.) The pay of senior staff should be trebled or quintupled. That wouldn't make it competitive with Wall Street, but it would make the contrasts less glaring. In exchange, regulators would need to accept that, once they had reached a certain level of seniority, a return to Wall Street would be prohibited for ten years. The revolving door would be locked shut.

In addition, regulators should be given much greater discretionary powers. Congress could lay out the broad principles by which Wall Street should be regulated, but regulators should be left to determine the detail by themselves. That wouldn't stop Wall Street lobbying like crazy every time regulation took an unwelcome turn, but it would place a substantial obstacle in the path of that lobbying effort.

And finally, regulation should come with teeth. It's true that the SEC and others have become much better at seeking, and securing, huge fines when rules are infringed, yet there's a kind of phony quality to those punishments. Who on the management team actually suffers? Who loses their job, who suffers financially, who goes to jail? The answer, almost always, is nobody at all. When a specific individual is forced to make a payment, the size of that payment is pitifully small. So, for example, the SEC brought aggressive action against Citigroup, alleging that the bank had failed properly to disclose some $40 billion of subprime assets on its balance sheet. A billion dollars is, as I've had cause to mention before, a lot of money. Forty billion dollars is a vast amount of money: a sum that the average American household would take 800,000 years to earn, a period roughly four times as long as the human race has been in existence. Citi settled that action at a cost of $75 million, an amount that inflicted some injury on its shareholders, but had only the most minimal of impacts on those who caused the damage. In addition, the company's chief financial officer for the period in question agreed to pay $100,000, without admission of wrongdoing. A hundred thousand bucks would take the average American household two years to generate, but for Gary Crittenden, the CFO in question, who wasn't an average American and whose household earned $10 million a year – before taking account of bonuses, pension contributions, and the like – a hundred thousand bucks was equivalent to about three days' pay. *That* was his penalty.[2]

Effective immunity of this kind simply has to go. If a firm commits a great wrong, its management must suffer proportionately. Its members need to be hit in the pocketbook and, if necessary, denied their liberty. It's crazy that we live in a world where poor, badly educated kids get incarcerated for relatively minor crimes against property, but Masters of the Universe are glossily untouched, no matter how grave their financial misdemeanors. Indeed, I'd like to propose that future enforcement actions are based on the Feierstein Scale. For every $1 million that a firm steals or conceals or mis-sells or misrepresents, it should pay a $1 million fine and someone from that firm should have to spend a year in jail. That's soft-hearted of me, I know: ordinary Americans who commit property crimes can generally expect much fiercer punishment. But that's me all over. Soft-hearted Mitch, all gooey on the inside.

One last word too, an important one. Anyone who deals with Wall Street – who trades foreign exchange, bonds, stocks, commodities, derivatives, or ETFs, or who buys M&A or due diligence advice, anything at all – needs to become a tougher, nastier customer. It's astonishingly rare for customers to drive a hard bargain with the major firms. To haggle on price and to go on haggling till the terms improve. A huge part of the reason why Wall Street makes the excessive profits it does is that its customers are somehow cowed from beating relentlessly down on the terms they're offered. I've seen large companies, famed for their ability to wring the best possible prices from their suppliers, go all wobbly-kneed when it comes to Wall Street. That's crazy. My own firm, Glacier Environmental, has a consultancy arm through which we offer to help clients negotiate terms with Wall Street. We don't charge a single

penny in fees, just take a share of what they save. It's easy for
me to make that promise because I know that we'll be able
to achieve excellent savings with every client we work
with.* A price-competitive Wall Street would be a leaner,
more efficient one.

❖

I have worked in the financial markets for thirty years now
and have been fortunate – or unfortunate? – enough to have
watched the evolution of Planet Ponzi from a front-row seat.
I have likewise been in a position to see its implosion in
every awful, lingering, destructive detail. So I'll close this
chapter by repeating what I said at the start. Change is possible. The last thirty years have been exceptional in American
history. The country managed for two hundred years with
finances that were, by and large, prudently managed, and a
financial system which, by and large, did what it was meant
to do. Other countries have been the same. Britain's history
of public finance is almost a hundred years longer than
America's and it too did fine for three hundred years.

Naturally, times change – but changing times don't
mean you have to change your principles. Even now, there
are countries that manage to handle their affairs – to educate
their kids, provide health care to their sick, pay pensions to
their elderly – without creating some tottering Ponzi scheme
of debt. The British government is seeking to creep back to
sound finances and sound banking right now. These things
are possible today. They're possible in America. Possible in
Italy, Spain, and France. And they need to happen.

* And if you happen to run a large firm or a middling-sized government, give me a call. I'll buy you lunch. We've got plenty to talk about.

TWENTY-FIVE

Gold, wheat, and shotgun shells

WHETHER OR NOT politicians will grapple in a timely way with the 'to do' list in the previous chapter is a moot point. Personally I doubt it. But whether they do or not, the next few years are going to be rocky, and you need to protect yourself and your family from the fallout. This chapter, therefore, contains your own personal 'to do' list. I've taken a safety first approach, because most people will want to ensure their safety before they start to consider more extravagant plays on the markets, but each investor will need to find their own balance. Do note, however, that my advice has, of necessity, to be somewhat generic. In part, that's because I'm a regulated investment professional and there are rules around what I can and can't say to individuals. I am very happy to share my own investment philosophy and to share my thoughts on how I expect to manage my own portfolio, but these comments are intended to stimulate thought and provoke discussion, not to act as personalized investment advice.

Also, you need to be aware that I'm writing this book a while before it will be published. I can't know the future state of the markets, nor do I know the status of your own portfolio, what your investment goals are, or what your investment horizon may be. Those things are of crucial importance in shaping your strategy and you cannot neglect them. You *must* figure these things out carefully for yourself before taking action. Indeed, unless you are already a sophisticated investor, I would urge you to take good, professional, and impartial advice before committing to any major decision. Such advice can be invaluable.

And in that spirit, I'll share with you two stories that encapsulate my own philosophy – and, I'm sure, the philosophy of any investor who has made money over the long term. Back in the late 1990s, when the NASDAQ was trading around 5000, I remember standing on the first tee of the Hills Course at Jupiter Hills Golf Club. There were three of us present that day. Myself, an investment banking friend of mine, and someone else who was joining us for that round of golf. He started talking about Yahoo's incredible stock market ascent from trading at a few bucks a share to several hundred dollars per share. 'All you Wall Street guys must have made a fortune on that,' he said. My friend smiled and shook his head. 'Nope. I do not own any Yahoo.' I said the same, adding that I never invested in things I didn't understand. A company with no earnings whose stock price rises like a spaceship blasting off for Mars was not a company I wanted any part of. Sure enough, that spaceship plunged back into the atmosphere in the course of the year that followed that conversation, leaving precious few survivors.

On another occasion, at another golf club on Eastern Long Island, a few of the members were discussing their investments with Bernie Madoff. One of the group said to me: 'You work on Wall Street. What do you think of this?' I had a listen and was interested enough to dig into Madoff's fund in a little more detail. I was baffled. I didn't get it. So I called the guy back and said, 'Sorry, I'm just not sure how Madoff operates and if I don't understand it, I don't invest.' I didn't think Madoff was a crook, I just didn't know how he made his money. That was enough to keep me away from what *looked* like a gold mine but *was* a beartrap. If you don't understand something, don't invest in it. It's a rule that has protected me for thirty years. It's a rule I urge you to follow yourself.

That said, the first and biggest moral of this book is that you need to throw out all the assumptions you'll have lived with to this point. Sovereign debt is no longer so safe you don't have to think about it. (Truth is, it never was.) Banks might fail, including large ones. Money market funds may 'break the buck' – that is, lose money. Equally, you need to shed some of your Ponzi-ish optimism. House prices have fallen, but they may fall further. Stock market prices have fallen, but they may fall further. Some bond prices have already collapsed, but they could collapse further. The dollar has collapsed against the yen (falling by a third, from $1 = ¥120 in 2007 to less than ¥80 at the time of writing). It could fall further. We may, indeed, be entering a period where the average investor will struggle to ensure that their money keeps pace with inflation. With inflation high, bond yields low, and equities suffering, there is no certainty that you can safely store your money in any way that will even preserve its value, let alone increase it. I'm sorry to say that nothing you assumed in the past should be considered certain knowledge today. Times have changed.

The moral that follows immediately from this one is that

you need to rethink what it means to keep your money safe. Personally, if safety were my priority, I'd play it very safe. I'd mostly avoid having money on deposit at banks, but to the extent I kept my money there, I would make sure that I held no account exceeding the FDIC insurance limits, using multiple bank accounts if necessary. Capital preservation needs to be your mantra.

I'd also check the creditworthiness of the banks I was investing in. Even if your deposits are government-insured, you don't want to go through the pain of watching your bank fold, particularly as the government insurance agencies may get overwhelmed at some point, in which case the settlement of claims may become slow and uncertain. It's easy enough to check credit ratings: you can simply go online. You'll need to register separately with the S&P, Moody's, and Fitch websites to gain direct access to their ratings, but registration is free, it takes just a few moments, and we are talking about your life savings here. It's worth a few moments. You also need to be very careful about taking internet shortcuts: looking at lists of credit ratings compiled by other internet sites. I've just looked at one list which showed ratings as much as twenty-seven months out of date and chock-full of dead links. Given how fast things are moving, you have to make absolutely certain you get the most up-to-date possible information, and that means going direct to the agencies themselves. And not just one; you need to check all of them, because a downgrade by one agency is likely to be followed by one or both of the others before too many months are out.

Do also be careful that you check the *right* credit rating. Any large bank will have numerous debt-issuing subsidiaries, each of which has its own specific credit ratings. If you are considering placing some savings in a particular bank, make sure you know which legal entity is going to be taking care of your money and check the ratings of that specific entity. If you're unsure, call the bank and ask. (You should also confirm the government insurance limits that apply to your intended account.) Don't be embarrassed to ask these things. It's your money. You have every right to look after it. Indeed, I'd advocate getting key information in writing and in language that you understand. In terms of what credit rating you should find acceptable – well, it's hard to say. Personally, I'd want to see ratings as close to that AAA gold standard as possible, but these days that gold standard is essentially unattainable. I'd say that AA- should be the lowest rating worth accepting, perhaps A+ if you have some strong reason for choosing a particular bank.

Under no circumstances accept a rating of BBB or below, *especially* if the bank in question is offering you a wonderful interest rate. In the current climate, a wonderful interest rate is a beacon, flashing danger: a strong signal that the bank is encountering funding problems and is scrabbling cash any place it can. Don't let that bank scrabble yours.

Finally – because I'm cautious and because I don't choose to put too much trust in the ratings agencies – I'd advise that you run a quick check on what the market at large thinks of the bank you've selected. Go to an online source such as Google Finance and look up your selected bank. For example, at the time of writing, the Royal Bank of Scotland – a very large British lender – enjoys credit ratings of AA- (Fitch), A (S&P), and A1 (Moody's).[1] That S&P rating should sound a note of alarm, I trust, but perhaps you feel reassured by Fitch's vote of confidence. So go over to Google Finance, or whatever other financial website you prefer, and enter the name of the bank, in this case RBS. You'll get a view of the stock price and various news stories, but you should also come across a section called 'Key stats and ratios' or something similar. Click through to that information and look for a ratio called 'price to book,' or something similar.* That ratio measures the value the stock market places on the firm as compared with the value that shows up in the company accounts. In happier times, you'd expect that ratio to be greater than 1.00 – that is, the bank should be creating value, not destroying it. In these times, however, it's rare to find any bank in that position, so I can't advise you to seek out such banks, much as I'd like to. Nevertheless, you should treat any bank with a price to book ratio of less than 0.60 as being under siege, any bank with a price to book ratio of less than 0.40 as in real trouble. The price to book ratio for RBS is currently 0.17 and there are rumors afoot of another possible government bailout.[2]

All this may sound like a lot of trouble: but if I'm even half right about the true financial status of the world's banks, then we are heading for one heck of a banking crisis and you would be insane not to spend an hour or so doing your homework. It could easily be the single most profitable hour you spend in your entire life. Get serious about it: it's your family's wealth at stake.

That, then, is one really strong option. You parcel your money out across several banks, choosing only the strongest, and making sure that no individual account exceeds the

---

* Google sources its data from Thomson Reuters, which is one reason I recommend it. Thomson Reuters is a highly trustworthy source, as is Bloomberg. If the data you're looking at comes from anyone else, just make sure you can rely on it.

relevant government insurance limit. If you do that, you'll be fine. Or at least, if you do all that and you're not fine, the world will be so bombed out that you should probably just buy some canned food and some shotgun shells and take yourself off to a cave until the world has found its sanity again. And it will. Just take plenty of food.

Another option – for readers in America, Canada, Britain, Germany, the Netherlands, and Scandinavia – is to buy government bonds. Personally, I'd avoid buying longer-term government bonds: the ten- or thirty-year maturities. The United States government is not about to default on its debt today (aside from, maybe, a technical default the next time our politicians behave like idiots). The same goes for the other countries on that list. All the same, the future is unknowable and we live at a time of unprecedented turmoil. That simple fact argues in favor of caution. Why commit yourself to a ten-year loan to a government, when you could lend for just a year, or even less? If everything looks fine in a year, you can reinvest your money without difficulty. If things look worse, you have an opportunity to reconsider your options.

As soon as we start to step away from these super-safe options, risks multiply; but so too do your chances of making some money. Investment in currency is speculative and can incur losses. The same goes for everything else that we're about to look at. Buyer beware!

Let's start by thinking about currency movements. Over the last five years, the value of the dollar has declined sharply against the yen. Over the same period, the value of the pound sterling has declined against the euro. The scale of these movements often dwarfs any interest rate differentials. (That is, you normally earn a higher rate of interest in the currency that's depreciating; the higher interest rates don't necessarily make up for the depreciation, however.) As a rough guide, I'd expect currency movements to become one of the major investment themes of the next few years. A currency is likely to decline if its government operates with unsound finances, if its central bank is printing money like crazy, if it has a large and vulnerable banking system, if it has a housing market that is declining from bubble-era levels, and if it is closely connected with countries that are in a similarly bad way. That, in effect, is the position of the United States and most other countries we've spoken about in this book. A currency is likely to appreciate in value if its government operates sound finances and sound money; if it has a strong economy with good growth prospects, a strong and stable housing market, and perhaps especially if it has abundant natural resources. Those things are not, alas, true of very many countries today, but exceptions do exist: Canada and the Scandinavian states, for example.

A natural diversification for American investors would be to switch some US dollar assets into Canadian dollars. North of the border, you have a government with sound money, untroubled banks, and huge natural resources. That's a wonderful recipe for a steadily appreciating currency. The Australian and New Zealand dollars look attractive for similar reasons. Hong Kong dollars and the Brazilian *real* also offer strong possibilities for currency gains.

Germany has a strong economy, but has tied itself into the euro. As a result, anyone investing in German government bonds is likely to get the worst of both worlds – low bond yields and a declining currency. It's certainly not an investment I'd choose to make at the moment.

Climbing upwards on the ladder of risk, we get to gold. I *like* gold. My two favorite objects at the moment are my $100 trillion Zimbabwean banknote and a gold Krugerrand – the coin being worth vastly more than the note. The underlying economic reality is that you can trash a currency simply by printing too much of it. It's a heck of a lot harder for a central bank to destroy the value of gold. If you review the graphs presented in chapter 13, 'A brief flash of reality,' you'll see why I like it so much. In times of grotesque debt accumulation and asset destruction, gold is the one investment buddy you can really trust. I have plenty of gold in my current portfolio and I can't see that changing while conditions remain as uncertain as they are.

Having said that, the price of gold isn't anchored by interest rates or dividend payments, or any of the other things which normally anchor the price of a security or physical commodity. That makes the gold price more than normally susceptible to swings of sentiment. So if you like gold, then buy carefully. Buy on the dips. Don't get suckered into buying when gold is on one of its periodic upsurges. And don't, of course, be stupid enough to plunge *all* your assets into gold. That's not responsible investing, no matter what asset you're investing in.

There are other physical commodities, however, which have an equally compelling attraction. Commodities such as wheat, rice, oil, copper, and other metals are supported by the most remorseless of all current trends: a swelling world population and powerful growth in the emerging market giants. These commodities offer huge potential for profit – but you do need to invest with caution. You need to research an opportunity hard before you invest, and be prepared to walk away if the prices turn against you. You do need to think strategically as an investor, but you can't afford to neglect tactics. In the long term, these are markets with wonderful upside potential; but a great opportunity at the wrong price is a deal you need to turn down.

By this point on our ladder of risk, we're a heck of a lot higher than we were when we started. The truth is that ordinary investors should avoid futures, options, and other complexities, but I do believe that all investors should have direct exposure to physical commodities. The best way to do this is via a managed fund (such as a mutual fund) which invests directly in such things on your behalf. There are ETFs that theoretically offer the same thing, but I personally would avoid them. Commodities are traditionally seen as high risk and indeed they do bring some volatility into a portfolio. I personally regard them as a lower-risk long-term investment, in the sense that a rising world population and strong growth in the emerging markets will over time force the price of physical commodities (including food) ever higher, especially as currency values erode due to debasement, inflation, and excessive debt (which ultimately will have to be monetized).

If you fancy treading still higher on the risk–reward ladder, there are additional steps which may appeal to a minority of confident investors. If you're inclined to explore these upper steps, go ahead and do so – but always bearing in mind that as the opportunity for reward increases, so the risk of loss increases too. You need to evaluate your investments against your own risk tolerance – very low, low, medium, high, or very high. In general, younger folk can afford to invest a small proportion of their assets in well-researched medium- to high-risk opportunities; but no matter who you are, if you are attracted to high-risk opportunities, make sure you never invest money you can't afford to lose.

I'd say there will be three major themes between now and the end of 2013, or thereabouts. The first will be acute trouble in the eurozone. Thus far, the damage done to the currency itself has been limited. The real damage has been to various specific risks within the currency zone, notably certain sovereign bond markets and the market for bank debt. In time, I'm confident that the region's debt problems will cause the currency itself problems as investors rush to get out of the euro. They will most likely buy US dollars, the traditional safe haven, as they exit. In the longer run, however, the debt problems, inflation, and monetary expansion in the US are going to accumulate to a point where that currency no longer feels safe either. So while I wouldn't want to be in the dollar for the long term, I personally am short the euro and long the US dollar for the time being. I'd expect to expand my position whenever attractive opportunities arise. If you don't know what shorting means, and if you're not sure how you'd go about shorting a currency – well, you may not be sufficiently expert to dabble in these things. The golden rule of investing is never to invest in an opportunity where you don't fully understand the full range of risks and the full range of possible outcomes.

The second major theme will be problems in the banking sector. As it happens, for technical reasons, most bank stocks are at such low levels today that there is no great upside in shorting them. Nevertheless, if there is any sustained rally in the banking sector and if that rally is not firmly based on solid capital increases and honest accounting for losses, I'll be looking to short the stock of individual banks. There is potentially a huge amount of money to be made here, but it's an area where you need some real depth of expertise if you're not to be burned.

Finally, the equity market is likely to go through a period of sustained volatility. On the one hand, investors are still stuck in Ponzi-ish thinking. They've spent twenty or thirty years relying on policymakers to support the markets whenever those markets have hit a roadblock. Investors *want* to believe that the current efforts of central banks and political leaders will make a difference, and we've already seen some huge (and unrealistic) 'relief rallies' at various stages since 2008. It still amazes me how gullible certain investors can be. Markets are meant to act according to reason and evidence, yet when a central banker comes out like a cheerleader, claiming that everything is getting better, the markets often trade up massively without any solid reason to do so. Experience shows that the only solid improvement will come from quantifiable deleveraging and solidly based growth, yet markets frequently ignore that knowledge in a lather of forgetting and false hope.

At the same time, professional investors aren't completely dumb, and when the cold, hard evidence points to a mounting crisis in both the financial markets and the real economy, the market will react. Emotions sway a market, but facts will end up determining it.

Those conflicting feelings will make for a turbulent ride in the equity markets. If you're adept at timing your entry and exit from the market, you should be able to make plenty of cash by riding the relief wave up and selling again for the surge down. The relief rally may well be substantial and it may well be prolonged, but that doesn't mean it's sustainable. Indeed, the current trading pattern in the markets –

abrupt, exaggerated movements in both directions – strongly suggests an unhealthy trading pattern and one where the underlying demand is weak rather than steady.

Because these things move so fast, I'll maintain a running update via my blog (planetponzi.com), but you can do a lot simply by making sure you have the right mindset to profit from markets in this state. The fundamental requirement for successful investing is that you keep a rigorous eye on the fundamentals, while also staying in touch with the market mood. In particular, you need to be aware that many individual investors end up feeling pressured by both the upswing and the downswing. At the top of the market, you'll read a lot of material in the mainstream media about the glorious prospects for equities, the strong upsurge, the great growth prospects, and so forth. Talking heads – usually with an undeclared buy-side interest – will try to talk the markets up. Inevitably, you may feel you need to be in the market to benefit from all these things. But remember that professional investors are always ahead of you. The mood reflected in the mainstream media is already dated, and by this point professional investors will be thinking about taking profits and protecting against a fall. If you do invest then, you risk finding that you've bought in at the very top of the market.

Likewise, when the market is low, it'll be that way because of a torrent of bad news, media bias, and grim prognostications for the future. You may well feel, if you do hold equities, that you were dumb for not selling them before but that you should at least cut your losses by getting out when you can. Again, that's precisely the wrong way to think. Just as you need to sell when the market mood is euphoric, you need to buy when the market mood is dire. You also need to be realistic about your own limitations. Investing your money can be scary. The pressure of negative headlines can be overwhelming and nudge you into making poor financial choices. If you do want to invest your money actively, you need to be confident that you have the right emotional makeup to do so calmly and rationally – even when the markets around you are at their most volatile and the news headlines are at their most frightening. But for those who do have the confidence to do this, the opportunities for profit will be very considerable. And as I say, do watch the website, as we'll maintain a running commentary on events there.

A final word about what *not* to invest in. You should certainly treat the entire area of exchange traded funds (ETFs) with suspicion. There are some very good and reliable ETFs, but there are far too many very poor ones. The simple test is only to invest in something you completely understand and feel comfortable with. If you are faced with a 1,000-page prospectus packed with legal terms that you don't understand, you should avoid the damn thing. That's not you being stupid, it's you being smart.

For the same reason, if an opportunity looks too good to be true – a great bank interest rate, some kind of structured product with apparently excellent returns – it is too good to be true. In successful investing, plain vanilla is the best flavor, for almost everybody, for almost all the time. And in times of uncertainty, you should prioritize safety and the preservation of capital above everything else. That's prudent investing. It's how you'll create and preserve your wealth.

TWENTY-SIX

Mr Smith goes to Planet Ponzi

THIS BOOK HAS NOT been optimistic in tone, but I remain an optimist. Not in the short term, admittedly – the short term is going to be horrendous – but in the longer term.

The simple fact is that there is only one proven model for long-term wealth creation. That model requires free markets, competition, democracy, free speech, an openness to trade, innovation, entrepreneurship, and a lot of hard work. It's a model based on enterprise and on calling authority to account. Those things aren't merely embedded in American DNA, they pretty much *are* American DNA. Although the economic model looks a little different in Europe and Japan – a little more government intervention, a little less entrepreneurship – the same basic recipe has fueled a dramatic increase in living standards right across the Western world. The froth created by Planet Ponzi is merely the foam on top of the wave – temporary, dazzling, but fundamentally irrelevant. The collapse of Planet Ponzi will simply restore our focus on the things that have mattered the most all along: strong companies competing fiercely.

What's more, countries can beat even the nastiest of

financial crises. Sweden did so during the 1990s. Britain is taking some of the right steps (albeit under far less propitious circumstances) today. The Latin American debt crisis of the 1980s and the Asian and Russian financial crises of the late 1990s also passed away, leaving relatively little trace behind.

And once a crisis is fixed, it doesn't need to recur. Sweden again is something of a poster-child for sound economic management, but so too is Canada. Australia (except for its crazy property market) is also well managed. So is New Zealand. Germany, though it's surrounded by profligacy and economic turbulence, nevertheless pumps out strong economic results with remarkable consistency.

So these things are possible. In a way, it's a mistake to get over-focused on all the bad things that have happened over the past few years. Although it's absolutely essential to understand those mistakes and their origins, it's easy to end up believing that Ponzi-ish thinking is so ingrained in our culture as to be effectively unavoidable. And that's simply not true. Planet Ponzi has been a twenty- or thirty-year aberration. The damage from the period of financial realignment that will follow its collapse will be severe enough to teach a lesson to everyone: politicians, regulators, and – most important of all – taxpayers and voters. If voters refuse to accept fiscally incontinent government, we will never again have fiscally incontinent government. If voters refuse government-by-lobbyist, we will have government-by-voters instead. If voters refuse to accept a Wall Street of vast political influence, minimal regulatory oversight, and lethal economic impact, Wall Street too will be tamed. That's how it used to be. That's how it can be again.

Indeed, although this book has presented a large

number of uncomfortable data, I see it as a fundamentally positive book. A motivational one. Although the political and financial situation around the world is dire, the power of change lies in our hands: yours and mine. And that change is starting to happen. The Western world has seen a surge in peaceful, popular protest movements, unparalleled for a generation or more. It's perfectly true that those movements often lack coherence, but movements do. The protesters in Egypt's Tahrir Square didn't present a closely argued set of political demands, nor did they need to. They gathered to express their rage at Mubarak's rotten regime and that regime duly crumbled, to be replaced, let's hope, by something better. We need our Tahrir Squares: the rage, the protest, and, in due course, the regime change too.

What's more, all the building blocks for a revived American economy are already in place. Leave aside the financial system for a moment. The US is still the richest, most innovative, most entrepreneurial nation on earth. We have the best universities, the best scientists, the strongest companies, and lavish natural resources. These are assets that will endure far beyond any financial crisis. They are assets which, even during the supremacy of Planet Ponzi, led to the success of Microsoft, Intel, Google, Apple, Amazon, eBay, Facebook, and countless others – to name only companies from a single economic sector.

And crises can be positive. Rahm Emanuel, President Obama's chief of staff, once commented: 'You never let a serious crisis go to waste. And what I mean by that is it's an opportunity to do things you think you could not do before.' He's right. The toxic political atmosphere in Washington has inhibited change for far too long. It's been impossible to secure real tax reform, real reform of Medicare or social security, a fundamental rethink of defense spending. Yet these things are essential. They've been essential for a long while, and it's taken a once-in-a-century crisis to force these issues on to the agenda. Naturally, it's not enough for these items to figure on a Washington agenda — we actually need to see change. That means legislators passing laws which their primary voters won't like. It means an administration taking actions that are right for the country, not just right for the next day's news headlines. It means voters acting wisely too: voters willing to use the opportunity brought by the elections of 2012 to enforce changes of the right sort.

The same goes for Wall Street. It was always going to be impossible to force through a fundamental reform of investment banking while those banks appeared to be highly successful at creating wealth. So it's entirely positive that circumstances have altered so abruptly. As banks tremble again on the verge of collapse, and as ordinary voters can see what wreckage Wall Street has inflicted on the economy, change becomes not merely possible, but imperative.

The same goes for Europe. The pain currently being inflicted on southern Europe is awful, but it ought to have the effect of compressing into a few violent years the economic reforms that should have been put in place over the past two decades or more. If the rage of people on the streets sweeps out one rotten set of politicians, there's no reason to think that set should not be replaced by a better, more truthful, more responsible set. Nor is there any reason why the economies of the south can't be as vibrant as those of the north. Italy, remember, had thirty extraordinary years of postwar growth, and that was despite its governments not because of them.

These things aren't idle hopes. The British government

– the same one which is slashing spending, raising taxes, and being tough with banks – is, broadly speaking, *not unpopular*. Still more bizarrely yet (to an American observer at least), the left-wing Labour opposition party isn't calling for anything so very different. The Labour leaders call for the austerity program to run a little more slowly, but even they explicitly support the need for entitlement cuts and tax increases. As a matter of fact, there isn't a single political party in the UK that does not support these things.

The Brits are a stoic sort of people, but it's not some weird ingredient in the British character which makes them willing to endure this kind of pain. It's simply that *their politicians risked being truthful*. They explained the facts and explained why the pain was necessary. That's all there was to it. That's all it would take in the United States, all it would take anywhere else in the world: truthful politicians, willing to take a risk. It's not much to ask – and as the gaudy palaces of Planet Ponzi collapse around us, it's going to be harder and harder to shy away from a return to truth-telling.

There's yet another positive aspect to all this. Our culture has become gradually poisoned by Ponzi-ish falsehoods. We've raised a generation of children to believe in a get-rich-quick culture, to believe that material success simply floats down from the sky, that it doesn't have to be earned by effort, risk-taking, and hard work. The super-materialists of Planet Ponzi – all those bankers who seemed to have a huge amount of wealth without having done anything tangible to deserve it – were terrible role models for our children, and at the same time so prominent that their example was hard to avoid. Yet as one set of role models collapses, another one endures: the older American one founded on a belief in hard work, invention, thrift, and excellence. The destruction of one culture will mean the return of the other. It can't happen too soon.

Finally, I don't believe at all in the idea that China is going to rise up and overshadow America and the Western way of life. The collapse of Planet Ponzi will be debilitating in the short term, but strengthening in the longer term: a tactical reverse that imposes a better strategy on the generals. Inevitably, of course, the Chinese economy will soon be larger than the American one. It won't be so many years before the same is true of India too. But these are dumb wins, not smart ones. In 2011, in the midst of our financial crisis, per capita GDP in the United States was $48,666. In the same year, Chinese per capita GDP stood at $4,833. The reason why the Chinese economy is going to exceed the American one has everything to do with sheer mass of population and almost nothing to do with its technological or economic sophistication.

And of course, this discussion hasn't yet mentioned the one thing that matters the most. The United States is a great democracy. China is not. The United States has unfettered freedom of speech. China does not. The United States allows anyone to do anything, talk to anyone, play with any new idea, start any company, sell any product, and pitch any service unless those things are specifically prohibited under the law. As Barack Obama's extraordinary rise to power has demonstrated, any American citizen can become President. In China, none of these things is true. Back in the 1930s, when Stalin's Great Purges were filling the Gulag, the Soviet economy grew at an astonishing pace, while the United States, stuck with the debris of its Great Depression, looked slow and creaking by comparison: but history would settle that particular contest with unarguable finality. Coercion works; autocracy works; repression, spies, informants, and secret police all work – but within limits. In another ten years or so, I reckon, China is going to reach those limits.

But enough of China and back to the home front.

For the most part, this book has presented a relentlessly negative picture. Almost wherever we've chosen to look, we've come across dumb governments, crazy spending, tax codes that make no sense, phony profits on Wall Street, bankers who get insanely rich from behavior that seems little better than fraudulent. But I'm an optimist. The disintegration of Planet Ponzi will be wrenchingly difficult, but is for the best. It'll turn America – and Americans – away from speculation, from debt addiction, from fiscal incontinence. The America that will emerge will have all the strengths we have today – the science, the companies, the innovation – but we'll join to that the rigor and solidity that used to be ours. America has an ugly present, and a glorious, prosperous, and un-Ponzi-ish future. The same can be equally true of Britain, and of Europe. The future is in our hands.

Either I'm dead right or I'm crazy.

Afterword

THE AFTERWORD TO the hardback edition of this book began thus:

> This book has been three years in the planning and almost as much in the writing. Perhaps that sounds a little dilatory, but in my defense I'd point out that I have an investment firm to manage and investors to look after. They, always, come first.
>
> In addition, though, events have nearly always run ahead of my pen. I've long known that the United States had a deficit problem, but each time I looked the problem seemed to have gotten worse. Likewise the euro. I knew the currency zone had problems which would likely prove lethal, but the scale of issues seemed to increase faster than my ability to write them down. My draft text constantly made reference to various shocking facts – only for me to find that, next time I looked, things had deteriorated further . . . When I began writing *Planet Ponzi*, I knew the book and its ideas were important. Now that I'm finishing it, I see they're essential.

I wrote those words in November 2011 and now, in August 2012, with another printer's deadline approaching, I find myself unsure of what more to say. Pretty much everything in the book has either been proved true or is in the course of coming true. Instead of writing an afterword, maybe I should just take a highlighter pen to everything I've written thus far, and add a giant note in the margin reading 'It's *like this, only more so.*' But since my publishers might not love that approach, I'll try to be a little more disciplined and update my survey in a few brief strokes.

We start with the euro crisis, currently the major headline grabber. Last year, in November, Spanish ten-year bonds yielded 5.5% on the international markets. That was already a frighteningly high rate of interest: simultaneously, a tax on the entire economy and a sign of the naked fear that stalked the bond markets. As you know, I felt back then that the Spanish story was at risk of getting much worse and that if the country's banks needed a bailout, the government did not have the funds to provide it. Sure enough, the banks demanded a monster bailout and the government was unable to come up with the cash. These problems are set to worsen. As the Spanish economy continues to buckle, the value of its real estate will fall further, thereby causing ever-larger problems for the nation's banks. As unemployment rises and tax revenues decline further, the debts mount and the economy shrinks.

There is, of course, a simple solution to the woes of the banks, namely bankruptcy. If a business fails, it should be left to fail. That's how capitalism works. Capitalism without bankruptcy is like Catholicism without hell. It's also a wonderful way to make sure that bankers remember those old virtues of prudence and risk-aversion. Nothing says *Do your homework* quite like the threat of total wipeout.

Needless to say, however, no one on Planet Ponzi gave a thought to that solution. Instead, some European money was magicked up (without consulting taxpayers, of course) and handed to the banks. Since the money wasn't a gift, but a loan, the whole debt pile just grew bigger. Bond markets were hardly pacified by that sight, so it wasn't too long before

Spanish bonds traded over 7.75%. (Indeed, if you sauntered along to your friendly neighborhood bank and asked for a loan, you might well, assuming you could provide some collateral, get a better rate than that. If so, you are more creditworthy than the Kingdom of Spain.) Interest rates of this level aren't an inconvenience: they are insupportable. I mean that in a literal, financial sense: a shrinking economy with debt fast climbing towards 100% of GDP cannot pay interest of almost 8%. A government asked to do so is essentially bankrupt. That bankruptcy may take time to play out, but it's not the time that matters, it's the destination.

I also, however, mean 'insupportable' in a looser, more emotional sense. The rate of unemployment amongst Spanish youth exceeds 50%. Just imagine how disenfranchised you would feel if you were a Spanish kid, unable to get a job, whose friends were also unable to start their careers or secure their futures – and you saw your government paying extortionate interest rates, simply with the aim of deferring the inevitable by another year. Why would you put up with that? Why should you? Why would you not, in fact, prefer to take to the city streets, with flags and placards, demanding change? Indeed, it's not even quite correct to say that the Spanish *banks* are being bailed out. The real beneficiaries are the creditors of those banks – German and French lenders, very often – who are being protected from the consequences of their own stupid decision-making. Why would any young Spaniard regard the interests of those overseas creditors as justifying the sacrifice of a generation?

The pain in Spain has grabbed the headlines, but the eurozone crisis afflicts a continent, not a nation. It will only take a bank failure or a bad economic number to put Italy (with its much greater debt load) into the spotlight again.

Italy, remember, has had four consecutive quarters of negative GDP growth. That's not a recession, it's a depression, and there's no glimmer of change visible on the horizon. Indeed, the shrinking economy leads to one inescapable conclusion: that Italy is insolvent, mathematically unable to pay its debt. The country is too large to rescue, so disaster is the only possible outcome.

France, until now, has stayed at the very margins of the crisis, but it has huge banks which are overexposed to the countries of greatest risk. It also has an old-fashioned socialist government which believes that taxing wealth-creation is a sure-fire way to avoid a fiscal crunch. Though Spain may continue to hog the headlines for a period, you shouldn't forget that there are other, larger countries in a position almost as precarious.

Meanwhile, although Germany is still regularly spoken of as though it was a fountain of infinite cash, the reality is far different. Moody's, the credit-rating agency, has placed Germany on credit watch for a possible downgrade in its AAA rating. It is, if you like, the first signal that the limits of bailout are being reached. Any more, and Germany too will start to stagger under the load. Fortunately, voters and politicians in these richer, more prudent northern countries are becoming ever more implacable in their resistance to further bailouts. For once, and in northern Europe only, politicians are getting things right.

The same cannot be said of the central bankers, who have been as culpable in this crisis as anyone. Mario Draghi, the ex-Goldman head of the ECB, recently declared that 'Within our mandate, the ECB is ready to do whatever it takes to preserve the euro. And believe me, it will be enough.' Those remarks caused a huge and (to my mind) inexplicable surge in world asset markets. The statement, implicitly, promised that the ECB would simply buy Spanish and Italian bonds without limit, printing money as needed to fund those purchases. That a supposedly sane central banker could make this promise – to support an over-indebted country in its quest to become ever more indebted, trashing an entire currency in order to do so – indicates just how deeply Ponzi-ish thinking has taken hold. Fortunately, however, the Bundesbank hasn't lost the power of reason and has, to its credit, insisted that the ECB act properly and within the law. That's banker code for saying that the ECB can't print money to buy sovereign debt, nor can it seek to achieve the same ends via some legal back-door.

In short, the European crisis is coming to a head. Greece needs another bailout and will ultimately default on its debts and exit the euro. Spain will also fail to repay its debts as scheduled. I don't know whether the rich northern countries will choose to exit the euro (Germany may exit first), or if the collapse will be forced on the southern countries first. But it doesn't matter. The euro will shortly not exist in its current configuration and Europe will be better off for its demise. Investors who lent money to governments, lazily assuming that sovereign debts will always be repaid, will receive the best of reminders to brush up on their financial history. That too is a good thing.

The next great issue to claim the world's attention will be the US's upcoming 'fiscal cliff'. That cliff arises because, on 31 December 2012, a host of income-tax cuts are due to expire and because, on 2 January 2013, a deep, automatic cut is due to be imposed on federal spending, totalling $1.2 trillion over ten years.

Now you know me well enough to realize that I want the

government to cut its deficit, so you would expect me to be strongly supportive of measures aimed at bringing taxation up to a realistic level and at cutting back on federal spending. But you have to be smart about these things. If you're speeding at 130 miles an hour on the freeway, you can't just slam on the brakes and hope for the best. Likewise, if you're a business needing to cut costs, you need to plan how and where to trim expenses so as to minimize disruption and maximize the benefits. Neither the scheduled tax cuts nor the scheduled spending limits have been constructed in that way. Quite the reverse. The spending cuts were purposely designed by Congress as a 'gun to the head', on the theory that such a threat would force partisan legislators to seek rational compromise.

No such luck. There is, even at this desperately late stage, no common plan of action, no thoughtful strategy around which Congress and the administration can cohere. The United States has never faced a more urgent peacetime challenge and our leadership – Democrat and Republican alike – are flunking it. What's worse is that they're not even trying. We get soundbites and attack ads and red meat tossed out to keep the party faithful happy, yet no action is taken on the one thing that really matters.

Indeed, it's actually worse than that. The Republican-controlled House of Representatives recently passed a bill that would have extended the Bush-era tax cuts. You might reasonably ask yourself how a party with some theoretical attachment to fiscal conservatism could pass such a bill, but leave that point aside for the moment. At least the House seemed to have noticed the approaching fiscal cliff and seemed ready to take action. But appearances deceive. The House knew perfectly well that the bill it had passed would stand no chance of approval in the Democrat-controlled

Senate. So, far from making a real attempt to solve a crucial problem, the House is deliberately spending crucial legislative and debating time on what it knows to be a pointless distraction: a blame game, nothing more.

I've said some harsh things in this book about the governments of Italy and Japan and Greece. The sad truth is, however, that the US government is as bad, or almost as bad, as these. The federal government has taken on commitments that amount to many times the size of US GDP. Because we cannot meet those commitments under any realistic future scenario, the government will be forced to default, either by breaking its promises to pensioners and those needing health care, or by runaway inflation, or both. Most likely both.

Lest you think I exaggerate, let me invite you to consider the 'super-committee' charged by the US Congress with finding $1.2 trillion worth of expenditure savings over ten years. A trillion dollars is a lot of money, even over ten years, but the annual amount still represents just 0.6% of American GDP, a minuscule fraction of the savings that are actually needed to fix the deficit.

In effect then, the so-called super-committee was there to do a rather ordinary job: to find the kind of cost and revenue improvements that any competent business manager would perform as an ordinary part of his or her regular duties. No manager I know would regard a cost saving or revenue enhancement of 0.6% of sales as being more than a routine operational issue. Something you fix, then move on from. Yet those super-powered committee members delivered nothing. The committee didn't save a dime, didn't find a nickel's worth of new tax revenue, didn't come up with a plan at all. By way of comparison, a recent IMF Working Paper suggested that to close the US's fiscal gap (and taking due account of the higher health and pension costs that are on their way) would require *all* taxes to increase by 35% and *all* transfers to be cut immediately and permanently by 35%. That's the scale of the necessary solution, yet the super-committee couldn't even take the first modest step.

As a consequence of all this, the US fiscal outlook has deteriorated sharply. It's gotten worse because each day that goes by without a solution is a day in which debt and debt service increase. That's not merely a financial issue, because millions of Americans continue to plan their lives on a health care, pension and taxation system which is fundamentally broken. The closer those Americans get to retirement, the more offensive it will be to dishonor the pledges that have already been made. So the problem mounts. And meanwhile, the rhetoric of politicians alters the climate. Reforms need broad popular consent if they are to endure. Yet the Tea Party right is making it increasingly hard for any Republican official to speak sanely about revenue increases. The Big Government left likewise makes it all but impossible for any Democrat to speak coherently about entitlement reform. Because these politicians hog the airwaves, there is not merely a legislative majority against reform, there is, increasingly, a popular one too. For a country which is already bankrupt, gridlock is a disastrous position to be in. It's genuinely difficult to exaggerate the feebleness of our politicians. If these guys had been in charge of running US operations through the Second World War, you and I would be speaking Japanese.

At the heart of this book stands an unholy trinity: Washington, Europe and the finance industry. On the first two counts, and almost a year on from first delivering a manuscript to my publishers, I can report that basically everything I thought was the case *is* the case, only worse. *It's like this, only more so.* When it comes to the finance industry, those words are true, but insufficient. In recent months, we've witnessed the calamitous failure of the Spanish banking industry, and civil unrest in Spain and Greece. Worse than that: we've seen a general deterioration in the sovereign bond market. If I had space to re-crunch the numbers on the solvency of the world banking system, the end result would be significantly worse than the data I presented in the main body of this book. You can't be *very* bankrupt any more than you can be *very* pregnant, but if you could be, the European banking industry would be. The British and American industries are not far behind.

There are different versions of bankruptcy, though. Financial bankruptcy is not, in itself, a dishonorable state. Plenty of fine entrepreneurs have come to grief. Many well-run companies have encountered a change in their markets which have resulted in failure. That's all fair enough. But our finance industry is morally bankrupt as well as financially insolvent.

Barclays has recently admitted that it had, for years and on a huge scale, manipulated the LIBOR market. Like many of the things in this book, that sounds technical but it really, really matters. Hundreds of trillions of dollars' worth of financial contracts are linked to the LIBOR rate. *Hundreds* of trillions. And Barclays – along with plenty of others – manipulated those markets to their own advantage: surely the biggest fraud in history.

But even when you think it can't get worse, it does. HSBC has, it turns out, laundered billions of dollars for drug cartels, terrorists and failed, dangerous states. The bank's Mexican operations moved some $7 billion into the US, and much of that money was tied to drug trafficking. Since

2006, almost 50,000 Mexican citizens have lost their lives as a result of that trade. A trade which HSBC helped to finance.

ING, a Dutch bank, recently agreed to pay a penalty of $619 million for processing billions of dollars on behalf of Cuban and Iranian clients. If employees failed to conceal the origin of the payments in question, they were threatened with dismissal. Other banks have also been punished for similar violations.

As I write, another British bank, Standard Chartered, stands accused of concealing some 60,000 illegal transactions with Iran. The bank has strenuously denied those charges (Barclays and HSBC both admitted to and apologized for the ones laid against them) and Standard Chartered itself may well be able to demonstrate its innocence. I don't know. Yet in a way, that not knowing is the point: as things stand today, we can take absolutely nothing on trust. When major international banks manipulate the world's largest financial markets and handle billions of dollars for some of the world's worst people, we simply have to conclude that the entire industry needs to be rebuilt from the ground up.

You wouldn't expect the world's major economies to thrive against a background such as this and indeed, they are struggling. Jobs growth in the US is desperately weak at a time when the economy is, notionally, recovering. Britain is in a recession that seems to be deepening, not ending. Europe's unique mixture of austerity and denial is driving even the best economies into the mire. The seas are rising – and the major dangers (fiscal mayhem in the US, currency collapse in Europe) still lie ahead.

And although consumer prices are not yet out of control, the danger signs are flashing red. Since March 2009, metals prices have risen some 76%. Food prices have surged, as have rents. The price of corn has roughly trebled over an only slightly longer period. Other commodity prices are rising too. These things shouldn't surprise you. If central banks print money without restraint, the only possible consequence will be inflation. If it doesn't get you now, it'll get you tomorrow. There is no alternative outcome.

Indeed, that inflation is already visible in the world's financial asset markets: stocks and bonds. It's hard to exaggerate the degree to which the central banks' wall of money has inflated these prices. Since the post-Lehman slump, US stocks are up over 100%; the NASDAQ is up over 130%. The bond markets are, if anything, even more dangerously inflated. As we've seen repeatedly through this book, such bubbles are unsustainable. A collapse will come and that collapse will, once again, wreak havoc on the plans and expectations of savers and pensioners. It's a cruel and quite needless blow to inflict.

All these things cumulatively lead to a breakdown of credibility. You and I no longer believe in our banks. We no longer believe in our governments. We no longer believe the promises of a better future. We're right to withhold our belief, because we've been deceived too often.

As a consequence of this loss of credibility, bailouts are barely working any more. In early 2012, the ECB plunged about €500 billion into the European banking system – a sum that bought peace for about six weeks. The €100 billion offered in the Spanish bailout bought peace for a matter of hours. Frankly, I'm surprised it lasted that long.

Loss of credibility, failure of bailouts: as the failure of trust becomes endemic, civil unrest is the inevitable conclusion. I don't think people *ought* to burn cars or break windows, but I *do* understand why it happens. I've more sympathy, by far, with the *indignados* of Madrid than with the people who govern them. And I've infinitely more sympathy with those protesters than with the banks who precipitated the calamity.

Yet none of these things are my central concern in this afterword. You've heard enough already. There's too much debt, too little action. Too much spin, too little truth.

The biggest point, really, is this. Democracy has taken a pasting. The Italian government contains *not a single elected official*. Berlusconi was a clown, but he was an elected clown. The government in place today has no discernible democratic mandate whatever.* A Greek prime minister was shunted out of power, following pressure from France and Germany, because *he wanted to consult his people*. On the board of the ECB, Jens Weidman, who represents the German Bundesbank, has to shout himself hoarse in an attempt to ensure that *the ECB obeys the law and its founding charter*.

Those things are wrong, and obviously wrong, yet the situation in the US is little better. We Americans pay our elected politicians to find solutions and yet a super-committee, charged with making modest progress on what is beyond question the most important issue of the day, has failed to make any progress at all. We face an election campaign in which we debate Mitt Romney's tax bill and Obama's views on gay marriage, while the greatest issue of our age receives barely any rational debate. The media, needless to say, are as culpable as the politicians, arguably more so.

I suppose the easy, cynical thing to say is that politicians only ever really care about re-election. As long as the dummies who voted them in the first time are prepared to do so a sec-

---

* Oh, and its prime minister is an alumnus of Goldman Sachs: yet another indicator of the malign interdependence of politics and Wall Street.

ond time, why would they care that their bad or non-existent decision-making was imperiling the nation's future? Yet in a way I'm worried that that conclusion isn't nearly cynical enough. A shocking recent study found that Congressmen and women make huge insider trading profits – 6% a year in the case of members of the House of Representatives, a stunning 10% a year in the case of Senators. I'm a pretty good investment manager myself. My investors have no cause to complain of the returns I've brought their way in recent years. But 10% a year? Every year? A portfolio that yields 5% a year for ten years will turn a hundred bucks into $163. A senatorial portfolio, boosted by that extra 10%, would deliver more than $400 over the same time period. If you've ever wondered why your elected representative is a heck of a lot richer than you are, there's part of the reason, right there. And although a bill has recently cleared Congress that notionally puts an end to these matters, it's notable that prosecutorial powers have been sharply reduced from an earlier draft bill. It's a telling amendment. After all, rules only matter if they're credibly enforced.

So let's keep our conclusion simple. Democracy matters. Big issues need to be transparently explained, then put to a vote. No one has ever voted for Planet Ponzi; we were led into it blind. A failure of democracy got us into this mess. We need to trust democracy to get us out.

But democracy isn't merely a question of voting. Democratic accountability means nothing unless you have transparency too. Transparency in government means honest figures. It means that governments need to present the kind of figures we've looked at in this book. Ones drawn almost entirely from official sources and yet which are routinely obscured and denied by people who should know better. If voters could see that a government's financial promises had become worthless, that government would not be re-elected. If voters properly understood that corporate lobbying had purchased hundreds of billions of dollars in tax favors and other perks, the politicians involved would be driven from office in disgrace.

These same two themes – accountability and transparency – need to be our watchwords for the financial industry too.

Transparency first. Banks must be obliged to draw up honest balance sheets. No games of 'extend and pretend'. No sovereign bonds held at face value, when the markets rate them as junk. No pretence that worthless collateral is anything other than worthless. A recognition that falling real estate markets will involve massive write-offs. Simply writing honest balance sheets would transform the banking industry.

We need transparency too when it comes to failures of other sorts. If a bank manipulates the LIBOR rate, the individuals involved – right up to the most senior level – must be publicly named. If a bank isn't prepared to do so voluntarily, it must be compelled to do so. And so with everything else: financing drug traffickers, moving money for terrorists, giving succour to Iran and Syria.

With transparency comes accountability. In most walks of life, bad people go to jail. The same rule needs to apply in banking too. Fiddle interest rates: go to jail. Finance drug-cartels: go to jail. Support international terrorism: go to jail. It's so simple, so obvious, yet it almost never happens.

Accountability would also vastly benefit the financial markets. Insolvent firms need to be left to go bankrupt. Possibly the most astounding single fact about the global financial crisis has been that *virtually no creditors have lost money*. How can that possibly be? What's so precious about these people that we defend them, at vast expense, from the consequences of their own dumb decisions? In what other industry, what other walk of life does this happen? Indeed, as with all things on Planet Ponzi, the truth always exceeds imagination. It's not merely that creditors have been *protected*. They have very often been *paid*, as bankers pocket huge advisory fees for sorting through the mess that they themselves created.

Once again, the right answers are the simplest ones. Accountability in the financial markets has to mean, above all, that people start to lose money. It also means that regulations need to be enforced properly, so that miscreants know they will be sent to jail if caught. The process of adjustment may be brutal, but it won't last for long – and once it's over, we'll have a global economy ready to march forwards once again.

Part of that rebuilding effort will need to involve the dismantling of the over-large, 'too big to fail' institutions that dominate both investment and retail banking. As rumours spread earlier this year of huge losses emerging on its proprietary trading book, JP Morgan's chief executive, Jamie Dimon, dismissed those concerns as a 'tempest in a teapot'. That tempest was later estimated to have cost the bank some $2 billion . . . except that as the final numbers were crunched, it turned out that the actual cost was closer to $6 billion. What's truly chilling about this incident isn't the size of the numbers, it's the fact that a well-regarded bank doesn't even notice when $6 billion goes walkabout. If a bank can't keep track of its assets to this extent, it has no right to exist. No right to demand the trust of creditors or the patience of regulators.

In fact, one of the bewildering things about our current mess is that the solutions are so simple. They're obvious. If a government is in deficit, it needs to cut government spending and eliminate tax loopholes and exemptions. If a bank is insolvent, it needs to be left to go bust. If creditors have made bad loans, they need to bear the consequences. These things are so obvious that it's bewildering there is any real debate about them. The fact is that there wouldn't be any debate, except that politicians and bankers have been so close for so long, the former have lost all power of rational thought. So here's one more thing for our wish list: walls of steel need to be erected between banks and politics. Erected, then electrified.

Above all, where excessive debt is the problem, there exists one and only one solution: less debt. If dumb creditors lose money, that's good, a positively beneficial outcome. Simply put: too big to fail is too big to exist. The failure of some creditors will remind all the others that credit discipline matters, just as it always has done, just as it always will.

In particular, we need to relearn an old lesson: that you cannot solve a problem of excessive private-sector debt by getting the government to take it over. Or by extending government guarantees to soften the hit. Or by ratcheting up government debt in a vain effort to re-charge the engines of growth.

Those lessons could usefully be relearned by the central banks too. It's not just a question of economics; it's also a matter of political *ethics*. Central bankers aren't elected, and have an appalling habit of concealing their actions, not merely from the public, but from legislators too. What right does the (Goldman-advised) Federal Reserve have to load its balance sheet with toxic assets generated by an irresponsible banking system? Why does the ECB feel it's OK to make loans to insolvent banks against collateral it knows to be rotten? Why does Mervyn King at the Bank of England feel justified in pouring newly printed money into the banking system?

The truth is that, as Albert Einstein remarked, we can't

solve problems by using the same kind of thinking we used when we created them. Our political leaders and central bankers are *precisely* mired in the thinking that brought us to this point. It's as though they've been poodles of the banking industry for so long, they've forgotten what it is to be a guard dog. As for the financiers themselves, they've profited so long from irresponsibility and a failure of integrity that it actually bewilders them to consider there might be (and once was) an alternative.

Simple lessons are good ones: we might actually end up remembering them. I said I'm an optimist and I mean it. Change is coming and crisis will only make it come sooner. This book is a part of that change. Your reading it is part of that change. So too is your anger, your passion, and your vote. The world needs those things. It needs them now.

M.F.
August 10, 2012

Notes

In keeping with my policy throughout this book, I've cited material that is as widely available as possible, and wherever possible from official or other highly trustworthy sources. In nearly all cases, you can use the notes below to retrieve the underlying data or information from freely available online sources. If you don't believe something I've said, please feel free to check. The truth is out there.

One practical point: I haven't given the full, long URLs in these notes for all web-sourced material because they tend to be very unstable. If you go to www.example.com and search for 'Article title and date' you'll always find the item you're looking for. And any good search engine will help you.

Chapter 1: The scheme

1 Mary Darby, 'In Ponzi we trust,' *Smithsonian Magazine*, Dec. 1998.

2 'The Madoff scam: meet the liquidator,' CBS News, *60 Minutes*, June 20, 2010. Note that there is still some uncertainty about the exact scale of the losses.

3 The Federal Bureau of Prisons is kind enough to make Madoff's exact projected release date available online. Just go along to their website – www.bop.gov – and pop the name 'Bernard L. Madoff' into their Inmate Locator.

4 'Bernie Madoff baffled by SEC blunders,' *New York Daily News*, Oct. 31, 2009.

5 I haven't sought to update The Economist's data. The relatively low number for Manhattan real estate is eye-catching, but you can verify this from the NYC FY12

Tentative Assessment Roll, published Jan. 14, 2011.

6 Graph available direct from the Federal Reserve, www.federalreserve.gov.

7 Data from Reuters, extracted Aug. 19, 2011.

8 All book value ratios extracted from Reuters, Aug. 16–19, 2011. For more on the possible further injection of state funds into RBS, see Robert Peston, 'If RBS needs capital, taxpayers will suffer,' BBC Business News, Oct. 7, 2011.

9 Laurence Kotlikoff, 'US is bankrupt and we don't even know it,' Bloomberg, Aug. 11, 2010 (www.bloomberg.com). The article is worth reading in full.

Chapter 2: The price of liberty

1 Alexander Hamilton, 'The first report on public credit,' 1790. The full text is available online in a number of locations.

2 You can piece this graph together for yourself from a number of public sources, but the relevant government standard data series runs only a century back, so you can't get the graph itself direct from an official source. The best place to find it is Christopher Chantrill's excellent website, www.usgovernmentspending.com. I've corresponded with Mr Chantrill on a number of points and have found his data to be carefully and intelligently constructed.

3 Joseph Stiglitz and Linda Bilmes, The Three Trillion Dollar War (Allen Lane, 2008).

4 Sen. Charles E. Schumer and Rep. Carolyn B. Maloney, War at Any Price?, Joint Economic Committee of the US Congress, Nov. 2007. Household data sourced from the US Census Bureau.

5 Christopher Chantrill, www.usfederalbailout.com. Other 'bailout counters' are available online, including ones from more prestigious news organizations, but I like Chantrill's monitor for its accuracy and up-to-date quality.

6 I need to confess: I've used an unofficial source (from Google Answers) for the thickness of a dollar bill, so my data might be a few feet out if you try to build that tower. You can get a lot of other data from the Bureau of Engraving and Printing, though, including the fact that dollar bills aren't made of paper at all. They're 75% cotton, 25% linen.

7 Dawn Kopecky, 'U.S. rescue may reach $23.7 trillion, Barofsky says,' Bloomberg, July 2009.

8 IMF, Global Financial Stability Report, April 2011, table 1.3: 'Sovereign market and vulnerability indicators.' Data are also available in a slightly more user-friendly format from www.EconomyWatch.com.

Chapter 3: Future-money in happy-land

1 Congressional Budget Office, Letter from the Director to the Hon. John Boehner and the Hon. Harry Reid, Aug. 2011.

2 See the Fiscal Year 2012 Budget of the US Government (available from www.whitehouse.gov), but also 'On the debt-ceiling deal,' *The Economist*, 'Democracy in America' blog, Aug. 2011.

3 See the Fiscal Year 2012 Budget of the US Government, p. 202.

4 'Service sector growth slows in July,' Reuters, Aug. 3, 2011.

5 'US GDP disappoints with 1.3pc growth,' *Daily Telegraph*, Oct. 29, 2011.

6 'Stopping a financial crisis, the Swedish way,' *New York Times*, Sept. 22, 2008.

7 'Sweden's experience on banking resolution and budget consolidation,' IMF, 'Public Financial Management' blog, May 2009. See also the OECD's useful paper on 'Fiscal consolidation: lessons from past experience,' available online but undated from www.oecd.org.

8 'There never was a surplus,' *The Economist*, 'Democracy in America' blog, July 27, 2011.

9 Information on holders of US Treasury bonds is available from The Treasury Department (www.treasury.gov), 'Major foreign holders of Treasury securities.'

10 Data available from the non-partisan Tax Policy Center (www.taxpolicycenter.org), 'Average and marginal federal income tax rates for four-person families at the same relative positions in the income distribution: 1955–2010,' April 2011.

11 Tax data alone are available from the OECD (www.oecd.org). This graph uses a broader measure of government revenue and is most easily available from Christopher Chantrill's website www.usgovernmentrevenue.com. He sources his underlying data from publicly available official sources – you just need to do a little hunting and crunching to obtain the overall data.

12 Data from the OECD, www.oecd.org.

13 Stephanie Kirchgaessner, 'Brutal battle looms over tax loopholes,' *Financial Times*, Jan. 26, 2011.

14 David Kocieniewski, 'G.E.'s strategies let it avoid taxes altogether,' *New York Times*, March 24, 2011.

15 'Analysis: 12 corporations pay effective tax rate of negative 1.4% on $175 billion in profits; reap $63.7 billion in tax subsidies,' Citizens for Tax Justice, Oct. 21, 2011, www.ctj.org.

16 'Study says most corporations

pay no U.S. income taxes,'
Reuters, Aug. 12, 2008.

17 National Taxpayer Advocate,
2010 Annual Report to Congress,
www.irs.gov.

18 David Lynch, 'Why corporate
tax reform is so tricky,' Bloomberg
Businessweek, April 7, 2011.

19 www.taxpayeradvocate.irs.gov/
files/ExecSummary_2010ARC.pdf.

20 'Building the U.S. tax code,
break by break,' *Washington Post*,
Sept. 18, 2011. The same source
provides a useful graphic detailing
the various breaks and
exemptions.

21 See Stockholm International
Peace Research Institute (SIPRI),
Military Expenditure database,
www.sipri.org/databases/milex,
data retrieved Aug. 2011.

22 See Robert Moeller, 'The truth
about AFRICOM,' *Foreign Policy*,
July 21, 2010; also Thomas
Eddlem, 'Can we cut "defense"
spending?,' *New American*, March
8, 2011. The quotation printed in
the text has been withdrawn from
the AFRICOM website.

23 Data sourced from the
AFRICOM website,
www.africom.mil, data extracted
Aug. 2011.

24 Calculated from Stephen
Trimble, 'F-35 strikes trillion-
dollar mark for maintenance bills,'
Flight International, June 6, 2011.

25 'The last manned fighter,' *The
Economist*, July 14, 2011.

26 Nathan Hodge, 'Gates takes
aim at navy, questions carrier
fleet,' *Wired*, May 3, 2010; also,
'Aircraft carriers and Chinese
missiles: time to rethink the U.S.
naval doctrine,' East West
Institute, Jan. 21, 2011.

27 Steve Schifferes, 'The dilemma
for US car workers,' BBC, Feb. 21,
2007, http://news.bbc.co.uk.

28 Timothy Carney, 'Tick, tick,
tick: the cost of Obamacare is a
time bomb,' *Washington Examiner*,
Jan. 16, 2011.

29 Congressional Budget Office,
letter from the Director to the
Honorable Nancy Pelosi, March
2010.

30 Jill Jackson and John Nolen,
'Health care reform bill summary:
a look at what's in the bill,' CBS
News, March 21, 2010.

31 Data available from the
Department of Finance, Canada
(www.fin.gc.ca).

32 Sally Pipes, 'RomneyCare's
unhappy anniversary,' Forbes,
April 26, 2011, www.forbes.com.

33 You can get the exact level of
the US debt by going to one of the
Treasury Department's websites –
www.treasury direct.gov – and
navigating to the page on 'The
debt to the penny and who
holds it.'

34 As you'd expect, there's a lot
of material available on this. See
e.g. Louise Story, 'U.S. inquiry is
said to focus on S.&P. ratings,'
New York Times, Aug. 17, 2011;
Zachary Goldfarb, 'Political parties
trade blame for downgrade in U.S.
credit rating,' *Washington Post*,
Aug. 6, 2011; for the Warren
Buffett comments, see Betty Liu
and Andrew Frye, 'Buffett says
S&P's downgrade mistaken, still
doesn't see another recession,'
Bloomberg, Aug. 6, 2011, but also
Alex Pollock, 'Was there ever a
default on U.S. Treasury debt?,'
American Spectator, Jan. 21, 2009
(or via www.aei.org), and
Catherine Rampell, 'Fearing
(another) U.S. debt default,' *New
York Times*, Jan. 4, 2011.

35 Jagadeesh Gokhale and Kent
Smetters, *Measuring Social
Security's Financial Problems*
(National Bureau of Economic
Research, Jan. 2005); also, 'The
$64 trillion question,' *Wealth
Manager*, Sept. 2007. The IMF
estimated world GDP at $61.8
trillion for 2010 (IMF, *World
Economic Outlook*, April 2011).

Chapter 4: A hole as big as the world

1 Robert Novy-Marx and Joshua
D. Rauh, 'The liabilities and risks
of state-sponsored pension plans,'
Journal of Economic Perspectives,
vol. 23, no. 4, 2009.

2 'State and municipal debt:
tough choices ahead,' Committee

on Oversight and Government
Reform, April 2011, Documents
for the April 14th Hearing.

3 'A gold-plated burden,' *The
Economist*, Oct. 14, 2010.

4 See data cited in Dennis
Cauchon, 'Government's mountain
of debt,' *USA Today*, June 6, 2011.
Note that federal debt appears
lower and federal pension liabilities appear higher than normally
quoted because of the way in
which federal pensions are funded.

5 *The 2011 Annual Report of the
Board of Trustees of the Federal Old-
Age and Survivors Insurance and
Federal Disability Insurance Trust
Funds*, May 2011, p. 67,
www.ssa.gov.

6 *The 2011 Annual Report of the
Boards of Trustees of the Federal
Hospital Insurance and Federal
Supplementary Medical Insurance
Trust Funds*, May 2011, pp. 130,
146, https://www.cms.gov.

7 US Census Bureau, 2011
(www.census.gov).

8 Evolutionary biology isn't my
strong suit, but I used a useful
article in the *New Scientist*
('Timeline: the evolution of life,'
July 2009). And I'll admit to making use of Wikipedia on this one
too.

9 See 10-Q filings for Fannie Mae
and Freddie Mac (or, more formally, the Federal National
Mortgage Association and Federal

Home Loan Mortgage Corporation). The filings are available at www.fanniemae.com and www.freddiemac.com respectively.

10 Lorraine Woellert, 'S&P lowers Fannie, Freddie citing reliance on government,' Bloomberg, Aug. 8, 2011.

11 FDIC, *Annual Report*, 2010, www.fdic.gov.

12 FDIC, *Annual Report*, 2010. The FDIC's liabilities exceed its stock of assets by some $7.4 billion. If, however, we take the corporation's total stock of assets and subtract only its *actual* (not contingent) liabilities, the corporation has net assets of approximately $10 billion. It's that $10 billion which underpins the contingent liability associated with support of the entire US banking system. If you need more help in understanding the logic of this arithmetic, I recommend studying the FDIC's balance sheet a little further. A cup of strong coffee might also help.

13 'The Budget and economic outlook: an update,' Congressional Budget Office, Aug. 2011.

14 Kotlikoff, 'US is bankrupt and we don't even know it.'

Chapter 5: How to win friends and influence people

1 Go to the CBO website (www.cbo.gov) and search for 'average after-tax income.' You have to do a little crunching to get the data in the graph, but nothing too challenging.

2 Data available from Center for Responsive Politics, lobbying database, at www.opensecrets.org/lobby. Data include partial data for 2011. Data retrieved Nov. 4, 2011.

3 Hui Chen, David C. Parsley, and Ya-wen Yang, 'Corporate lobbying and financial performance,' April 28, 2010, available from the Social Science Research Network (www.ssrn.com).

4 See ch. 3 above, nn. 14, 15, 16, 20, 24, and 25; also Mark Knoller, 'White House exults in General Motors repayment,' CBS News, April 21, 2010, and William Greider, 'The AIG bailout scandal,' *The Nation*, Aug. 6, 2010.

5 See also 'U.S. bailout recipients spent $114 million on politics,' Reuters, Feb. 4, 2009.

6 Jeffrey Birnbaum, 'Clients' rewards keep K Street lobbyists thriving,' *Washington Post*, Feb. 14, 2006.

7 Matt Miller, 'Make 150,000% today!,' *Fortune*, Jan. 27, 2006.

8 Jacob Hacker and Paul Pierson, *Winner-Takes-All Politics* (Simon & Schuster, 2010), p. 25.

9 'Pinched,' *The Economist*, Sept. 17, 2011.

10 Tax Policy Center, www. taxpolicycenter.org.

11 'IMF finds "trillions" in undeclared wealth,' Tax Justice Network, March 2010, www.taxjustice.net.

12 Warren Buffett, 'Stop coddling the super-rich,' New York Times, Aug. 14, 2011.

13 See the full breakdown at www.forbes.com.

14 'Treasury preserves bank payday with AIG rescue cash,' Bloomberg, March 24, 2009.

15 Graham Bowley, 'Strong year for Goldman, as it trims bonus pool,' New York Times, Jan. 21, 2010.

16 Gretchen Morgenson, 'An A.I.G. failure would have cost Goldman Sachs, documents show,' New York Times, July 23, 2010.

17 Bradley Keoun, 'Morgan Stanley speculating to brink of collapse got $107 billion from Fed,' Bloomberg, Aug. 23, 2011. I also recommend a data visualization by Bloomberg ('The Fed's secret liquidity lifelines'), made available online at www.bloomberg. com/data-visualization/federal-reserve-emergency-lending.

Chapter 6: The $50,000,000,000 egg

1 Chris McGreal, 'What comes after a trillion?,' Guardian, July 18, 2008.

2 'Zimbabwe rolls out Z$100tr note,' BBC News, Jan. 16, 2009.

3 www.cnbc.com/id/42551209 /Inflation_Actually_Near_10_Using _Older_Measure.

4 See Williams's discussion in his August 2006 newsletter, available at www.shadowstats.com.

5 The results are online at www.shadowstats.com if you care to take a look.

6 P. J. Huffstutter, 'Cheap food may be a thing of the past in U.S.,' Los Angeles Times, March 16, 2011.

7 On Nigeria, see e.g. 'Nigerian army clashes with militants in oil delta,' Reuters, May 11, 2011. On Venezuela, see e.g. 'Oil leak,' The Economist, Feb. 24, 2011.

8 www.indexmundi.com/ commodities. Data extracted Aug. 19, 2011.

9 You can get the data from the Federal Reserve Bank of New York (www.newyorkfed.org). Look for the page entitled 'Historical changes of the target federal funds and discount rates.'

10 You can get a good long-term historical graph of long-term rates at www.multpl.com/interest-rate.

11 Joe Weisenthal, 'Dallas Fed chief: the Fed is monetizing the nation's debt for the next 8 months,' Business Insider, Nov. 8, 2010.

12 Stephanie Kirchgaessner, 'Perry compares Fed stimulus to treason,' *Financial Times*, Aug. 16, 2011.

Chapter 7: After Beachy Head

1 Phillip Inman, 'Bank of England governor blames spending cuts on bank bailouts,' *Guardian*, March 1, 2011.

2 Inman, 'Bank of England governor blames spending cuts on bank bailouts.'

3 Robert Chote, 'Post budget presentations: opening remarks,' Institute for Fiscal Studies, June 2010, www.ifs.org.uk.

4 Nick Mathiason, 'Hedge funds, financiers and private equity make up 27% of Tory funding,' Bureau of Investigative Journalism, Sept. 30, 2011, www.thebureauinvestigates.com. *See also* Lucy Keating, 'Tory tax breaks for the wealthy,' Bureau of Investigative Journalism, Sept. 30, 2011, www.thebureauinvestigates.com.

Chapter 8: A statistical anomaly

1 All value-added data in this chapter are from Bureau of Economic Analysis (www.bea.gov), 'Gross domestic product (GDP) by industry data.'

2 'Forty years on,' *The Economist*, Aug. 13, 2011.

3 A junk bond is the common term given to any non-investment-grade debt security – that is, one rated BBB– or lower. The market is also known as the market for 'high-yield debt.'

4 'Gross value-added in the financial sector,' Deutsche Bank Research, March 2007, www.dbresearch.de.

5 Bureau of Economic Analysis, 'Corporate profits by industry.'

6 Greta R. Krippner, 'The financialization of the American economy,' *Socio-Economic Review*, vol. 3, no. 2, May 2005, pp. 173–208.

7 Steven Levitt and Stephen Dubner, *Freakonomics* (Allen Lane, 2005).

Chapter 9: A house for Joe Schmoe

1 You can view the entire document for yourself. Just go to the Senate Committee on Homeland Security and Governmental Affairs (www.hsgac.senate.gov) and search for 'Timberwolf.'

2 'How panic gripped the world's biggest banks,' *FT Magazine*, May 8, 2009. The *FT* article comprises an edited extract from Gillian Tett's worthwhile *Fool's Gold* (Little, Brown, 2009).

3 Maurna Desmond, 'IMF: subprime losses could hit $1

trillion,' Forbes, April 8, 2008.

4 It's strangely hard to get precise figures for this filing. Your best bet is probably to enter 'Lehman Brothers bankruptcy filing document – EPIQ systems' into a search engine and review the data that come up. Note that there are a small amount of nonfinancial liabilities to be included, as well as the (much larger) quantum of financial ones.

Chapter 10: How to hide a neutron bomb in ten easy steps

1 Landon Thomas Jr, 'Greek rail system's debt adds to economic woes,' New York Times, July 20, 2010.

2 Menelaos Tzafalias, 'Greece to call time on cushy pension deals for "unhealthy" jobs,' Independent, May 21, 2010.

3 You can get a full view of historical Greek rates by going to the Bank of Greece website (www.bankofgreece.gr) and searching for 'drachma money market rates.'

4 Manuela Saragosa, 'Greece warned on false euro data,' BBC, Dec. 1, 2004.

5 Or check a good online resource such as Investopedia (www.investopedia.com). Search for 'Advanced bond concepts: yield and bond price.'

6 Emma Charlton and Keith Jenkins, 'German bunds slide

most in 8 weeks; Greek two-year notes rise,' Bloomberg, Sept. 17, 2011.

7 Search Bank of International Settlements (www.bis.org) for 'Amounts outstanding of over-the-counter (OTC) derivatives.'

8 Fawn Johnson, 'SEC queries firms on repos,' Wall Street Journal, March 30, 2010.

9 Tett, Fool's Gold, p. 241.

10 Eric Dash and Sewell Chan, 'Panel criticizes oversight of Citi by 2 executives,' New York Times, April 8, 2010.

11 See JP Morgan Chase's financial statements, most easily accessed via http://investor. shareholder.com/JP Morganchase/earnings.cfm.

12 James Kirkup, 'The path to Northern Rock's nationalisation,' Daily Telegraph, Jan. 14, 2008.

13 Kirsty Walker, 'Northern Rock chief's offer to resign,' Daily Mail, Oct. 16, 2007.

14 'Northern Rock bosses: a board profile,' Daily Mail, Sept. 18, 2007.

15 Ashley Seager and Angela Balakrishnan, 'Rock liabilities added to the national debt,' Guardian, Feb. 8, 2008.

16 For a scarily huge number, see table on p. 192 of JP Morgan's

annual report for 2010, accessible at http://investor.shareholder.com/jp morganchase/annual.cfm. Total derivatives notional amounts: $78,905 billion. That number is not a misprint.

17 Patrick Jenkins and Megan Murphy, 'Banks brace for hits on Greek bonds,' *Financial Times*, July 21, 2011.

18 Data for Maryland's GDP from the Bureau of Economic Analysis. Data for Greece from IMF, *World Economic Outlook*, April 2011.

19 Hugh Son, 'BofA posts record quarterly loss on costs of bad home loans,' Bloomberg, July 19, 2011.

20 'Strife of Brian,' *The Economist*, Sept. 17, 2011.

21 Text available from www. propublica.org. Search for 'Squared CDO 2007-1 Ltd. Prospectus.'

22 Linda Sandler, 'Lehman paid bankruptcy lawyers, managers $27.1 million in fees in April,' Bloomberg, May 23, 2011. For a taste of some of those uncertainties, see also Peter Henning, 'Legal fees keep surging in Lehman class-action suit,' *New York Times*, Aug. 1, 2011.

23 'Too big a fail count,' *The Economist*, June 2, 2011.

24 Tom Lauricella, Kara Scannell, and Jenny Strasburg, 'How a

trading algorithm went awry,' *Wall Street Journal*, Oct. 2, 2010.

25 'Too much of a good thing,' *The Economist*, June 23, 2011; 'Explosive,' *The Economist*, June 23, 2010.

26 Javier Blas, 'High-speed trading blamed for sugar rises,' *Financial Times*, Feb. 8, 2011.

27 Peter Guest, 'Volatility will go on in world's largest cocoa supplier,' CNBC News, April 28, 2011.

Chapter 11: Collecting nickels in front of steamrollers

1 Michael Lewis, *The Big Short* (Allen Lane, 2010), p. 62.

2 Lewis, *The Big Short*, p. 61.

3 Lewis, *The Big Short*, p. 63. See also Max Abelson, 'Mr. Bubble bounces back,' *New York Observer*, Sept. 7, 2011.

4 See an interesting discussion by Steven Malliaris and Hongjun Yan of the Yale School of Management: 'Nickels versus black swans: reputation, trading strategies and asset prices,' March 2009. Document available online via www.ssrn.com. Also see Reuters, 'Nickels and black swans,' May 26, 2009.

5 'Many unhappy returns,' *The Economist*, Aug. 20, 2011.

6 Roger Lowenstein, 'Long-Term Capital Management: it's a short-term memory,' New York Times, Sept. 6, 2008. See also 'The story of Long-Term Capital Management,' Canadian Investment Review, Winter 1999, accessible via www.investmentreview.com.

7 Alternative payment models could be envisaged. See e.g. Larry Harris, 'Pay the rating agencies according to results,' Financial Times, June 3, 2010.

8 Rupert Neate, 'Ratings agencies suffer "conflict of interest", says former Moody's boss,' Guardian, Aug. 22, 2011.

9 Gillian Tett, 'Rating agencies in a bind as pressures mount,' Financial Times, Dec. 16, 2010.

10 'One non-default Greek rating enough for ECB – report,' Reuters, July 5, 2011.

11 Financial Stability Board, 'Principles for reducing reliance on CRA ratings,' Oct. 2010.

12 Andrew Ross Sorkin, 'Revolving door at S.E.C. is hurdle to crisis cleanup,' New York Times, Aug. 1, 2011.

13 George Packer, 'A dirty business,' New Yorker, June 27, 2011.

14 Project on Government Oversight, 'Revolving regulators: SEC faces ethical challenges with revolving door,' May 2011, www.pogo.org.

15 Arthur Levitt, Take on the Street (Random House, 2002), p. 236.

16 Jean Eaglesham and Victoria McGrane, 'Budget rift at CFTC pulls plug on alarm,' Wall Street Journal, Feb. 25, 2011.

17 Sewell Chan and Eric Dash, 'Financial crisis inquiry wrestles with setbacks,' New York Times, April 5, 2010.

18 Chan and Dash, 'Financial crisis inquiry wrestles with setbacks.'

19 John King, 'Starr investigation costs just shy of $30 million,' CNN, April 1, 1998.

20 'NASA puts cost of shuttle inquiry, cleanup at $400 million,' Los Angeles Times, Sept. 12, 2003.

21 IMF, 'Fiscal implications of the global economic and financial crisis,' June 2009.

22 Andrew Haldane, 'The $100 billion question,' Bank of England, March 2010.

23 See www.planetponzi.com.

24 Transcribed from YouTube video, '2010-11-09 Greenspan Admission,' or enter: www.youtube.com/watch?v=731G71Sahok&feature=player_embedded#!

25 'Banks to pay victims of botched foreclosures in settlement with regulators,' Bloomberg, April 2011.

26 Lorraine Woellert, 'BofA, JP Morgan among 17 banks sued by U.S. for $196 billion,' Bloomberg, Sept. 13, 2011.

27 'Securities regulators expected to reach settlement with banks,' Wall Street Journal, April 17, 2011.

28 'Nevada, U.S. regulator challenge BofA on mortgages,' Reuters, Aug. 30, 2011.

29 Francesco Guerrera, Henny Sender, and Justin Baer, 'Goldman Sachs settles with SEC,' Financial Times, July 15, 2010.

30 Chris Dolmetsch, 'Morgan Stanley sued by Allstate on mortgage claims,' Bloomberg, July 6, 2011.

31 'Madoff trustee defends $19 billion suit against JP Morgan,' Bloomberg, Sept. 2, 2011.

Chapter 12: I'm short your house

1 Senate Committee on Homeland Security and Governmental Affairs, April 2011, Levin–Coburn Report on the Financial Crisis, http://hsgac.senate.gov/public/_files/Financial_Crisis/FinancialCrisisReport.pdf.

2 To source this quote, you need to bring up the press release which announced the publication of the Levin–Coburn report (cited in n. 1 above). At the end of that release, there's a link to pp. 5460–901. Click that link and search for the text quoted.

3 Simon Goodley, 'Markets meltdown leads to surge in City addictions,' Guardian, Sept. 9, 2011.

4 Robert Shiller has made his data available at his website www.irrationalexuberance.com – an excellent resource. There are also some useful notes on the house price index at S&P's website, www.standardandpoors.com.

5 You can source data on owner's equivalent rent (and a fuller explanation of what that term means) from the FHFA (www.fhfa.gov): search for the FHFA's report on 'Housing and mortgage markets in 2010' and take a look at figure 10.

6 You can get the most recent data release from the Bureau of Labor Statistics (www.bls.gov). Just search the site for 'Latest releases.'

7 FHFA report on 'Housing and mortgage markets in 2010,' figure 12.

8 Paul Davidson, 'Construction hiring regains some vigor in September,' USA Today, Oct. 9, 2011.

9 FHFA report on 'Housing and mortgage markets in 2010,' figure 13.

10 FHFA report on 'Housing and mortgage markets in 2010,' figure 14.

11 FHFA report on 'Housing and mortgage markets in 2010,' figure C-1.

12 'New CoreLogic data reveals Q2 negative equity declines,' CoreLogic, Sept. 2011. You can get more recent information by searching the CoreLogic site at www.corelogic.com.

13 'Self harm,' The Economist, Sept. 3, 2011.

14 FHFA report on 'Housing and mortgage markets in 2010,' figure 16.

15 Justin Fox, 'A slow-motion wreck for commercial real estate,' Time, Jan. 18, 2010.

16 John Gittelsohn, 'Shiller says U.S. home-price declines of 10% to 25% "wouldn't surprise me",' Bloomberg, June 9, 2011.

Chapter 13: A brief flash of reality

1 Amos Tversky and Daniel Kahneman, 'Judgment under uncertainty: heuristics and biases,' Science, vol. 185, no. 4157, Sept. 1974, pp. 1124–31.

2 Tali Sharot, Alison M. Riccardi, Candace M. Raio, and Elizabeth A. Phelps, 'Neural mechanisms mediating optimism bias,' Nature, vol. 450, Oct. 2007, pp. 102–5.

3 Go to the UK Treasury website (www.hm-treasury.gov.uk) and search for 'Optimism bias.'

4 Goldman Sachs, Global Economic Outlook 2011, Dec. 2010. You can access the report via Goldman's website, www.goldmansachs.com.

5 I've sourced the data using my own (paid) feed from Thomson Reuters (http://thomsonreuters.com/), but there are numerous free data sources available on the internet.

6 'Buffett's Bank of America warrants soar in value,' Reuters, Aug. 25, 2011.

Chapter 14: Planet Ponzi comes to London

1 Andrew Haldane, Simon Brennan, and Vasileios Madouros, 'The contribution of the financial sector: miracle or mirage?,' in 'The future of finance: the LSE Report,' London School of Economics, July 14, 2010.

2 Mary Jordan and Karla Adam, 'For London's new super-rich, no whim need go unfulfilled,' Washington Post, March 8, 2007.

3 Julia Vitullo-Martin, 'Keeping New York competitive,' Manhattan Institute's Center for Rethinking Development, Jan. 2007, www.rpa-cui.org.

4 Jordan and Adam, 'For London's new super-rich, no whim need go unfulfilled.'

Chapter 15: The rise and rise of Planet Ponzi

1 GDP data are drawn from IMF, *World Economic Outlook*, April 2011; British household data from 'Household wealth grows five-fold in the last 50 years,' BBC News, May 16, 2010.

2 Data from Microsoft's 2010 10-K filing, available online via www.microsoft.com/ investor/SEC/default.aspx.

3 Market cap sourced Sept. 5, 2011. Balance sheet data from 10-K filing (effectively an annual report), period ending Sept. 25, 2010. Both pieces of data easily found online via http://investor.apple.com.

4 Bureau of Economic Analysis, 'U.S. net international investment position at yearend 2010,' www.bea.gov.

5 You can source the data from the Office for National Statistics (www.ons.gov.uk): search for 'The UK's international investment position.' The statistical issue referred to in the text is that foreign direct investment (FDI) is valued at historic cost not market value. Because the UK is an enthusiastic direct investor overseas, its true holdings of FDI are likely to be understated, by as much as 50%.

6 There's good economic theory behind the remarks in this paragraph. You can get a layman's discussion of these themes from George Monbiot, 'It's in all our interests to understand how to stop another Great Depression,' *Guardian*, Oct. 10, 2011.

7 Data available from HM Treasury (www.hm-treaury.gov.uk), 'Whole of Government Accounts: unaudited summary report for the year ended 31 March 2010,' July 2011. GDP data from IMF, *World Economic Outlook*, April 2011.

8 I am particularly grateful to Stéphenie Peyet and Spencer Wilson, both of the OECD, for resolving these points for me. I wouldn't have got there without them. Obviously the personal opinions expressed are mine not theirs.

9 Data available from the OECD (go to www.oecd-ilibrary.org). Search for data on 'Household wealth and indebtedness as a percentage of nominal disposable income.'

10 This illustration isn't quite fair – GDP per capita is different from salary, and of course that 90% of GDP figure applies at a national level, not just to those about to enter retirement. But still: 90% is too low. The Netherlands has pension assets equal to around 135% of GDP, which is roughly where all other countries ought to be.

11 Irving Fisher Committee of the Bank for International Settlements (www.bis.org),

'General government pension obligations in Europe, 2007.'

12 'Debt and deleveraging: the global credit bubble and its economic consequences,' McKinsey Global Institute, Jan. 2010.

Chapter 16: Giants unicycling on clifftops

1 David Oakley and Peter Spiegel, 'Greek rating now the worst in the world,' *Financial Times*, June 13, 2011.

2 S&P release, available from www.standardandpoors.com. You may need to register to access the release, but registration is free. Enron recovery data available from Enron Creditors Recovery Corp. (www.enron.com). Visit 'Press Room' and search 'Recent releases.'

3 Michael Leister, quoted by Bloomberg, 'Greek bonds fall to record lows on concern bailout redundant; Italy slides,' Sept. 6, 2011.

4 Stephen Fidler, 'What future for Greek bond swap?,' *Wall Street Journal*, Sept. 23, 2011. For a bulletin from the November 2011 death-spiral, see Paul Dobson and Lucy Meakin, 'Italian 10-year yield surges to record on debt, growth concern,' Bloomberg, Nov. 7, 2011.

5 Data from IMF, *World Economic Outlook*, April 2011. Data include estimates for 2011/12.

6 IMF, *World Economic Outlook*, April 2011.

7 For the identities of Portuguese bondholders, visit www.epp.eurostat.ec. europa.eu (even the website address is bureaucratic). Search for 'Structure of government debt breakdown by bondholder.'

8 GDP data from IMF, *World Economic Outlook*, April 2011. Comparative size of Italian bond market from 'Pub skittles, the Italian version,' *The Economist*, 'Schumpeter' blog, July 8, 2011.

9 Shiyin Chen, 'Stocks decline, euro weakens on Italian vote concern; Swiss franc slides,' Bloomberg, Nov. 7, 2011.

10 IMF, *World Economic Outlook*, April 2011. Also John Prideaux, 'Oh for a new Risorgimento,' *The Economist*, June 9, 2011; OECD, *OECD Economic Surveys: Italy*, May 2011.

11 For this paragraph and the preceding one, see 'Berlusconi's bung,' *The Economist*, July 7, 2011.

12 Global Fortune 500, available at www.money.cnn.com. Data correct as of Sept. 27, 2011.

13 'Among the dinosaurs,' *The Economist*, Aug. 27, 2011.

14 Kim Willsher, 'France's socialists have a candidate,' *Los Angeles Times*, Oct. 16, 2011.

15 Lisa Abend, 'Protests: has the revolution come to Spain?,' *Time*, May 23, 2011. Youth unemployment figure from 'Left Behind,' *The Economist*, Sept. 10, 2011.

16 'Chest pains,' *The Economist*, Aug. 27, 2011.

17 There's a good (English language) interview with Ms Lagarde in the international edition of *Spiegel Online* (Sept. 4, 2011). Go to www.Spiegel.de/international/ and search for 'Interview with IMF chief Christine Lagarde.'

18 Susan Pulliam and Liz Rappaport, 'Goldman takes a dark view,' *Wall Street Journal*, Sept. 1, 2011.

19 For the numbers, see Bloomberg (www.bloomberg.com/data-visualization/federal-reserve-emergency-lending). For the boasting and the influence, see Alex Brummer's fine, angry piece in the *Daily Mail*, July 18, 2009, 'As Goldman Sachs posts huge profits from the economic crisis, the question is: Did it cause the problems in the first place?'

20 Elena Logutenkova and Aaron Kirchfeld, 'Deutsche Bank's Ackermann bets investors will choose returns over capital,' Bloomberg, Dec. 21, 2010.

21 'Banks would not survive sovereign debt devaluations,' BBC News, Sept. 5, 2011.

22 'Ackermann spurns Lagarde call for mandatory European bank recapitalization,' Bloomberg, Sept. 2011.

23 'Lloyds warns of £10bn loss at HBOS after hefty write-offs,' *Independent*, Feb. 14, 2009. See also 'Lloyds HBOS merger gets go-ahead,' BBC News, Jan. 12, 2009.

Chapter 17: The *aureus* and the *as*

1 Catherine Rampell, 'Fearing (another) US default,' *New York Times*, Jan. 4, 2011.

2 Greg Lucas, 'So you think the California budget deficit is dire?,' *Capitol Weekly*, March 24, 2011.

3 David Skeel, 'Give states a way to go bankrupt,' *Weekly Standard*, Nov. 29, 2010.

4 'State bankruptcy bill imminent, Gingrich says,' Reuters, Jan. 2011.

5 Public Policy Institute of California, 'When government fails: the Orange County bankruptcy,' March 1998, www.ppic.org.

6 Sam Roberts, 'When the City's bankruptcy was just a few words away,' *New York Times*, Dec. 31, 2006.

7 The EU has put together a

useful FAQ paper on the EFSF, available at www.efsf.europa.eu.

8 'After the fall,' *The Economist*, Sept. 17, 2011.

9 Keith Richburg, 'Worldwide financial crisis largely bypasses Canada,' *Washington Post*, Oct. 16, 2008.

10 Energy Information Administration, 'World proved reserves of oil and natural gas, most recent estimates,' March 2009, http://38.96.246.204/international/reserves.html.

11 'Moody's reassesses German Landesbanks' ratings,' Reuters, May 10, 2011.

12 Gavin Finch, Elisa Martinuzzi, and Charles Penty, 'EU bank stress tests missing sovereign defaults fail to convince analysts,' Bloomberg, July 18, 2011.

Chapter 18: Choosing second

1 The CIA World Factbook (available at www.cia.gov) has an easy to use ranking. Just search for 'country comparison: exports.' The data refer you to merchandise exports at current exchange rates.

2 Department for Business Innovation and Skills (www.bis.gov.uk), 'UK trade performance over the past years,' 2011 (month of publication not clear from the document).

3 www.weforum.org/news/us-competitiveness-ranking-continues-fall-emerging-markets-are-closing-gap.

4 Bond yields from *Financial Times*, Dec. 2, 2011.

5 IMF, *World Economic Outlook*, April 2011.

6 'Darling reveals Labour crisis row,' *Guardian*, Sept. 4, 2011.

7 Data here and in the next paragraph are drawn from HM Treasury, *Spending Review 2010*, Oct. 2010. See also BBC News, 'Spending Review in graphics,' Oct. 20, 2010.

8 Office for Budget Responsibility, *Economic and Fiscal Outlook*, March 2011, http://budget responsibility.independent.gov.uk/.

9 Independent Commission on Banking, *Final Report*, Sept. 2011, http://bankingcommission.s3.amazonaws.com/.

10 Department for Communities and Local Government, 'Dramatic simplification of planning guidance to encourage sustainable growth,' July 2011, www.communities.gov.uk.

11 See www.redtapechallenge.cabinetoffice.gov.uk.

12 You can get a transcript of the relevant moment at http://blogs.Channel4.com. Search for 'Fact check: ask the

Chancellors.' The debate itself can be viewed on Channel4.com – search for 'Ask the Chancellors.'

13 Alan Travis and James Ball, 'Three-quarters charged over riots had previous criminal convictions,' *Guardian*, Sept. 15, 2011.

Chapter 19: A van for Fukushima

1 Debt and GDP data from IMF, *World Economic Outlook*, April 2011. For the government's champions, see JP Morgan, 'Japan's debt trap: who's in the trap?,' June 2011, www.jpmorgan.com.

2 IMF, *World Economic Outlook*, April 2011.

3 'Rebuilding Japan – or ruining it,' *The Economist*, April 28, 2011.

4 'The domino that never falls,' *The Economist*, July 21, 2011.

5 Data from the *Financial Times*, collected Sept. 18, 2011.

6 'Don't sit on your hands,' *The Economist*, May 12, 2011.

7 'Moody's uncertain about Japan's growth, likely to downgrade outlook,' www.Firstpost.com, May 2011.

8 'The good bureaucrat,' *The Economist*, Sept. 14, 2011.

9 'Game on,' *The Economist*, March 5, 2009.

10 'Stepping Out,' *The Economist*, 'Banyan' blog, June 23, 2011.

11 'Spain's *indignados* summon spirit of 1968,' www.Channel4.com, May 2011.

Chapter 20: The man who ate a supermarket

1 Aditya Chakrabortty, 'Athens protests: Syntagma Square on frontline of European austerity protests,' *Guardian*, June 19, 2011.

2 'Europe grapples with youth unemployment,' *Financial Times*, Feb. 16, 2011.

3 James Boxell, 'Chirac and de Villepin accused over cash,' *Financial Times*, Sept. 11, 2011.

4 See Robert Rubin profile on Bloomberg Businessweek (www.businessweek.com). For Hank Paulson, see David Davis, 'The great bailout,' *Spectator*, Feb. 20, 2010.

5 Timothy Burger and Kristin Jensen, 'Summers earned millions in D. E. Shaw salary, bank speech fees,' Bloomberg, April 4, 2009.

6 Burger and Jensen, 'Summers earned millions.'

7 Jesse Hamilton, 'Ex-Goldman exec started SEC job after earning $57 million,' Bloomberg, Sept. 1, 2011.

8 Donal Griffin, 'Pandit's payouts climb toward $200 million as top

bailout recipient slips,' Bloomberg, July 1, 2011.

9 Louise Armitstead and Harry Wilson, 'Bob Diamond bites back at Treasury Select Committee,' *Daily Telegraph*, Jan. 12, 2011.

10 Andrew Grice, '£850bn: official cost of the bank bailout,' *Independent*, Dec. 4, 2009.

11 Thomson Reuters, http://thomsonreuters.com/, or widely available online.

12 Jill Treanor, 'No bank should be a burden to the taxpayer, says Barclays' Bob Diamond,' *Guardian*, Feb. 21, 2010.

13 Ann Busby, 'Fuel protests: UK government gets the blame,' CNN.com, Sept. 12, 2000.

14 Esmé Deprez and Alison Vekshin, 'Anti-Wall Street protesters march from NYC to San Francisco,' Bloomberg Businessweek, Oct. 6, 2011.

15 For a useful survey, see 'The Middle East in revolt,' *Time Specials* (via www.time.com/time/specials/), 2011.

16 Sangim Han, 'Saudi Arabia uncomfortable with crude oil price, Aramco's Al-Falih says,' Bloomberg, April 26, 2011. See also 'Running dry,' *The Economist*, June 9, 2011 and International Energy Agency, *Oil Market Report*, Oct. 12, 2011, http://omrpublic.iea.org/currentissues/.

17 For a reminder that all is not well in the Emirates, see 'Arab unrest puts focus on UAE's northern emirates,' Reuters, July 6, 2011.

18 'North Caucasus: guide to a volatile region,' BBC News, Jan. 25, 2011.

19 Adam Nossiter, 'Western officials seek softer approach to militants in Nigeria,' *New York Times*, Aug. 30, 2011.

20 John Collins Rudolf, 'Mexico oil exports could end within decade, report warns,' *New York Times*, April 29, 2011.

21 'Oil leak,' *The Economist*, Feb. 24, 2011.

22 'Ex-chief says FEMA readiness even worse,' *Boston Globe*, April 1, 2006.

23 Julie Ann Dobbs, David W. Held, and T. Evan Nebeker, 'Status of Mississippi gulf coast Live Oak trees after Hurricane Katrina,' *SNA Research Conference*, vol. 51, 2006.

24 'No safety net,' *The Economist*, Sept. 8, 2005.

25 'El Niño doubles risk of civil wars: study,' Reuters, Aug. 24, 2011.

26 Henry Ridgwell, 'Japan tsunami damage cost could top $300 billion,' Voice of America, March 25, 2011.

27 'Japanese urge "farewell" to nuclear power six months after quake,' Reuters, Sept. 19, 2011.

28 'Bright ideas needed,' *The Economist*, Sept. 17, 2011.

29 Stuart Biggs and Yuriy Humber, 'Tepco failed to disclose scale of Fukushima radiation leaks, academics say,' Bloomberg, May 27, 2011.

Chapter 21: Doing a Caporetto

1 Ron Suskind, *Confidence Men* (Harper, 2011). See also 'A cantankerous crew,' *The Economist*, Oct. 1, 2011; 'Critics slammed Ron Suskind's "Confidence Men." But how closely did they read it?,' *Washington Post*, Sept. 30, 2011.

2 I don't know which exact article is being referred to either, but see e.g. Mark Pittman and Bob Ivry, 'U.S. taxpayers risk $9.7 trillion on bailout programs,' Bloomberg, Feb. 9, 2009.

3 Go to www.youtube.com and search for 'Alan Grayson: is anyone minding the store at the Federal Reserve?' Your jaw will drop as you listen.

Chapter 22: Crunching the numbers

1 Haldane, 'The $100 billion question.'

2 Data available via www.banker.com. You need to register to access the data, but registration is free.

3 'Banks disclosed 80 pct of subprime losses – Fitch,' Reuters, May 14, 2008. See also IMF data presented later in this chapter.

4 For Fuld's non-apology, see 'Dick Fuld testimony: no apologies here,' *Wall Street Journal*, Sept. 1, 2010. For Fuld's compensation, see Brian Ross and Alice Gomstyn, 'Lehman Brothers boss defends $484 million in salary, bonus,' ABC News, Oct. 6, 2008. I'm not going to reprint Cayne's outburst here, but unshockable readers can expand their vocabulary by checking out Heidi Moore, 'Bear Stearns' Jimmy Cayne's profane tirade against Treasury's Geithner,' *Wall Street Journal*, March 4, 2009. For Cayne's compensation, see Forbes, 'CEO compensation for James E. Cayne,' May 3, 2007.

5 Data available from the Federal Reserve. Go to the website (www.federalreserve.gov) and search for 'Mortgage debt outstanding.'

6 Gittelsohn, 'Shiller says U.S. home-price declines of 10% to 25% "wouldn't surprise me".'

7 'Rooms with a view,' *The Economist*, July 7, 2011.

8 Mortgage data from European

Mortgage Federation. Go to the website (www.hypo.org), click on 'Facts and figures,' then look for 'Value of mortgage debt.' The data in the table are for 2009, the most recent figures available. I've used an exchange rate of €1 = $1.371 to convert to US dollars.

9 Tracy Alloway, 'Under-reported – and non-performing – assets at US banks,' *Financial Times*, 'Alphaville' blog, June 17, 2011. If you want more bad news, you might want to explore PWC's June 2011 study, summarized online under the title 'Non-performing loans balloon for European banks as coverage slips' (via www.pwc.co.uk/eng/publications/european-outlook-for-non-core-and-non-performing-loans.html, but you need to register before you can download the report).

10 'Major Japanese banks' asset quality and capital levels remain a concern,' Fitch, Dec. 3, 2009.

Chapter 23: The end of days

1 'Strife of Brian,' *The Economist*, Sept. 17, 2011.

Chapter 24: What is to be done?

1 You can get the full text of the document online, from – why not? – www.marxists.org.

2 Kara Scannell, 'SEC pushes Citi

toward $200m settlement,' *Financial Times*, Sept. 15, 2011.

Chapter 25: Gold, wheat, and shotgun shells

1 Data sourced from RBS website (www.rbs.co.uk) and checked against data supplied by the three agencies in question.

2 Patrick Jenkins, 'UK government fears new RBS bail-out,' *Financial Times*, Oct. 7, 2011.

Afterword

1 'A downgrade for Congress,' *The Economist*, Nov. 26, 2011.

2 Nicoletta Batini, Giovanni Callegari, and Julia Guerreiro, 'An analysis of U.S. fiscal and generational imbalances: who will pay and how?,' IMF working paper, April 2011.

3 Bloomberg. Data sourced Nov. 28, 2011.

4 'Euro-Govt-Italian yields ease after sale; Bunds dip,' Reuters, Nov. 29, 2011.

5 Mark Gongloff, 'Germany's bond-auction fail: here's what it means,' *Wall Street Journal* blog, Nov. 23, 2011.

6 Bloomberg. Data sourced Nov. 28, 2011.

7 'Beware of falling masonry,' *The Economist*, Nov. 26, 2011.

8 Peter Griffiths, 'UK to return to recession, more QE needed – OECD,' Reuters, Nov. 28, 2011.

9 'Germany seems to have slipped into mild recession: OECD,' Reuters, Nov. 28, 2011.

10 Griffiths, 'UK to return to recession.'

11 Bob Ivry, Bradley Keoun, and Phil Kuntz, 'Secret Fed loans gave banks $13 billion undisclosed to Congress,' Bloomberg, Nov. 28, 2011.

12 Roger Lowenstein, 'Corzine forgot lessons of Long-Term Capital,' Bloomberg, Nov. 2, 2011.

13 Jonathan Weil, 'MF's missing money makes you wonder about Goldman,' Bloomberg, Nov. 25, 2011.

14 Barak Ravid, Amos Harel, Zvi Zrahiya, and Jonathan Lis, 'Netanyahu trying to persuade cabinet to support attack on Iran,' Haaretz.com, Nov. 2, 2011.

15 Robert Worth, Rick Gladstone, and Alan Cowell, 'Britain evacuates diplomats after Tehran embassy attack,' New York Times, Nov. 30, 2011.

16 Jack Shenker, 'Tahrir Square stands united after week of bloodshed and betrayal,' Guardian, Nov. 25, 2011.

17 Neil MacFarquhar and Nada Bakri, 'Syria calls Arab League sanctions "economic war,"' New York Times, Nov. 28, 2011.

18 'Russia PM Vladimir Putin booed at martial arts fight,' BBC News, Nov. 21, 2011.

19 'German President questions legality of ECB bond purchases,' Spiegel Online International, Aug. 24, 2011.

20 Matthew Brockett, 'ECB stepped up bond purchases last week as crisis worsened,' Bloomberg, Nov. 28, 2011.

21 Alan J. Ziobrowski, James W. Boyd, Ping Cheng, and Brigitte J. Ziobrowski, 'Abnormal returns from the common stock investments of members of the U.S. House of Representatives,' Business and Politics, vol. 13, no. 1, 2011, article 4. I should be clear that I am using the term 'insider trading' in an informal sense, not a legal one. Because of the way that insider trading legislation is drafted, those representatives and senators aren't committing an offense by trading on the basis of their legislative knowledge. Funny, that.

Index

Page numbers in *italics* refer to figures and tables.